More praise for

In Love with the World

"With this book, we enter into the interior life of a remarkable young Buddhist teacher. After setting off by himself on a wandering retreat, he immediately encounters fear, aversion, sickness, and near death. Yet the same emotional and physical difficulties that would throw the average person for a loop become opportunities for Mingyur Rinpoche to work with his mind, and to deepen his commitment to transforming adversity into awakening. His willingness to describe this process in such intimate detail has been an immense help to my own path and makes this one of the most inspiring books I have ever read."

—PEMA CHÖDRÖN, author of *When Things Fall Apart*

"Yongey Mingyur Rinpoche's life-changing adventure carries us with him and teaches us how to find the unshakable heart amid it all."

—JACK KORNFIELD, author of *A Path with Heart*

"In this vivid, compelling account, Mingyur Rinpoche reveals his own struggle and awakening as he faces the loss of worldly identity and the threat of dying itself."

—TARA BRACH, author of *Radical Acceptance* and *True Refuge*

"On the path to enlightenment, Mingyur Rinpoche had to escape from the sanctity of a Buddhist monastery, where he lived a privileged cossetted life, to find himself in the down-and-out railway stations, malodorous toilets, and flophouses of India. His misadventures along the way make for a rollicking travelogue. And yet this slim book also moved me and left me with a better appreciation of Tibetan Buddhism than so many weightier tomes that I've struggled to understand."

—BARBARA DEMICK, author of *Nothing to Envy*

"Through the unfolding wisdom of his personal story, Mingyur Rinpoche shows us the true value of investigating and freeing our minds. A courageous trailblazer, he illuminates a clear path, making it more accessible for others."

—TARA BENNETT-GOLEMAN, author of *Emotional Alchemy*

"Part thriller, part deeply personal autobiography, and part Buddhist teachings on how to live a meaningful life, this is an extraordinary book. It is a cliffhanger that recounts the journey of a modern wandering yogi who courageously gave up everything to challenge his mind and heart and live in the most difficult of circumstances. A gripping narrative of how the process of dying, letting go of our fixed selves and constraining habits, can liberate the human spirit and promote flourishing, this book has something profoundly important to teach each of us."

—RICHARD J. DAVIDSON, bestselling author of *The Emotional Life of Your Brain,* co-author of *Altered Traits,* and founder and director, Center for Healthy Minds, University of Wisconsin-Madison

"I'm in love with *In Love with the World.* This artfully told spiritual adventure casts a spell—you can't put it down, and you don't want it to end."

—DANIEL GOLEMAN, author of *Emotional Intelligence*

In
Love
with
the
World

SPIEGEL & GRAU

NEW YORK

In
LOVE
with
the
WORLD

A MONK'S JOURNEY
THROUGH THE BARDOS
OF LIVING AND DYING

Yongey Mingyur Rinpoche

WITH HELEN TWORKOV

Published in the United States by Spiegel & Grau, an imprint of
Random House, a division of Penguin Random House LLC,
New York.

SPIEGEL & GRAU and colophon is a registered trademark of Penguin
Random House LLC.

Grateful acknowledgment is made to Ken McLeod for permission to
reprint an excerpt from "Thirty-Seven Practices of a Bodhisattva"
from *Reflections of Silver River: Tokmé Zongpo's Thirty-Seven Practices
of a Bodhisattva* translated by Ken McLeod (Windsor, CA: Unfettered
Mind, 2014). Reprinted by permission of Ken McLeod.

Quote on pages 127–128 is from Shantideva from
The Way of the Bodhisattva. Translated by the
Padmakara Translation Group (Boston: Shambhala, 1997).

LIBRARY OF CONGRESS CATALOGING-IN-PUBLICATION DATA
Names: Yongey Mingyur, Rinpoche, author. | Tworkov, Helen, author.
Title: In love with the world: a monk's journey through the bardos of
living and dying / by Yongey Mingyur Rinpoche with Helen Tworkov.
Description: New York: Spiegel & Grau, [2019]
Identifiers: LCCN 2018037052| ISBN 9780525512530 |
ISBN 9780525512554 (ebook)
Subjects: LCSH: Yongey Mingyur, Rinpoche, 1976– | Buddhist
monks—Biography. | Near-death experiences—Religious
aspects—Buddhism. | Intermediate state—Buddhism. |
Spiritual life—Buddhism.
Classification: LCC BQ998.O54 A3 2019 | DDC 294.3/923092 [B]—dc23
LC record available at https://lccn.loc.gov/2018037052

Printed in the United States of America on acid-free paper

randomhousebooks.com
spiegelandgrau.com

246897531

FIRST EDITION

Book design by Simon M. Sullivan

Contents

PART TWO

RETURNING HOME

•

Prologue

FINISHED WRITING THE letter. It was past ten o'clock on a hot night in Bodh Gaya in north-central India, and right now no one else knew. I placed the letter on a low wooden table in front of the chair that I often sat on. It would be discovered sometime the following afternoon. There was nothing left to do. I turned off the lights and pushed back the curtain. Outside, it was pitch black, with no sign of activity, just as I had anticipated. By ten thirty, I began pacing in the dark and checking my watch.

Twenty minutes later I picked up my backpack and left the room, locking the door behind me. In the dark, I tiptoed downstairs to the foyer. At night, a heavy metal bolt secures two thick wooden doors from the inside. Narrow rectangular push-out windows parallel each door, and are almost as long. I waited for the watchman to pass. Once I calculated that he was the farthest from the front door, I opened a window and stepped out onto the small marble porch. I closed the window, flew down the six steps to the brick walkway, and quickly moved behind the bushes to the left.

A high metal fence surrounds the compound. The side gate on the alley stays open during the day, but at night it's locked and a guard sits nearby. The front gate is rarely used. High and wide, it opens onto a bypass that connects the main roads that run parallel to each other. The two metal panels of the gate are secured by a heavy chain and a large padlock. To leave without being noticed, I would have to stay out of the watchman's sight for his next round. I waited in the bushes for him to pass, once again calculated his distance, and ran the hundred feet to the main gate.

I threw my backpack over the gate, aiming for the grassy area to the side of the blacktop so that it would land quietly. Besides, my father had always told me: *When you're on a journey and you come to a wall, always throw your pack over first, because then you will be sure to follow.* I unlocked the padlock, pushed back the gate, and slipped through.

My heart burst with fear and exhilaration. The darkness of night seemed to light up and absorb all my thoughts, leaving just the shocking sensation of being on the other side of the fence, in the dead of night, alone outside in the world for the first time in my adult life. I had to force myself to move. I reached around through the bars to close the padlock, then I picked up my pack and hid on the side of the road. Two minutes before eleven, and I was in-between one life and the next. My breath thundered in my ears; my stomach tightened. I could hardly believe that so far the scheme had worked perfectly. My senses intensified and seemed to extend far beyond my conceptual mind. The world suddenly became luminous, and I felt as if I could see for miles . . . but I could not see the taxi.

Where is the taxi?

It had been ordered for eleven P.M. I stepped out onto the bypass to search for headlights. Despite strategizing like a jailbird, I had shared my plan with no one, and no getaway car was waiting. On the other side of the fence, now behind me, sat Tergar, a Tibetan Buddhist monastery . . . and I was its prestigious thirty-six-year-old abbot.

A year earlier, I had announced my intention to enter an extended retreat. This had not sounded any alarms. Three-year retreats are common in my tradition. However, it was assumed that I would seclude myself in a monastery or a mountain hermitage. In addition to Tergar in Bodh Gaya, I have monasteries in Tibet and Nepal, and meditation centers throughout the world, but no one anywhere had imagined my true intentions. Despite my revered position—or more precisely, because of it—I would not vanish into an institutional or isolated dwelling. I had set my sights on following the ancient tradition of sadhus, the wandering Hindu ascetics who give up all their belongings to live free of worldly concerns. The earliest heroes of my own Tibetan Kagyu lineage had followed in the footsteps of their Hindu predecessors, taking shelter in caves and forest groves. I would die to my life as a privileged tulku—a recognized incarnation of a spiritual adept. I would discard the mantle of being the youngest son of Tulku Urgyen Rinpoche, the esteemed meditation master. I would live without attendants and administrators and would exchange the protections granted by my role as abbot and lineage holder for the anonymity that I had never known but had long yearned for.

My wristwatch read ten after eleven. My plan was to take the midnight train to Varanasi; the train left from the Gaya station, just eight miles away. I had ordered the taxi earlier that evening while coming home from the Mahabodhi Temple, the historic site that commemorates the Buddha's great awakening under a bodhi tree. An offshoot of the original tree marks the heart of this sprawling temple complex, and pilgrims from all over the world come to sit under its leaves. I went there often, but this particular evening I specifically went to do kora—ritual circumambulation— and to offer butter lamps as a way of praying for my retreat to go well. I had been accompanied by my longtime attendant, Lama Soto.

Headlights appeared and I stepped onto the road. A jeep drove past. After another ten minutes, I once again saw headlights. When a large cargo truck came barreling toward me, I jumped back and slipped in a mud puddle. When I pulled my foot out, one of my rubber flip-flops got stuck. I retrieved it, then continued to hide, my hands wet with slimy muck. My enchantment vanished, and agitation rolled in like fog. Anyone who frequented this road would recognize me. No one had *ever* seen me unaccompanied, not at this hour, not at any hour. I had taken the taxi for granted. I had no idea what I would do after I reached Varanasi, but at this moment it seemed critically important not to miss the train. I had no backup plan. I began walking quickly toward the main road, sweating from heat and excitement.

Earlier in the evening, Lama Soto and I had been driven to the Mahabodhi Temple in the Tergar jeep, a distance of about two miles. We had passed the small shops that line the main road: convenience stores that sell dry goods, a few restaurants, computer cafés, souvenir and trinket shops, and travel bureaus. Cars and taxis, bicycles, and rickshaws crowded the road, along with tuk-tuks, the three-wheeled motorized contraptions that make a racket. As the road approaches the temple entrance, beggars line the streets, holding out their alms bowls. On the way back to Tergar, we had stopped at the office of a travel agent, where I had ordered a taxi to come to the main gate of the monastery at eleven o'clock. We had spoken in English, so Lama Soto, who spoke only Tibetan, knew nothing of this arrangement.

I was on the bypass halfway toward the main road when the taxi finally appeared. After thirty minutes in the world on my own, the confines of a car provided unexpected comfort. Several times each day since I was little, I had recited prayers that included: *I take refuge in the Buddha; in the dharma—the Buddha's teachings; and in the sangha—the enlightened assembly.* Now I noticed that I was taking refuge in this taxi, and was grateful for its shelter.

I found myself thinking about Naropa (circa 980–1040 CE), the learned abbot of the Buddhist university Nalanda. I knew that he had left his exalted position to seek a higher level of wisdom than he had yet accomplished, but I had never before thought about the circumstances of his departure. *I wonder if he started out totally alone. Perhaps an attendant was waiting outside the gates with a horse. That's how Prince Siddhartha escaped from his father's kingdom: He had confided in his charioteer, and they had made a secret arrangement.*

As the taxi sped toward Gaya, my body went forward as my mind went backward. The carefully constructed departure suddenly felt jarring. During the previous weeks, I had envisioned how the events of this evening would unfold. Now I watched the same movie in reverse, starting in the present and going backward, and accepting that there are different ways to say goodbye.

Lama Soto and I had returned to Tergar from the Mahabodhi Temple by seven o'clock, and I had gone straight to my private rooms on the second floor of my house. My apartment consists of a large reception room for meeting guests, which leads to a second room, where I practiced and slept. The house sits behind the central temple, which is the size of a village block. Traditional ornamental designs cover every wall, each column, and the entire ceiling of the temple. A huge golden Buddha rises from the shrine and directly faces the main gate and, beyond that, the Mahabodhi Temple. Earlier in the day I had circumambulated the marble portico that runs along the outside walls, and had gone upstairs to the balconies that overlook the main room, all the while silently saying goodbye. Adjacent to my house are the guesthouse and administrative offices. Behind these buildings are the dormitories and classrooms for about 150 young monks who range in age from nine to twenty. I had passed by every room, walked down every corridor, not quite believing that I might not see any of this again for a long time. I planned to stay away for at least three years. I had done everything I could to ensure the continued welfare and training of the monks. I hoped I hadn't missed any important details.

Lama Soto had come to my room at about nine o'clock to check if I needed anything before he retired. Originally from

Kham, an area of eastern Tibet known for its strong, tough men, he had been my attendant for the last ten years, since I was twenty-six, and had shielded me in a crowd like a bodyguard. His room was on the first floor of my house. The door to my private rooms had creaked so loudly that in preparation for sneaking out, I had greased its hinges. Two weeks earlier, I had informed Lama Soto and the monastery administrators that I was not to be disturbed before noon each day. This unusual request suggested that I would be practicing meditations that should not be interrupted. But really, this would allow me to be far away before my absence was discovered.

What most appealed to my sense of mischief was obtaining a key to the front gate. I traveled frequently between my monasteries in India and Kathmandu, and during a previous visit to Bodh Gaya, I had informed the head of maintenance that the gate needed a more substantial padlock and that I would purchase one on my next visit to Delhi. To this end, Lama Soto and I had gone to Old Delhi one afternoon, ambling through a section of the market that featured locksmiths. When I returned to Bodh Gaya, I accompanied the maintenance supervisor to the gate in order to replace the old lock. The new lock came with three keys, and I handed him two but kept one. This also provided me with a chance to swing the gate back and forth in order to test its weight and the noise it made.

The Mahabodhi Temple was now barely out of sight, yet I already knew something of the need to nourish the steady awareness of buddha-mind. When I had entered the taxi, the agitation in my voice had made the driver accelerate to dangerous speeds. Temples and stupas—buildings that house sacred relics—reflect the heart and mind of the Buddha. Respecting outside forms of Buddha nourishes our own innate wisdom. Yet the true buddha, the awakened essence of mind, exists within each one of us.

My heart was beating fast. Between the speed of the taxi and the darkness, I couldn't see anything out the window. Images moved through my mindscape faster than the speed of the taxi. According to scientists, fifty to eighty thousand thoughts pass through the mind in one day, but it felt like that many in one minute. The faces of relatives appeared before me: my mother, Sonam Chödrön, and grandfather, Tashi Dorje, in their quarters at Osel Ling, my monastery in Kathmandu. I imagined monastery officials and nuns and monks meditating in formal shrine rooms; I saw friends sitting in European cafés, or in Hong Kong eating at large round tables in noodle restaurants. I imagined their astonishment on learning of my disappearance: Jaws would drop; faces would fall forward, leaning into the news. I watched amused, but my amusement did not extend to my mother. When I saw her face, I knew how worried she would be, and I just had to trust in my father's advice.

In 1996, I had visited my father at Nagi Gompa, his hermitage on an isolated mountainside outside Kathmandu. He had been sick with diabetes, but no change in his physical condition indicated that he was close to dying. As it turned out, he died two months later. We were in his small room, a space of not more than ten by ten feet that sat perched on the roof of his house; his retinue resided on the lower floors. The room had a big picture window that looked out over the valley. He was the abbot of a small nunnery, and for his teachings, the nuns crowded into this little space.

He sat on a raised rectangular box. This is where he slept, and it was from here that he taught. His lower body was covered with a blanket. I sat before him on the floor. As usual, he initiated the conversation by asking, *Do you have any issues to discuss with me?*

I told him that I wanted to do a wandering retreat.

He looked down at me. *Ami,* he said, using a Tibetan term of endearment. *Listen to me, ami, are you sure? Really sure?*

I told him, *Yes. I am sure. I have wanted to do this since I was a little boy.*

Then my father said, *Wonderful. But if you really want to do this, I have one piece of advice: Just go. Don't tell anyone where you're going, including our family members. Just go, and it will be good for you.*

I had not forgotten his advice, even though fifteen years had passed before I used it. For decades, as part of the daily liturgy, I had repeated: *All things are impermanent; Death comes without warning; This body too will be a corpse.* The more I matured in my view, the more I intuited that I had not fully absorbed the deepest meaning of this phrase, but even so, the possibility of this impermanent body becoming a corpse without my realizing my aspirations had never strayed far from my concerns. I had waited a long time to do this retreat, waited until it became a do-or-die proposition—or perhaps it would be more accurate to say do *and* die. I would be leaving behind everything I knew—with no more certainty of what might come next than if I were on my deathbed.

In addition to leaving my mother, leaving Lama Soto was also sad, for he had been ill, and I knew we would never see each other again. He would be the one to discover my absence, and I took no pleasure in picturing his distress as the implications of the letter I had left behind became clear:

> By the time you read this letter, I will have begun the long retreat that I announced last year. As you may know, I have felt a very strong connection with the tradition of retreat since I was a young boy growing up in the Himalayas. Even though I didn't really know how to meditate, I would often run away from home to a cave nearby, where I would sit quietly and chant the mantra "om mani peme hung" over and over again in my mind. My love of the mountains and the simple life of a wandering meditator called to me even then.

PART ONE

ADDING WOOD
TO THE FIRE

1

•

Who Are
You?

Are you Mingyur Rinpoche?

My father asked me this question soon after I began
studying with him, when I was around nine years old. It was so
gratifying to know the correct answer that I proudly declared, *Yes,
I am.*

Then he asked, *Can you show me the one thing in particular
that makes you Mingyur Rinpoche?*

I looked down the front of my body to my feet. I looked at my
hands. I thought about my name. I thought about who I was in
relation to my parents and my older brothers. I could not come up
with an answer. He then made looking for the *real me* sound like
a treasure hunt, and I earnestly searched under rocks and behind
trees. When I was eleven years old, I began my studies at Sherab
Ling, a monastery in northern India, where I brought this search
inside myself through meditation. Two years later, I entered the
traditional three-year retreat, a period of intense mind training.
During this period, we novice monks did many different exercises, each one deepening our understanding of subtler levels of
reality. The Tibetan word for meditation, *gom,* means "to become
familiar with": familiar with how the mind works, how it creates
and shapes our perceptions of ourselves and the world, how the
outer layers of mind—the constructed labels—function like
clothing that identifies our social identities and cloaks our naked,

nonfabricated state of original mind, whether that outerwear consists of business suits, jeans, uniforms, or Buddhist robes.

By the time I set off for this retreat, I understood that the value of the labels shifts according to circumstances and social consensus. I had already affirmed that I was not my name, title, or status; that the essential me could not be defined by rank or role. Nonetheless these same designations, empty of essential meaning, had circumscribed my days: *I am a monk; a son, a brother, and an uncle; a Buddhist; a meditation teacher; a tulku, an abbot, and an author; a Tibetan Nepali; a human being. Which one describes the essential me?*

Making this list is a simple exercise. There is only one problem: The inevitable conclusion contradicts every cherished assumption that we hold dear—as I was just about to learn yet again. I wished to go beyond *the relative self*—the self that identifies with these labels. I knew that even though these social categories play a dominant role in our personal stories, they coexist with a larger reality beyond labels. Generally we do not recognize that our social identities are molded and confined by context, and that these outer layers of ourselves exist within a boundless reality. Habitual patterns cover over this boundless reality; they obscure it, but it is always there, ready to be uncovered. When we are not constricted by habitual patterns that define how we see ourselves and how we behave in the world, we create access to those qualities of mind that are vast, that are not contingent on circumstances or concepts, and that are always present; for these reasons, we call it the ultimate, or *absolute* mind, or the mind of absolute reality, which is the same as the mind of pure awareness and which expresses the very essence of our true nature. Unlike the intellectual and conceptual head and the boundless love of an open heart, this essence of reality has no association to location or materiality of any kind. It is everywhere and nowhere. It's somewhat like sky—so completely integrated with our existence that we never stop to question its reality or to recognize its qualities. Because awareness is as present in our lives as the air we breathe, we can access it anywhere, anytime.

I had developed some capacity to hold the relative and absolute perspectives at the same time. Yet I had never known a day without people and props that mirrored the stitched-together patchwork that became known to me and to others as *Mingyur Rinpoche:* unfailingly polite, quick to smile, with a somewhat reserved demeanor, tidy, clean-shaven, wearing rimless glasses with gold frames. Now I wondered how these identities would play out in the Gaya station. I had been there many times before, but always with at least one attendant. This meant that I was never without a reference to rank, and was never challenged to depend solely on my own internal resources.

Tibetans have an expression for deliberately increasing the challenges of maintaining a steady mind: adding wood to the fire. Generally, people go through life taking note of those experiences that recurrently enflame our anger or anxiety or fear—and then we try to avoid them, telling ourselves things like, *I can't watch scary movies. I cannot be in big crowds. I have a terrible fear of heights, or of flying, or of dogs, or the dark.* But the causes that provoke these responses do not go away; and when we find ourselves in these situations, our reactions can overwhelm us. Using our inner resources to work with these issues is our only true protection, because external circumstances change all the time and are therefore not reliable.

Adding wood to the fire deliberately brings difficult situations to the forefront so that we can work with them directly. We take the very behaviors or circumstances that we think of as problems and turn them into allies. For example, when I was about three or four years old, I went by bus on a pilgrimage tour of the major Buddhist sites in India with my mother and grandparents. I got very sick on the first bus ride. After that, every time we even approached a bus, I became fearful and nauseated, and inevitably got sick again. At the age of about twelve, after a year of living at Sherab Ling Monastery in northern India, I was going home to see my family. The attendant who would be traveling with me arranged for us to take a bus to Delhi, an all-night ride, and then a plane from Delhi to Kathmandu. I had been looking forward to the visit, but for weeks I had dreaded the bus ride. I insisted that the attendant buy two seats for me so that I could lie down, as I thought this would settle my stomach. But once the trip started, and I was stretched out, I discovered that lying down made me feel worse. My attendant implored me to eat something or to drink juice, but my stomach was too distended to swallow a sip. When the bus stopped en route, I refused to get up and walk outside. I did not want to move, and didn't for many hours. Finally, I left the bus to use the restroom and have some juice.

When I returned to my two seats, I felt much better and decided to try to meditate. I started with a body scan, bringing my awareness to the sensations around my stomach, its bloating, and the nausea. This was very uncomfortable, a little disgusting, and initially made the sensations worse. But as I slowly came to accept these sensations, I experienced my entire body as a guesthouse. I was playing host to these sensations, as well as to feelings of aversion, resistance, and reaction. The more I allowed these guests to inhabit my body, the calmer I became. Soon I fell sound asleep, and woke up in Delhi.

This experience did not put to rest all of my anxieties about riding buses; the fear recurred with subsequent trips, although with lessening effect. The big difference was that after this, I welcomed bus rides. I did not seek them out, in the deliberate fashion that I had arranged for this wandering retreat, but I was grateful for the challenge of working with my mind in order to overcome adversity.

When we add wood to the fire, instead of trying to smother the flames of our fears, we add more fuel, and in the process gain confidence in our capacity to work with whatever settings we find ourselves in. We no longer avoid situations that have disturbed us in the past, or that evoke destructive patterns or emotional outbursts. We begin to rely on another aspect of mind that exists beneath our reactivity. We call this "no-self." It's the unconditioned awareness that reveals itself with the dissolution of the chattering mind that talks to itself throughout the day. Another way of saying this is that we switch mental gears from normal awareness to meditative awareness.

The normal awareness that guides our everyday activities is actually quite cluttered. We generally go about our days with minds filled with ideas of what we want, and how things should be, and with reactive responses to what we like and do not like. It's as if we are wearing different pairs of glasses without knowing it, and have no idea that these filters obscure and distort our perceptions. For example, if we have motion sickness, the extra glasses are the feelings of disgust from the smell and the embarrassment we feel from causing others to be disgusted by us. The fact that someone might notice adds to our physical discomfort.

Let's say we look at a mountain with normal awareness. Our mind is facing out and following our eyes to the mountain, and perhaps we're thinking about the last time we saw this mountain, or any mountain, and who we were with at that time, or if the climate or time of day for seeing the mountain was better before or now, or if we are hungry or happy. Or think of the times when we use normal awareness to collect our keys and phones before leaving the house. We might notice that this process often includes anxiety about being late or about what route to take to an appointment, or we might fantasize about returning home before we have even left.

With meditative awareness, we try to remove these filters and reduce the projections. We face inward and recognize awareness as a quality of mind itself. When we look at the mountain, there is less mental traffic between us and the mountain, fewer concepts and ideas. We see things about the mountain that we had not noticed before: the way the ridges are outlined by the shape of the trees, the changes in vegetation, or the sky that surrounds the mountain. This clear mind of awareness is always with us, whether we recognize it or not. It coexists with confusion, and with the destructive emotions and cultural conditioning that shape our ways of seeing things. But when our perception shifts to meditative or steady awareness, it is no longer narrowed by memory and expectation; whatever we see, touch, taste, smell, or hear has greater clarity and sharpness, and enlivens our interactions.

Shortly after I started studying with my father, I received teachings from him on meditative awareness. One day I was hanging out on the roof of my house, just looking around in a kind of distracted, casual way, and I noticed that partway up Shivapuri, the mountain behind Nagi Gompa, there was a road crew repairing a footpath that cut through the side of the mountain. About six people were using shovels, pickaxes, and wheelbarrows to level the path and clear dirt and stones that had fallen from above. I sat down and watched them work from the roof. Then I thought, *I should be meditating.* Following my father's instructions, I turned my mind toward itself without moving my eyes. I continued to see the people working, and hear the sound of pickaxes breaking rock, and watch the wheelbarrow dumping dirt over the side. But suddenly, I also saw the beautiful blue sky and the clouds passing overhead, and I saw leaves move in the wind and felt the breeze on my skin and heard birds singing. Before, with normal awareness, my focus had narrowed, and I did not feel or see anything but the road crew. Meditative awareness—also called steady awareness—introduces us to looking at the nature of awareness itself.

Once we become familiar with steady awareness, we still often move between this state and normal awareness. Despite the difference between them, both types of awareness exist within a dualistic construct: There is something watching and something being watched—the experience of awareness recognizing itself. When this duality is eliminated, we drop into what we call pure—or non-dual—awareness. Non-duality is the essential quality of awareness, yet when we speak of three types of awareness—normal, meditative, and pure—we are speaking of a gradual experiential process that takes place from dualistic to non-dualistic states, from very cluttered minds to minds that are increasingly liberated from habitual reactivity and preconceptions about how things are supposed to be. These categories of awareness are not sharply delineated, and our recognition of pure awareness also has many gradations. We can have glimpses or flashes of it, with differing degrees of depth or clarity. I knew something of pure awareness. Part of my intention for this retreat was to intensify my relationship to this aspect of reality, and I had hoped to accomplish this by stepping outside of my normal life.

Who was about to step into the Gaya railway station in the middle of the night? My maroon robes, yellow shirt, and shaved head identified me as a Tibetan Buddhist monk, a lama by profession—a perfect disguise for the disorderly mix of curiosity, anxiety, and confidence that accompanied my every heartbeat—and who in so many ways was still seeking the answer to my father's question: *Who is Mingyur Rinpoche?*

I had attained skills in recognizing awareness—within monastic enclosures and shrine rooms, and on my meditation mat, always within my comfort zone, and always near disciples and attendants. Even though I had been meditating for my entire life, and had spent many years in Buddhist monasteries, I was now starting out on a different kind of retreat. My titles and roles would get tossed onto the pyre. I would burn up the coarse, outer social protections and strategies in order to be free—not *of* life but *for* life, for living every day with a newly born engagement with whatever would arise. I would not just revert to the rewarding paths that I knew so well. I had some inkling that these roles had become deeply embedded, and I could not work with them until some degree of fracture had brought them to the surface.

I had set off on my own to intentionally seek this disruption through what I had been thinking of as an ego-suicide mission. I wanted to explore the deepest depths of who I really was out in the world, anonymous and alone. I wanted to test my own capacities in new and challenging situations. *If I can truly disrupt my established routines, find my own edge and then keep going, let's see what happens to my recognition of awareness, see what happens to the virtues of patience and discipline when no one is watching, when no one even knows who I am; when perhaps I don't even know who I am.*

The taxi squealed to a stop. It was time to find out. I paid the driver and left the cab. As if to affirm that every worldly refuge is as fleeting as smoke, I paused in front of the station and turned to watch the taxi disappear.

2

•

Acknowledge
the Wave
but Stay with
the Ocean

DAY AND NIGHT the Gaya station teems with travelers, beg-gars, pilgrims, and crying children. Entire families sit on top of their belongings, or stretch out on the platforms either waiting for trains or because they have no place else to be. Porters balance heavy cases on their turbaned heads. Meandering cows, pigeons, and dogs make their way among floor dwellers, caged birds, and tethered goats. A public announcement system blares track and schedule information. Venders hawking tea and snacks scream and push their way through the crowds. Men and women chew betel nuts and then spit out the red juice, which hits the ground like blobs of blood. It's noisy, tumultuous, and dirty, all features familiar to me only from afar. In the past, I would have remained in an exclusive lounge while an attendant-monk purchased tickets and arranged for a porter. Now I steered through throngs cast in shadow by dim overhead bulbs.

I had never once bought a ticket for anything, and had never had more weight in my backpack than a bottle of water, perhaps sunglasses, and a hat. Now my backpack also contained two Buddhist texts that I had chosen to take on this journey. The ten thousand rupees that I carried (about $150 US) had come from the many small envelopes placed on the table in my room as offerings from visitors. Lama Soto routinely collected these before retiring each evening, but for several weeks I had hidden a little money each day. I studied the chalkboards to figure out the correct queue for the train to Varanasi. This would be my first ride in the lowest class. I was given no seat assignment. Once I had my ticket I stood near the wall of the crowded platform, improbably hoping that the train would arrive on schedule. Thin curls of smoke from small cooking fires choked the air and heightened a cinematic vision of an underground world. As the atmosphere became increasingly claustrophobic, pressing in like a physical weight, the plan to add fuel to the fire steadily became a reality— and this was just the beginning. Exploring the true nature of my being was causing the flames to burn a bit sooner than I had anticipated.

By habit we perceive ourselves and the world around us as solid, real, and enduring. Yet without much effort, we can easily determine that not one aspect within the whole world's system exists independent of change. I had just been in one physical location, and now I was in another; I had experienced different states of mind. We have all grown from babies to adults, lost loved ones, watched children grow, known changes in weather, in political regimes, in styles of music and fashion, in everything. Despite appearances, no aspect of life ever stays the same. The deconstruction of any one object—no matter how dense it appears, such as an ocean liner, our bodies, a skyscraper, or an oak tree—will reveal the appearance of solidity to be as illusory as permanence. Everything that looks substantial will break down into molecules, and into atoms, and into electrons, protons, and neutrons. And every phenomenon exists in interdependence with myriad other forms. Every identification of any one form has meaning only in relationship to another. *Big* only has meaning in relation to *small*. To mistake our habitual misperceptions for the whole of reality is what we mean by *ignorance,* and these delusions define the world of confusion, or samsara.

Life is change and impermanence—that was another core tenet of my training. *Change and impermanence. Impermanence and death.* I had joyfully anticipated the death of my roles, and of transforming into an itinerant yogi, alone in the big chaotic world; but the change from always having an attendant to being totally alone struck me like a thunderbolt. I already missed Lama Soto's broad shoulders and his firm, wide stance. Standing alone did not feel safe. *Acknowledge the wave but stay with the ocean. This will pass . . . if I let it.*

I stood very erect, a little primly—as was my habit—and looked down onto vagrants who had settled in for the night, some sprawled like drunks. *I could have traveled first class, and waited in the lounge with the ceiling fans. But this is what I asked for . . . circumstances so unfamiliar as to make me unfamiliar to myself. I have been away from my monastery for an hour. Have I already reached my limit? Of course not.* Shyness and vulnerability were not new to me, but they had not surged with such unexpected impact in decades. I wanted to hide, but I had nowhere to go. I could feel the tension and resistance in my body, and I acknowledged how much the surface of my mind was getting stirred up by discomfort and judgment. At the same time, a sense of stability, cultivated by a lifetime of practice, was also present—but it felt fragile in a way that I was not used to.

I had never imagined that it would be easy to beg, or to sleep on the street. I had chosen this type of retreat for its difficulties. I had studied the beggars that lined the road to the Mahabodhi Temple and envisioned myself among them. I had projected my reactions to strangers who avoided my alms bowl. In my imagination, I sometimes met their indifference with genuine concern for their coldheartedness; at other times, I responded with anger. I had wondered how far I would go to get food. I had pictured rooting through garbage like a wild pig. I was a vegetarian and ate few sweets, but for the past few weeks I had seen myself chomping down meat and savoring discarded cookie crumbs. I had even wondered if hunger would induce me to eat raw fish guts, like the Indian adept Tilopa.

Tilopa (988–1069 CE) had sought anonymity in remote lands far from monasteries. Yet his occasional encounters with seekers had left a trail of wondrous stories that only increased his reputation. When word of Tilopa's exceptional wisdom reached Naropa, the great pundit of Nalanda immediately recognized his own limitations and abandoned his high seat in pursuit of a master who knew more than he did. He finally caught up with the eccentric yogi on the banks of a river in Bengal. Tilopa was completely naked, eating raw innards tossed to him by the fishermen after they gutted their daily catch. This encounter was the first of many tests for Naropa, but his faith in this provocative mystic sustained his trials, and eventually led to his own enlightenment.

I had projected the possibility of eating fish guts, and had used my imagination to become familiar with extreme hunger, cold, and loneliness . . . but somehow I had missed envisioning the train station and experiencing the agony of standing alone in this murky, throbbing squalor, feeling so apart from the travelers brushing against my robes that I might as well have been on the moon. It did not take long for me to experience the indifference shown to a man of no rank. Even though I was wearing my robes, I felt myself to be the object of scrutiny but not respect. Monks are not respected in India. Even the Hindu sadhus are not respected in the cities, only in the villages. It was different in Old Tibet, where people who devoted themselves to spiritual activity were revered. Children grew up venerating monks and nuns. Buddha is not only a historical figure but also a living presence embodied by robes; for this reason, public displays of disregard always made me a little sad.

• • •

When the train pulled in, passengers grabbed their children, their animals, their big suitcases, their enormous cloth sacks tied with ropes and strapped around their foreheads, and pushed and shoved to get into the car. My backpack kept getting snagged and I had to lurch forward to disengage it. I was the last one in, and began the train ride in terror, squashed flat against the door, my head, torso, and legs pressed between the door and human bodies. I could see nothing but took note of the awful smell. I had to open my mouth and suck in whatever air was available. For the next several minutes, I could not keep my mind from feeling overwhelmed.

My training had introduced me to the spacious awareness of my natural mind. We compare this awareness to open skies and oceans—references meant to invoke immeasurable vastness, even though awareness is more immeasurable than skies and oceans combined. Once we learn to recognize the ever-present quality of awareness, to let go of the conditioned and contingent mind and recognize that we *are* this spacious awareness, then our thoughts and emotions manifest as waves or clouds inseparable from awareness. With recognition, we no longer get carried away by the stories that keep our minds spinning in repetitive cycles, or jumping around like a crazy monkey. If we keep our minds entangled with these stories, then it's hard to recognize awareness. As we all know, the weather systems within awareness often become quite stormy. But the more familiar we are with awareness as an innate quality of mind, the less effect the weather has on us. Waves arise, and clouds move by; when we are not stuck inside them, they lose their impact. Our sensitivity deepens, and we learn to trust the knowingness of the aware mind. I had known waves of hurricane strength in my life—but not for a very long time; and now, on the jam-packed train, I was not quite sure if my constricted breaths came from the pressure on my face or the fear in my heart.

After a few minutes, the strong energy of fear began to sub-side. My breathing slowed. At the same time, spacious awareness presented itself—as if to meet the wave. Sometimes this happens. It's as if the force of the turbulence itself allows awareness to be recognized more easily than at other times, and big emotion leads to big skylike mind. I was no longer swept away by the wave, and no longer felt like I was drowning. What I had to do was: Let it be. There was no point in trying to run away. The wave was there. Though I would have preferred to be somewhere else, I could now just acknowledge that, and stay with the situation—the spacious awareness *and* the unpleasant sensation. When we stay with a reality vaster than the skies, the destructive impact of our wild and disturbed reactions automatically diminishes. But clouds—or waves—don't disappear; they dissolve and rise again.

With each stop of the train, people pushed their way off, and more people boarded. I inched farther forward until I was able to take a spot on the floor and sat cross-legged with my pack in my lap, another entirely new experience. Within Tibetan culture, re-incarnated adepts like myself take higher seats than others, and it's taboo for tulkus to sit on the floor. Seeing me like this would have distressed Tibetan people. But no one here cared about me or my status, and anyway, to stick with my intentions I would have to shed a lot of social customs.

I was not habituated to first class, but I was keenly aware of my discomfort with this utterly new environment. The walls and benches were a kind of putrid green, and in the dingy light everything looked like it was growing mold. *I arranged this,* I reminded myself, *to travel with people who are deemed unimportant in the world and who are not valued by society. So who is experiencing such discomfort: The esteemed Rinpoche? The privileged abbot? The fixed mind holding these revered titles in place?*

My eyes were not in neutral gear. They were not just seeing,

not just resting on objects. Instead, figures around me were becoming alien creatures, *others, those over there.* Their dirty clothes
obscured my heart. I was faulting their cracked bare feet, yet
soon my own would look just as filthy. Their body odor was repel-
lent, even though the humidity and the heat and the absence of
air-conditioning must have left my body smelling just as bad, for
the shirt under my robe was glued to my torso with sweat.

Once again, my body was in one place, my mind in another.
One was wrapped in a monk's persona, but my experiences were
shaped by judgments of the most ordinary kind. It was like a waking dream. This dream had the strangeness of an environment
that is familiar but somehow different. Or maybe it was me who
was different. I felt out of place. I *was* out of place in this new
world. It was almost as if I had walked into someone else's
dream—and the dream did not want me in it, as much as I did
not want to be in the dream. But here I was. It was my dream,
after all, and it was the dream I had chosen. *I don't have to like
this dream. Just let it be. Don't get stuck in it. Let it take care of
itself.*

I didn't feel any connection with these people. Despite years
of practices that activate spontaneous compassion, I had to reach
back in memory for basic reminders: *Everyone wants happiness;
no one wants suffering. These people too have known joy and distress, just like me. They too have lost loved ones. They too have
known fear and kindness. They too will die, just as I will.* For a few
minutes, I repeated these reminders with genuine sincerity; then
aversion again resurfaced.

Until this night, I had imagined my retreat landscape in terms
of caves and pristine mountain lakes and village lanes. A friend
who rode the lowest-class trains had described the rides as very
pleasant: *The benches are hard, and sometimes the cars are crowded,
but the windows stay open and fresh air comes in and you can buy
tea at every stop.* That sounded fine to me. I had never imagined
anything like this.

For the next few hours I became both teacher and student, reviewing lessons as if I were back in monastery kindergarten. *Where did this aversion come from? How did it arise? Did it come from my mind, my body, or the outside world?* My breathing was more shallow than usual. I intentionally slowed and deepened my breath. But my mind continued to question and comment, making judgments about every little detail. Noticing this, I understood that I had to turn my attention to the judging mind itself. *Are my reactions true? Are my assumptions correct? Where did they come from?* I was asking myself questions that my tutor had asked me at the beginning of my first three-year retreat.

When I was thirteen, my tutor Saljay Rinpoche had asked me to identify pleasant and unpleasant sensations in my body. I kept trying to use concepts to bring about feelings: *Thinking about chocolate creates pleasant sensations. Thinking of garbage creates unpleasant sensations.*

But these particular images were ordinary, with no surprise value, and they had no impact on my body.

Saljay Rinpoche said: *You do not need to think. Just feel. Feel what is in your body.*

I could not, and asked what to do: *Should I bite my tongue or dig my fingernails into my palms?*

No. You do not need to create sensation. Just as you are now, feel what is pleasant and unpleasant.

I couldn't get it.

One day, Saljay Rinpoche began the lesson by telling me: *I have some good news. Tomorrow, classes are canceled. We have time off and can go on an outing. What should we do?*

Time off! I loved picnics and suggested a particularly beautiful area called Manali, to the north of Sherab Ling, at the base of the Himalayas. It reminded me of my hometown in Nubri, a district in northern Nepal just south of the Nepal-Tibet border. Sal-jay Rinpoche thought this was a grand idea.

Are you happy? Saljay Rinpoche asked.

Yes! I exclaimed.

How does it feel, in your body?

Wonderful, I told him. *My heart feels open and happy and this feeling is radiating like the sun and spreading into my limbs.*

That is pleasant sensation, explained Saljay Rinpoche.

Wow! I'd finally gotten it. More joy! More pleasant sensation!

Both a picnic and chocolate are mental images; but in my particular case, one made a stronger impact on my body. I ate chocolate only occasionally, but it was not a rarity, not like a day off from classes with a picnic included. Actually, there is always sensation in the body in response to attraction and aversion—even when it occurs at a level that is too subtle for us to detect. For example, flowers generally create positive sensations. They are objects of beauty and appreciation, used to celebrate weddings and honor the dead. Birthdays are observed with flowers, and we bring them to sick friends to cheer them up. Flowers are life enhancing and uplifting, and flower offerings communicate love, care, and devotion. By the time we reach adulthood, these associations dominate our relationship to flowers; and when this happens we stop noticing the presence of sensory response. The mind becomes so caught in its own circular history with flowers that it pays no attention to the body. And yet when we pay close attention to the body, we find that sensation is always present, no matter how subtly.

When I started working with sensations, I needed exaggerated triggers. For example, after Saljay Rinpoche had created a decidedly pleasant sensation, he then said, *Actually, we cannot go. I was just kidding.*

My lower lip stuck out in a pout and I suddenly felt heavy and sad.

Tell me now, said Saljay Rinpoche, *what is the sensation in your body?*

My heart feels closed and tight. My jaw is clenched, and this unpleasant sensation of tightness is spreading throughout my body.

I started laughing. I finally knew sensation without thinking.

Sitting on the train floor, I could see that I needed to reexamine this lesson, for I had *imagined* this train ride but I had not *felt* it . . . until now. I had conjured the outside world, but I had excluded sensation; yet the parallel universes of body, mind, and outside phenomena are always interdependent. Sensation is the link between the object and the mind; and part of mind training is becoming aware of the subtler sensations—connecting the mind with them, and seeing how they influence us. Then we can get some distance on our reactivity, and this leads to liberation. Without this awareness, we can get completely lost in the outer world.

Do not run away from these unpleasant feelings. Do not manipulate them into pleasant feelings. Stay with what is, with whatever arises. I was trying . . . but the newness of everything all at once, and especially the shock of being alone, kept knocking me back. *Pretend you are an old man watching children play,* I suggested to myself. *Just watch, delighted, even though you know the obstacles, the heartbreaks, the sorrows, the jolts. You know these things. Now is your time to stand at the edge and watch the water flow by. Just watch, without getting caught in the current.*

3

·

Born
with a
Silver Spoon

To use an expression I learned in the West, I was *born with a silver spoon in my mouth*—by Nepali standards. I had struggled with personal issues when I was young, including severe panic attacks; yet the difficulties faced by most people had never touched my life. It wasn't just extreme deprivation, to the degree that appeared to beset my fellow travelers; I didn't even know about things like purchasing a train ticket or standing in line. Ordering the taxi and paying the driver were novel experiences. I tried to observe how others were buying their small, disposable cups of chai, in case I wished to buy one for myself.

Adding wood to the fire would yank the spoon out of my mouth, even though at this moment, as I sat rigid and upright in the midst of this bad dream, every cell in me seemed to protest my surroundings. With each stop passengers got off, and more got on. Not one among them had shown a nod of respect for the Buddha's robes.

As the train jerked from side to side, people making their way down the aisle to use the toilets could not help stepping on or falling against those of us sitting on the floor. Each time this happened I recoiled. *Perhaps it was more conceit than aspiration that had prompted this venture. After all, I had spent my entire life in one gated community after another. What arrogance to think I could immediately play in the waves of this midnight adventure.*

The unusually protective environment I was raised in did not feature the gilded palatial residences and luxurious comforts of a god realm, but it offered some of the same isolation and protections. When I was little, I divided the year between my grandparents' simple home in Nubri and my father's modest nunnery. Within these unpretentious circumstances, I enjoyed plenty of food, warm clothing, and abundant security and love. *Realm* is a term that we use in my tradition to describe negative emotions. In the god realm, the dominant emotions are pride and an excessive desire for pleasure and comfort, which can be expressed in many different ways. For example, those who live in the god realm—or who wish to—are often lulled by fantasy and seduced by ease. The form of this realm might be a penthouse, a social media preoccupation, or a slothful outlook. Whatever the form is, when we fall prey to the indulgences of a god realm mindset, we lose the impulse to search for meaning, and this leaves us with self-satisfied ignorance.

My monastic training was designed to counter the afflictions that characterize this realm. The monasteries that I grew up in were pretty spare, with none of the conveniences associated with the modern world—no hot water, no heat, a limited diet. Although this life was far removed from the world of pleasure and comfort, it also separated me from the kinds of problems that many people face. I knew nothing of hunger, or caste prejudices, or racism; I had not lived through war or reigns of terror. I knew none of the challenges faced by so many people in today's world, such as leaving home for school or employment. I had never had to find a place to live, or concern myself with paying the bills or buying a car. Many people work while raising children, and often live great distances from their families. I never had those responsibilities. Some of my friends are divorced parents who live apart from their children, and this alone creates stress and sadness.

Others have struggled through alcohol and drug addiction, or encountered financial setbacks or family disharmony—all common trials of modern life that I only know about through people I have met on my teaching tours around the world. Everything had always been taken care of for me due to my role and status.

As a child, I was small and shy, and my nature was compliant and respectful. I wanted to be robust like my extroverted brother Tsoknyi Rinpoche, but compared with him I looked puny and a bit pathetic. My size and demeanor must have suggested that I could not have survived without extra precautionary measures, for I always had more protection than I needed. One time my mother, an attendant-monk, and I left Samagoan—our village in Nubri—to take a long bus ride to Gorkha, the administrative city in our district. I needed a stamp from the passport office for an upcoming trip to Tibet. My mother knew an official in the office and hoped that going in person would speed up the process. When we reached Gorkha, she deposited me at a restaurant, ordered my meal, and told me to stay put until she and the attendant-monk returned. Half an hour later, the monk came back to make sure that I had received my meal. He explained that my mother was meeting with the officials and that he needed to go back to her, and that I should wait in the restaurant. After a while, I got bored and wandered out into the street. Then I went into the administrative building and found my mother. She was alarmed to see me. *What happened! Why are you walking alone?* Then she berated the attendant-monk. *Why did you let Rinpoche walk alone?* But the thing is, I was not seven years old. I was seventeen.

To break the mold of my conditioning, I had needed to do something a little extreme. In order to break through our conditioning and confront old habits, we might deliberately reverse a common pattern, at least for a limited time: If we habitually pick up a cup with our right hand, we commit to using our left hand; or we vow not to check our media devices more than once an hour; or for one week we promise never to exceed the speed limit when driving. I do not drive, but I have been told that this can be quite difficult. Anything that interferes with mindless repetition can function as a wake-up call, and an antidote to automatic, mindless behavior and habitual fixations. To encourage curiosity and flexibility, it's important to discover our limits, and then stretch a bit further. In terms of lifestyle, a wandering retreat for me was a very big stretch, no doubt about it. But because I had gained a degree of confidence in working with my mind, and had overcome the severe panic attacks of my childhood, I had left Tergar with confidence in my capacity to overcome obstacles. That's how I'd ended up on this train, all alone, in the middle of the night.

Naropa must have left his monastery with confidence. I feel sure of it. I wonder if he started out with any money. The remains of Nalanda University are now a pilgrimage site near Rajgir, in the state of Bihar, only a few hours by car from Bodh Gaya. I have been there many times. This train route would pass close by. At the time of his departure, Naropa was a renowned scholar. *I wonder if he took classic texts with him. I wonder if being alone was difficult for him. I wonder where he spent his first nights . . .*

The people surrounding me would probably have preferred first class. But I was here by choice. Some people choose to be homeless, but often they are quite disturbed, maybe crazy, and not welcome anywhere. This was not my story. Some people disrupt their lives because of depression, or they have a midlife crisis. My life had been exceptionally wonderful. Practicing meditation, exploring the nature of suffering and liberation, and teaching what I had learned from my lineage and my experiences were my passions. There was nothing else I wanted to do—except to learn how to go deeper with what I was doing. This wandering retreat was about deliberately making trouble for myself—and perhaps I had underestimated how much trouble I would encounter so quickly.

Though I was aware of the many safety nets that had buttressed every aspect of my life, I had not always been ready to demolish them. I had devised this retreat convinced that their enormous value had been used up, and that the time had come to know the world without them. I was also not immune to the appeal of social standing, and enjoyed my role within the community. As much as I had idealized an anonymous life, to be suddenly ignored by everyone around me was disorienting.

Well, I thought, *this won't last forever. This retreat is a precious interlude between monastic responsibilities. I am not doing what Naropa did. He never intended to return to his monastery. I have never considered staying away forever. I will return and re-inhabit my roles. I will return to my responsibilities, and to my rank.* In addition to my father's status, my mother's father, Lama Tashi, was himself a great meditator who traced his heritage to King Trisong Detsen. In the eighth century, this king used his royal authority to establish Buddhism in Tibet. Being the youngest child in this prominent family bestowed numerous privileges. Then I was recognized as a tulku—a reincarnated lama—which conferred even more status onto my already entitled condition. From then on, I was pampered and indulged, and grew up as protected as a hothouse orchid.

I once visited a European country where friends showed me a documentary about their royal family. Their princess was never allowed to walk down the street by herself, and I thought, *Just like me.*

I too am royalty, a pedigreed dharma prince. Whatever possessed me to spend my first night in the world alone, imprisoned in a sweltering train? I can get off and buy a new ticket for first class . . . Well, that's a silly thought . . . I need to figure out how to deal with the discomfort.

According to custom, once a child is recognized as a tulku, he is watched over like a baby bird, closely observed even when the mother flies away. During the months of the year that I spent in Nubri, I would sneak out of the house to explore the nearby caves, or to play with other kids. Somehow, my grandmother always knew where to find me. I had never cooked a meal or cleaned my rooms or washed my clothes. The education of a tulku concentrated on enhancing the potential for spiritual awakening—an intensely focused training of the mind. If I had to do it all over again, I would choose no other path, for in just the past few hours I had felt rescued by my training more than once, even though that same training had ensured the practical life skills of a lapdog.

4

•

Impermanence
and Death

I'D HEARD ABOUT impermanence and death long before entering the monastery at the age of eleven. Traditional Tibetan culture was so closely merged with Buddhist values that the attempt to introduce children to reality started early, especially if one grew up, as I did, within a dharma household. Say you are crying because your brother hit you, or your friend took away your toy. You might be told, *Chiwa mitakpa! Impermanence and death! Don't be such an idiot. If you don't think about impermanence and death, your life will never amount to anything!* This might be comparable to a Western parent saying to a child: *Don't cry over spilled milk.* However, in Tibet, the recognition of impermanence and death was used as the measure of what was truly important.

One day I saw a red bicycle in the marketplace in Kathmandu. My eyes fastened on it and it parked itself inside my head. *Chiwa mitakpa*, my father told me. *That toy will fall apart; it will die. To fasten so tightly to an object that has no lasting quality is like trying to hold air in your hands. This cannot bring you real happiness.*

I understood that the toy might die, but that had nothing to do with me. I also wanted to grow big and strong like my older brothers, but growing up had nothing to do with growing old. Not only would this body of mine never die, but I was sure that my idea of *me* would not change. I would simply acquire grown-up attributes as *Mingyur Rinpoche.* I held to the assumption that individuated personhood was a process of solidification; like wet clay, my size and shape would change but that would not influence the *essential* me, the *real* me, even though I had no idea who that was. Nor would I ever know who that was—not in the terms I had assumed. Even after our cars die and our computers crash, and we have cared for dying pets and family members, we cannot bear to apply the certainty of impermanence to ourselves.

Let go of the toy. Don't cling to it, my father had told me. *When we cling to things that do not last—whether it is toys, or favorite foods, or special friends or places—we are wasting our lives.*

I am not wasting my life, I imagined explaining to my father. *I am not clinging to the role of monk, tulku, teacher, or abbot— though they feel like they have a life force of their own, separate from my aspirations. But now I will be able to see them better. I already know their essential emptiness; I know that they are not lasting, not solid, and that they do not exist as independent entities. I did not know that with the bicycle.*

Emptiness refers to the fact that things are not as solid and real as they seem. Something that we hold in our hands might appear completely solid and unchanging, but that's an illusion. Whatever it may be, it is changing all the time, and when we investigate, we find change and fluidity where before we assumed permanence and solidity. This does not make the phenomenal world *nothing*; at the same time, its essential nature is not what we usually think it is. The sustained recognition of emptiness—of the knowing, luminous clarity that exists beyond concepts—is called the awakened or enlightened state. This state of mind transcends words and concepts. Because this state cannot be described by words and cannot be imagined by the conceptual mind, it lends itself to many different names and descriptions; it is a paradox that while our true essence is empty of conceptual thinking, we need concepts to express that very emptiness. Everyone has dimensions to their minds that are luminous, spacious, and empty. The issue is whether we recognize these aspects or not. Liberation arises only with recognition, not just from having these natural qualities.

The recognition of emptiness does not mean that we walk away from our roles in society, or live without worldly responsibilities. But we have a choice about where to place our awareness. With the wisdom generated by the recognition of emptiness, we can change our relationship to circumstances, even to those that cannot be changed. And although our dissatisfactions are inherently temporary, insubstantial, and essentially empty, that doesn't mean we can wave a magic wand to make cancer disappear, or restore a romance or a reputation, or earn a higher salary. To use emptiness in order to justify abandoning everyday responsibilities can be a big trap. Tibetans have an expression that my teacher Guru Vajradhara Tai Situ Rinpoche often repeats: *Keep the view as vast as space. Keep your actions as fine as flour.*

The quality of emptiness that we are referring to was never born; likewise, it cannot die. This essential nature of our lives is unborn—like space itself. Space provides no place to abide, no foothold in which to secure our steps. In skylike emptiness, we cannot be stuck. Yet here we are, alive in this wondrous world of appearances, which can always benefit from wise discernment. With particularity as fine as flour, we discriminate between actions that intend to relieve suffering for ourselves and others and those that intend to cause harm.

Even though I was wearing the unadorned robes of a Buddhist monk, I now saw that I was probably the best-dressed person in the railcar. My rubber sandals made me one of the few passengers wearing footwear. I thought about my lay students and wondered how they might deal with this situation. But I suspected they mostly traveled in the intermediate class, not the very least expensive.

I lowered my gaze, straightened my back, and asked: *What am*

I feeling right now? My entire body felt racked by tension. I engaged in a body scan, an exercise that I often do at night once I lie down to sleep. I brought my attention to the top of my head and worked down very slowly, lingering to loosen specific knots. I spent time on my forehead, and the area immediately above my eyes, and especially the edges of the brows closest to each other. They had felt so pinched, as if held together by a safety pin. Then I moved to my nostrils, where I kept the attention until they relaxed from flaring out. The area where the jaw connects to the head always required some time. I moved the jaw up and down to release that resistant knot, then explored the midpoint between slack and clamped, which at the same time unclenched the teeth. The shoulders were another area of frequent tension that always took time. And then I traveled down to the feet. I could not feel tension in my feet but spent some time with them as a way of bringing the energy down from my head. I spent about ten minutes going from top to bottom. Then I just rested for several more minutes, feeling less agitated than I had for hours.

The exercise had the effect of pulling my sensory receptors back in. My ears and eyes remained alert but stopped roaming like cellphone locators. I dozed off for a few minutes—until I was jerked awake by a yowl that sliced the night like lightning. In the split second that it took for me to recognize that this was the train's own whistle, I had already been trapped by an angry mob or attacked in a terrorist explosion. The sound was not *just* sound. It was a gunshot or a bomb that announced harm and destruction. I could hear my projections, but I could not hear the sound itself. Ironically, though the sound was so loud that it felt all-consuming, it had not stopped my interpretive mind. I thought about the deep, resonant blasts made by the eight-foot-long brass horns used in Tibetan rituals—sounds more akin to foghorns than instruments of classical melody, and which seem to reverberate from the bottom of volcanoes. During rituals at the monastery, I would sometimes grow bored and restless and start to daydream. Then suddenly a blast of the horns would completely cut through the muttering mind. The sound would invade my mind and body with such explosive impact that for a few seconds, I had no mind and body, and would become the sound itself. *Why didn't that happen with the train whistle?*

Wait a second . . . I need to recollect more accurately, for it did not always happen this way, especially when I was little. Sometimes during rituals that used many instruments, I would start to panic. My throat would begin to close, and I would have to run out of the shrine room. Was this like those times, when my body refused entry to the sound, and the fixed mind held fast to fear?

The five senses always report neutral information. To the ear, sound is always *just* sound, nothing more. Like and dislike are shaped by the interpretive mind that remembers, adds, modifies, and spins: The interpretive mind creates entire fictions around *just* sound, *just* sight. The voice that provides this running commentary is the monkey mind. It chatters away, jumping from one sense object to the next, overly active and quite excitable.

I have a student who once rented a cabin for a week on the coast of Oregon. Every morning he woke up and lay in bed listening to the sounds of waves coming ashore and rolling back to sea. Swoosh, swoosh, again and again. He told me he had never heard a more soothing sound, and that the sound itself made him feel embraced by a universal love. On his last day, he packed his car and headed to the highway, planning to spend a night on the road. Sometime after dark, he followed signs to a motel. He checked in, exhausted, and fell asleep. In the morning, he could not believe his good luck to wake one more time to the soothing rhythmic swoosh of waves. When he got out of bed and went to the window, he saw a highway with six lanes of rush-hour traffic.

Misidentifications of sense perceptions happen all the time and make the body the best laboratory for learning about our minds. What had just happened on the train? My ear had detected a sound, not a good sound or a bad sound, just sound, just contact between the sense organ and the object. Then what? My mind had gotten swept up in a negative story to such an extent that I had forgotten that the words, images, and impressions that created the story were not true to any reality other than what was in my head. My student's mind had gotten swept up in a positive story, but in both cases, getting hooked by a story means that we have lost touch with awareness. Both associations obscured the simplicity of *just* sound. This is why we say: *The body is the home of the grasping mind.*

Misunderstandings about the source of sensation occur because the perception and the interpretation arise almost simultaneously, so close together that the strong but incorrect impression is created that the interpretive reality—good–bad, attractive–aversive—is lodged within the object itself and not in the mind. It can be very difficult to accept that the source of what we like or do not like arises in our mind. When we get our heads stuck in the clouds—pretty clouds, ugly clouds—we cannot see that they are impermanent, that they have a life of their own, and that they will pass on, if we let them. When we relate to the world with a mind full of preconceptions, we erect a barrier between us and reality *as-it-is*.

Holding misconceptions in place with a rigid mind is the same as grasping. We grasp on to what we know, or to what fits with our limited experience, and this distorts direct, immediate perception. When we feel threatened by change, we try to hold things in place—which is another way of describing the aspect of self that refuses to let old patterns die. But if we cannot consciously allow patterns to die, then we cannot take advantage of the energizing benefits of regeneration.

Impermanence—like emptiness—is an inherent characteristic of phenomena. Recognizing impermanence corrects misperceptions of permanence; but recognizing emptiness directly is even more helpful for working with attachment. Recognizing the fluidity of all forms disempowers the false claims of the fixed mind. In turn, this expands our sense of who we are and what we can do. It can be very liberating to know that our stories about train whistles, or our anxieties about our relationships or reputations, are not inherently rooted within us, and to know that we have an innate capacity for transformation. But understanding impermanence as the outer layer of death can be even more effective for cutting through our irrational mental habits. For transformation to occur at the deepest levels, we do not just acknowledge the continuity of change; we recognize that the process of dying and regeneration underlies the truth of impermanence. This is the greatest encouragement for our liberation. Yet our dread of physical death makes us resist the very idea of dying every day. We confuse the renewable deaths of our mental states with the ultimate death of our bodies. When we do this, every form of death and dying looms on the horizon as an inevitable nightmare, something that we spend our lives wishing will not happen. Actually, with some investigation, we can learn that what we dread as a future event is happening all the time.

A conversation that took place between two American women describes this intimate relationship between physical and immaterial forms of dying. One of these women came to see me soon after her only child, a twenty-year-old son, died from an accidental drug overdose. We spoke of ways to help her live with this tragic loss. About two years later, this woman's best friend found herself struggling through a very painful divorce. The first woman explained to her friend: *My son is never coming back. I entertain no fantasies about this. My relationship to myself and to how I relate to the world has changed forever. But the same is true for you. Your sense of who you are, of who is there for you and who you will travel through life with, has also changed forever. You too need to grieve a death. You are thinking that you have to come to terms with this intolerable situation outside of yourself. But just as I had to allow myself to die after my son's death, you must die to a marriage that you once had. We grieve for the passing of what we had, but also for ourselves, for our own deaths.* The profound misfortune of the death of this woman's son opened her heart to an exploration of impermanence and death that went far beyond her own personal story. She could push the boundaries because, as she explained, *After I lost my son, I had nothing left to fear.* She turned her heartbreak into wisdom.

We can learn from her without needing to relive her tragedy. The death of the small self cannot be accomplished in a lasting or effective way if we deny or circumvent the fear of physical death; yet working with small deaths can loosen the intense anxieties that surround physical death. There is a natural path between impermanence and death, and if we remain unwilling to follow it through, then we short-circuit the remarkable benefits of continuous dying. To approach the finality of our bodies while paying no attention to the mini-deaths of daily life is like confusing diamonds with pebbles and throwing them away. Nothing endures but change, and accepting this has the potential to transform the dread of dying into joyful living.

I was dying now, on this train, having started this journey. I was dying to my old life. I was doing what I had planned to do. I had taken the taxi to Gaya and bought a ticket on my own for Varanasi. Now the challenge was to let go of the resistance to the very changes I had arranged for, and to accept that the sounds and smells of this train could be as much an occasion for joyful living as any other circumstance that I had ever known.

5

.

Letting
Wisdom
Arise

ONCE WE MOVE from the belief that things are unchanging to the experience that everything is transitory, the tension between our expectations and reality as-it-is begins to dissolve; then we can know that the disturbance of this moment will pass, and that if we stay with recognition of awareness, the problem will transform on its own. It doesn't need any help from us in order to move on. The inherent nature of *everything* is change. It's our preoccupation with a problem that nails it in place. Yet leaving it be is easier said than done. We are not familiar with abiding in the nonconceptual aspects of our minds, and staying with our direct experience. We are so used to identifying with our ideas of who we are, and merging our identities with people and places, and with objects such as our cars and houses, that the experience of the natural mind liberated from all this familiar matter can be frightening. It can be misinterpreted as nothingness, as a kind of annihilation; and if we do not recognize this as our basic home, then we scramble to get away as quickly as possible and seek somewhere to land—which means we seek some familiar identity to reemerge with. What can be most helpful here is to lightly rest the mind on the qualities of awareness. Emptiness and spacious awareness have qualities of cognizance, or knowingness. This is not nothingness. In the same way that the breath can support awareness practice, qualities of spacious awareness can themselves support resting the mind in nonconceptual states.

Because of my interest in knowing more about how my students manage their lives amid irregular schedules, traffic jams, student loans, crying children, housekeeping, and so forth, I again returned to wondering what kind of practice they might apply to my current situation. I decided that the most reliable exercise for steadying the mind in the midst of circumstances that were being experienced as aversive was probably a simple awareness meditation. The idea is to gather the distracted mind by placing it lightly on one sense object. Because I had been agitated by sounds, I chose sound as the object. This awareness practice uses sound as support for meditation: The object *supports* our recognition of awareness but does not remain the focus of it.

For about one minute I took stock of all the different sounds around me. Then I selected the most dominant: the grinding chug of the train's wheels. I directed my mind to lightly rest on this sound.

Be with the sound.

No commentary.

Befriend this sound.

Let the thoughts, the fears, the stress drain out into this sound.

Use just this sound to gather the mind.

If thoughts come, that's okay. Just let them go. They are clouds passing through. Return to the object.

Rest.

After about five minutes, I withdrew my mind from the object—the chugging sound—and allowed my awareness to remain open, to let my mind acknowledge various sounds—the wheels, coughing, talking—but alighting on none of them. We call this open awareness, or shamata without object.

Let it be.

Whatever arises, let it be.

Stay with awareness. Notice the sound arising within the recognition of awareness.

Do not go toward it. Do not withdraw from it.

Do not pick and choose.

Stay aware.

Rest.

Soon enough, sounds that had been disturbing became soothing. After about twenty minutes, I was able to get some distance between myself and my unease. My expanded sense of self grew bigger than the problem. It was able to accommodate the negative reaction to sound within a larger sphere, so that I was no longer the exact size and shape of my discomfort. The unease was still there. It didn't disappear, but I was no longer trapped inside it.

Awareness is the essence of our existence. It is within our reach all the time, and yet most of us do not recognize that. A Tibetan legend tells of a poor family who lived in a mud hovel with a small firepit in the center, and a smoke hole through the thatched roof. Twigs and grasses were set in the gap among three flat rocks, which were placed just far enough apart for one small pot to rest on top. One day a treasure hunter came to the village and went from door to door looking for bargains. The woman laughed when he showed up, explaining, *We are the poorest family and have nothing that would interest you.* Suddenly the man sprang from the doorway to the firepit, his eyes wide with surprise. He examined the rocks and told her, *Can't you see? These rocks are laced with diamond crystals! I will sell them for you and you will be the richest people in the district.* He left with the precious gems, and several months later he returned with enough gold coins to turn the paupers into wealthy landowners. They had been rich all along but had not known it. Our awareness is our greatest treasure and we already have it, but we do not know it.

. . .

I felt restored by having been able to use my mind constructively, but this did not last long. All my life I had engaged in awareness practices within meditation halls, on plane rides, in cars, during lectures and meetings. Yet the thought kept emerging that I had never known an atmosphere more disagreeable than this train. This was the monkey mind at work, trying to convince me that there was a problem with the sound, not with my mind.

Through the practice of shamata meditation, the tumultuous habits of mind calm down; and then we can investigate the characteristics of the calm waters beyond the monkey's control. This is called vipashyana—or insight—meditation. I knew monkey mind intimately. I also knew that when we dismiss any value to knowing this monkey, it's like owning a car without knowing how to drive. The less we know about the chattering, muttering voice in our heads that tells us what to do, what to believe, what to buy, which people we should love, and so forth, the more power we grant it to boss us around and convince us that whatever it says is true.

Despite the relief that I had enjoyed from sound meditation, intermittently sounds were again conditioned by fear, and I continued to hover between abiding calm, an uncontrolled monkey in my mind, and contemplations of sound. *Right here*, I thought, *right now, is where the suffering arises. Between the sound and the projection, between things as-they-are and things as-we-want-them-to-be. This is what the Buddha taught: To misperceive reality is to suffer.*

But why, I wondered, *is it so hard to get it right? On this train, I have experienced fear more acutely than I have known it for many years. And I have felt my body constrict around the resistance to being where I am. I know that the fear of letting go of familiar identities—of one's ego—is fear of freedom itself. And I am trying . . .*

My father used to tell me: *If you do not recognize the truth of impermanence, you cannot attain genuine realization. You must allow the illusion of ego to die. Only then can true wisdom arise. Only with the death of this ego can we know freedom.* This was, after all, why I was on this journey. But I had not anticipated so much newness all at once.

The term *ego*—or *ego-self*—is frequently used to describe the self-centered, fabricated outer layer of self, and we often speak of letting go of the ego, or dissolving it, or transcending it. I myself had thought of *adding wood to the fire* as an ego-suicide mission. However, the common usage of *ego,* both within Buddhist teachings and in the world at large, makes ego sound like an entity that has a shape and a size, and that can be extracted like a tooth. It doesn't work that way. Ego is not an object; it's more like a process that follows through on the proclivity for grasping, and for holding on to fixed ideas and identities. What we call ego is really an ever-changing perception, and although it is central to our narrative story, it is not a *thing.* It therefore cannot really die, and cannot be killed or transcended. This tendency for grasping arises when we misperceive the constant flow of our body and mind and mistake it for a solid, unchanging self. We do not need to get rid of the ego—this unchanging, solid, and unhealthy sense of self—because it never existed in the first place. The key point is that there is no ego to kill. It is the belief in an enduring, nonchanging self that dies. The term *ego* can still provide a useful reference; but we need to be careful not to set ourselves up for battling something that is not there. Ironically, when we go into combat with the ego, we strengthen the illusions of self, making our efforts to awaken counterproductive.

Because ego is frequently identified in negative terms, especially among Buddhists, my father made a point of reminding me that we also have a healthy ego—or a healthy sense of self. This relates to aspects of self that intuitively know right from wrong, that can discern between protection and harm, that instinctively know what is virtuous and wholesome. We trip ourselves up only when we become attached to these basic instincts and create inflated stories around them. For example, I had used ego in a positive way to explore, and then maintain, monastic discipline. But if I were to think, *Oh, I am such a pure monk, I maintain my vows so perfectly,* then I would be in trouble.

When I examined my difficulties with *too much newness all at once,* I could see ego-self as a process, not as a solid thing. I was not able to allow all my previous identities to die at once. I needed time. I needed to work through the layers. I accepted that the roles I wished to toss onto the pyre were fabricated, not inherent to my being. But they could not be extracted as if with a surgical procedure. I had grown into them, and I needed to grow out of them.

As the train rumbled through the night, I continued to feel oddly cut off from my fellow travelers, from myself, and from yesterday's life. I kind of understood what was happening but had never had such a visceral experience of it. I had wished to peel off the outer layers—but they do not peel back like adhesive tape. Neither do they remain passive in the process, but rather they fight to stay intact, as if saying: *If you do not respect the Buddha's robes, I will wear them more proudly. If you cannot acknowledge that I am a man apart, then I will isolate myself, even at the risk of more misery.* Oh, the treacherous monkey—what a happy time it was having. Its main job is to convince us that deep in the jumble of this glued-together fabrication lies the *real* me, the essential true self that cannot change, that must keep faith with its fiction, and with its neurotic habits.

I frequently returned, with mantra-like repetition, to critical reminders. *Mantra* means "to protect the mind," and this is just what I was trying to do, protect it from straying too far into fixed associations to fear. But this effort was foiled by my inability to truly transcend my own reaction to my circumstances, meaning that *I* was praying for *them*—those wretched others on the train. Again I descended into an ice-cold realm of constriction. I did not want these unblessed strangers with their torn clothes and matted, lice-crawling hair to fall against me every time the train lurched. *Yes, I aspire to be a happy yogi in all situations . . . but these crying babies . . . and the stench of the overflowing toilets . . . Who am I now? Who allowed these prickly eye, ear, smell, touch sensations to spin a web that is leaving me diminished, irritable, and alone?*

At one stop, I had been able to move from the floor to a wooden bench, and I now sat with my back pressed into the wooden slats of the seat. I knew that if I really wanted to become more flexible, I would have to drop down to a place beneath the separation of heart and mind. I sat up straight and lowered my gaze. For a few minutes, I just remained still and did my best to relax my body and mind.

First, I directed my mind to rest lightly on the breath and to follow it.

Then I brought my awareness to the sensation at the rim of the nostrils, where the air enters.

Awareness of the coolness of the air on entering.

Awareness of the warmness of the air on exhaling.

Awareness of the heart beating.

Awareness of the blood circulating.

Awareness of the belly expanding.

Contracting.

Awareness of the chest expanding.

Contracting.

After a few minutes, I added contemplative reflection. This means thinking with the heart more than the mind. I remained aware of sensations but added the dimension of change. *My body* is moving . . . changing . . . this breath is coming in and going out . . . changing. I am breathing in new air, changing, I am breathing out old air, changing.

I am part of this universe. This air is part of this universe. With each breath, the universe changes. With each inhale, the universe changes. With each exhale, the universe changes.

Each inhale fills my lungs. Each inhale brings oxygen to my blood. Changing. Body changing.

Each sensation is temporary. Each breath temporary, each rising and falling temporary. All changing, transforming.

With each exhale, the old me dies.

With each inhale, a new me is born.

Becoming, renewing, dying, rebirth, change.

As my body is changing, so are those of everyone I know. The bodies of my family and friends are changing.

The planet is changing.

The seasons are changing.

Political regimes are changing.

My monasteries are changing.

The whole universe is changing.

In. Out. Expansion, contraction.

I continued to maintain awareness of the movement and sensations and then added whatever came to mind: *This train is changing: Its parts are getting worn down every minute. Gaya station is slowly crumbling, that man across the aisle in the plaid shirt is aging, the baby held by the woman in the red sari is growing, the little monks at my monastery are learning new lessons.*

After about ten or fifteen minutes, I just rested with the sensations. After a few more minutes, I took my mind off the sensations and just rested with the awareness itself—the alive, sentient quality that registers sensations with a pristine clarity beyond concepts—and I remained like that for another ten or fifteen minutes.

The confusion that arises when we cling to our beliefs and

expectations obscures the innate clarity of our awakened minds; at the same time, this confused conceptual mind simply does not have the capacity to understand mind beyond concepts. We use language to describe awakening, awareness, emptiness, spacious luminosity, enlightenment, realization, and all sorts of other concepts that defy description. Words can point toward the way, and we can definitely experience our own inner wakefulness; but we cannot conceive of it, and every idea that we have about waking up remains far removed from experience. This becomes obvious once we begin to work with our minds.

Most beginners start with the idea that meditation is supposed to be peaceful. If they feel peaceful, they conclude that they are doing things right. Soon enough a disturbing thought or emotion erupts, and this is identified as a problem. We do not like disturbances. We start off with this dualistic preference. We want smooth ocean waters with no waves. When the waves come, we say we cannot meditate; or we assume that the presence of waves means we are not meditating correctly. But the waves keep coming anyway, always. It is how we perceive them that changes. We can relate to these waves as threatening monsters and try to push them away. We can apply certain mental techniques to subdue them; or we can pretend not to notice them or try to deny their presence. But there is no liberation in trying to get rid of the waves; and actually, if you examine the mind that is trying to get rid of the waves, you will discover that it's stuck on the problem. It is making a mountain out of a molehill. We can also tell ourselves intellectually, *These waves are essentially empty.* We can play with the ideas and concepts of emptiness and use intellectual logic to convince ourselves that the wave is not *really* a monster. But our hearts still *feel* the threat, and react to protect ourselves from it. This describes the first stage of working with the mind.

In the next stage, we are introduced to resting the mind in the spacious, nonconceptual aspect of mind that transcends the limited self. The waves might still be terrifying, but we begin to glimpse the boundless expanse of water beneath the surface, and this gives us more confidence to let them be. We do not yet see them as *just* waves, but our perspective has become so much bigger than the waves. Our personal stories of fear and loss, of rejection and self-recrimination are there—but they do not pervade every bit of space in our heads. Our fixed minds have loosened up a little; and once we recognize that our own version of reality exists within a vast impersonal experience of reality, these same stories do not disturb us as much. We might begin to think, *Oh, there's a wave forming on the surface of my mind.* Or, *There's a monster in my head. Okay, no problem.* We can acknowledge the problem without reacting to it. We see it, but we do not *feel* it as much as we did earlier. The understanding of emptiness is dropping from the intellectual head to the experiential, feeling heart. The ratio is shifting: The more we rest in recognition of the spacious empty mind, and the more we embody the wisdom of emptiness, the less impact the disturbances have. The wave is there, but now it is just a tiny movement in the vastness of the ocean. But at this point, we still get stuck on the surface with the waves, and lose touch with the ocean beneath.

In the third stage, the wave no longer appears as a problem. It's still a wave—big or small—but we don't get stuck in it. We have become comfortable resting within the ocean itself.

The ocean does not become calm and still. That is not the nature of ocean. But now we have become so familiar with the full expanse of the ocean that even the biggest waves no longer bother us. This is how we can now experience our thoughts and emotions—even those we have spent our lives trying to be free of. Every movement of the mind, and every emotional reaction, is still just a small wave on the vast surface of the awakened mind.

Although the mind is always free, it remains imprisoned in constraints of its own making. Concentrating on a sense object can protect the mind from feeling overpowered by the waves. For example, focusing the mind on a flower, or on watching the smoke from a stick of incense, can protect the mind from obsessing on marital discord, or on a business scheme. This type of focus may provide temporary relief. Still, it does not allow us to experience freedom. When we connect to our own awareness, then we can accommodate whatever arises: the big waves of loved ones dying and relationships ending, and the ripples of crashed computers and delayed flights. No wave stays the same shape; all crests fall. Let it be. Let it pass. Become bigger than the thought, bigger than the emotion. Everything is *always* in flux; by letting it be we simply allow for inherent movement. We can notice preference and desire, but chasing after them blocks the flow of change. Awareness contains impermanence, not the other way around. But they have this in common: Our liberation comes from recognition.

Let it be makes it possible to see that our true nature is free from problems, distress, and suffering—and that it always has been. When we stop trying to make the surface calm—and accept that the very nature of ocean is change—we begin to experience this inner freedom.

But this is not freedom *from* distress and anxiety. It is freedom that can be experienced *with* stress and anxiety. We are liberated from suffering by correctly perceiving reality; this means that we have the insight and experience to know that our minds are so much vaster than we generally think they are. We are not the size and shape of our worries. To recognize reality as-it-is makes recognition and liberation simultaneous. On the train, as many times as my mind got carried off by strong winds, I used the continuity of change to bring myself back to unconditioned perceptions. *Let it be*. If I had not totally trusted, through my own experiences and the teachings I had received, that change is constant and that we are never separated from the spacious skylike mind, my courage to continue might have faltered. Now more than ever, with no friends, no shelter, no attendant, no student, no teacher role, my mind was my only protection. And I had to trust that death leads to rebirth even when, in the process of dying, this trust can elude us.

Most of us have experienced regeneration through loss many times. A divorce that feels like death itself can lead to a happier, healthier relationship. The nightmare of getting fired ends up being the best thing that ever happened. A debilitating illness that is initially met with alarm and refusal transforms into new dimensions of compassion. But we tend not to trust that these seeds for rebirth exist within the change, within the loss, and within the death of circumstances. I continued to trust that the fires I had deliberately fueled would lead to positive transformations, but at this moment, I had no idea how that would happen.

On the train, I sometimes recalled conversations with students as a way to teach myself.

One day a young friend from Hong Kong came to see me. Not too long before, she had made a big career move, leaving the corporate world for a position in an international NGO. But she found that her old job had been more congenial. Staff roles and assignments had been better organized and her goals had been accomplished with greater efficiency. She had felt more productive in her old role, and could not stop comparing her new situation with the old one and finding fault with the job that she had.

It sounds like you are not giving the new job a chance, I said.

She agreed that she could not let go of what was most familiar.

I asked, *What about thinking of this time as a kind of grieving period. Something has died, and you are mourning the loss. You stay present to the feelings of this loss, and once you sense some resolution, then you can move on.*

She told me, *I understand the benefit of acknowledging change and impermanence, but to see these changes as a kind of dying feels like inviting death.*

I told her, *Yes, invite death. Serve tea and make friends with it. Then you won't have anything more to worry about.*

She laughed but promised to try.

I myself had invited death. Identity-death. Self-consciously, deliberately, I had wished to leave behind my old job and burn up external identities. But like the woman who had changed jobs, I was resisting my new situation. *What will I do in the bardo?*

6

·

What Will You Do
in the Bardo?

What will you do in the bardo? my father had asked.

One of my older brothers had moved down to the densely populated city area of Kathmandu, and after a few months he came to visit us at Nagi Gompa. My brother complained about the cars that honked and backfired, and the dogs that barked all night. He winced describing Hindi love songs blasting from transistor radios, and fake gurus who sermonized through loudspeakers.

I cannot meditate, I cannot maintain any mental composure. My sleep is fitful and I feel stressed all the time, he explained.

With genuine concern, my father had gently asked, *What will you do in the bardo?*

What I remember from this exchange is that the city sounded exciting and I could not wait to visit my brother there; and even though I had no idea what *bardo* meant, I intuited that my father was reproaching my big brother, and found their exchange very amusing.

In my tradition, we explore six stages of life and death transitions known as the bardos. Impermanence frames the entire cycle and is particularly prominent in the natural bardo of *this life,* the span from first to last breath. Until we accept the truth of impermanence, ignorance and confusion will darken our days. To provide a brief introduction: The bardo of this life includes the bardos of *sleep* and *meditation*. In these first three stages of the bardo map—this life, meditation, and sleep—the emphasis stays with becoming familiar with the mind during the day and during the night. During this lifetime, nothing takes greater advantage of our precious human existence than familiarizing ourselves with our own minds—and essentially meditation is the most effective tool with which to accomplish this. Following this life, we enter the fourth bardo—the bardo of *dying*, which begins with the irreversible decline of our bodies. The fifth bardo, called the bardo of *dharmata*, is a dreamlike passage that leads to the last bardo, the bardo of *becoming*. At the end of this sixth bardo, we take birth in a new form, and the bardo of this life begins again.

In colloquial usage, when my father asked, *What will you do in the bardo?* he was referring to the bardo of becoming, the stage between dying and rebirth—an intermediate period fraught with difficulties for those who have cultivated no mental equanimity in this lifetime. Yet as my brother's predicament suggested, *intermediate* also applies to a disturbed mind within this life. My brother was *in-between* a quiet rural life and a noisy urban experiment; he was in-between the old and familiar and the new and unknown; in-between past and present.

My father's question, addressed to each of us, is: *What will you do in the midst of frightening sounds? Or on a crowded, reeking train? Or in a terrorist attack, or in a war, or, or . . . in any one of life's countless unwanted events: a diagnosis of ill health, a flat tire, a perception of being slighted, or disrespected, or rejected? What will you do when you experience your life as being interrupted by undesired circumstances? Will you maintain a steady mind that can accommodate what you don't want, and actually be of benefit to yourself and others? Or will you implode through fear, anger, or loss of control? How do we act when we do not get what we want, or when we do not want what we have?*

• • •

I am in the bardo of becoming right now, between the death of the old me and the birth of whatever comes next. Becoming and becoming, always in the bardo of the unknown, the uncertain, the transient.

For conventional Tibetans, the bardos categorize stages from physical birth to rebirth. But many teachers, including my father and Saljay Rinpoche, transmitted bardo teachings as an inner journey of the mind, and this is now my own understanding. In the conventional version of the bardo of becoming, we enter a stage in-between the physical death of this body and rebirth into a new form; the mind loses its lifelong mooring and continues beyond the death of the body. But with a broader application, we don't need to wait until we physically die in order to know the bardo of becoming. Most of us have had plenty of experience with feeling sane and stable—and then sometimes we fall apart. We cannot hold it together; the patchwork unravels, and the ground beneath us drops out. We find ourselves in-between one state of mind and another. In extreme cases, we find ourselves in totally unfamiliar and frightening mental landscapes. These experiences of falling apart commonly occur with traumatic events that include shock and upheaval. Everyday occurrences of heartbreak and loss can be so wrenching and unexpected that they interrupt familiar ideas that we have about ourselves. This is the same kind of experience that might happen when we step into a hellish railway station the very first time we are alone in the world. The rupture knocks us off our feet, and we feel like we are falling or drowning, going down; we desperately strive to get back on firm ground, to feel safe and supported—even when we identify safety as a small isle of familiar mental territory that is habituated to misperception.

Bardo can be understood to mean "this very moment." The nowness of this moment is the continual suspension (or pause) in-between our transitory experiences, both temporal and spatial, such as the tiny halt that exists between this breath and the next; or the arising and fading of this thought and the next. The interval can also be experienced as the in-between of two objects: the gap between two trees or two cars—the space that provides definition; or we can understand this interval as the emptiness that allows us to see form. Actually, *everything* is in-between. However minuscule the interval might be, it always exists, and it is always bracketed. Everything in the whole world system exists in-between something else. From this perspective, the exclusive reference of *intermediate* to the state between death and rebirth emerges as the prototype for transitions that occur within this life cycle; the bardo stages then illuminate how these iconic death-to-life transitions emerge in everyday experience.

Without some understanding of the natural transitions, it's easy to get stuck. Many years ago, I read an article in a newspaper about a woman who filed for divorce after thirty years of marriage. Unlike the more common complaints of infidelity and abandonment, this woman explained to the judge, *He's not the man I married.*

What if, I now asked myself, we could enter relationships more like we enter a train? We know that the train will move, then stop, and move again, through changing landscapes and weather systems. What if we enter relationships knowing that the thrill of new romance, or the excitement of a new business partnership, or the initial encounter with a spiritual mentor will not be the same in the future as it is in the beginning? What if we expected new positive circumstances to change rather than wished they would stay the same? The train makes many stops. We do not try to prolong them, and we do not expect the train to stay in one place. It passes through places just as we pass through the bardos. The bardos show us that everything is always in transition. And whether *becoming* applies to transitions between mental identifications within this lifetime or over many lifetimes, the challenge remains the same: to liberate ourselves by letting go of grasping on to our self-constructed narratives.

Even though we cannot pinpoint the exact beginning or ending of anything, including the bardo stages, nonetheless the gathering together of things into categories can be helpful. Each bardo gathers together characteristics that are particular to each stage of our journey. The characteristics of the natural bardo of this life offer opportunities for waking up that are interdependent, although not the same, as the opportunities for waking up when we are dying. To become familiar with the characteristics that lend themselves to waking up in each stage means to recognize heightened opportunities for turning confusion into clarity.

With the help of the breathing exercises, the speed of the grasping mind slowed, allowing me to connect with the subtle level of constant change. Every instance that brings attention to change helps us stabilize the understanding of impermanence as the immutable condition of our lives. As a path toward liberation, intellectual acknowledgment of impermanence must become integrated with embodied experience; then we can gain more support for giving up grasping at those things we cannot hold, whether that means our own bodies or those of people we love, or our roles, or our prestige.

Even on the train I had known glimpses of naked awareness, free from waves; not entirely free, but mostly free. Glimpses of pristine awareness can be transformative, but it takes work to stabilize the view. This is why we say, *Short moments, many times.* Many, many times. Yes, I had learned something about impermanence, and I had definitely embodied the benefits of my training—but within familiar enclosures, with protection, and with safeguards.

7

•

Lessons
from Milarepa

GOING FORTH INTO the homeless life diverges from convention, yet I was following in the footsteps of Tibet's most cherished saint, Milarepa, as well as Tilopa and other adepts in my
own lineage. Throughout my years of wandering, these predecessors were my companions; and on the train to Varanasi they visited frequently, especially Milarepa, my boyhood hero.

Milarepa had wandered through a landscape that looked like
my own district of Nubri. My village sits at the base of Mount
Manaslu, the eighth-highest mountain in the world. I had shud-
dered at the possibility of eating fish guts like Tilopa did, but even
though Milarepa had turned green from a steady diet of nettles, I
still wanted to do what he had done—sleep under stars and feel
at home in the wild. Mila, as he's affectionately called, had so
many incarnations in one lifetime that his path intertwined compassion and violence, abundance and poverty, misery and mercy.
Nothing about my understanding or my adventures adds up to a
thimble compared with Milarepa's, yet the expanse of his life—
what we know from his beginning to his end—widened the gates
of possibility for me.

As a child, Mila sustained hardships that I would never know.
His father was a successful wool trader who died when Mila and
his younger sister were children. At that point an aunt and uncle,
taking advantage of a powerless widow, claimed the family's lands

and forced the rightful owners into bondage. Mila had to get down on his hands and knees to convert his back into a seat for his aunt, as if she were the empress of China; in the same position, he became a mounting block for his uncle to step on when climbing onto his horse. Mila's mother witnessed these humiliations, and when her son became a teenager she encouraged him to learn black magic from a local sorcerer. A year later, during a wedding party attended by the wicked aunt and uncle, a hailstorm conjured by Mila brought down the house, crushing thirty-five revelers.

At this point Mila had already been born into wealth, reborn into servitude, and reborn again into retribution. The destruction of their enemies made his mother jubilant, and she circled the village in a one-person parade to proclaim her victory. But Mila did not participate in these celebrations. He soon left the village, having been reborn yet again into the life of a seeker, determined to atone for causing so much suffering.

As kids, we learned from Milarepa that happiness does not depend on circumstances. His infinite contentment in freezing weather, with no food and no clothes, turned him into a god-being; but his human story made his life approachable—even if his summit remains unattainable. Despite this, and despite the extremes of Milarepa's story, death and rebirth characterize everyone's story. We are all transformed through love and loss, through relationships, work, kindness, and tragedy. But we get scared of change, because when we identify with a pattern of behavior, giving it up can feel like death itself. Often the inarticulate dread of distant physical death gets mixed up with a closer, daily, more pressing—though unacknowledged—fear of the disintegration of the self. On some level, we know that the labels that construct our identities are not real; and we may fear—perhaps more than physical death itself—that these labels might fall off, like a series of dissolving masks, exposing us in ways that we are not willing to risk. So much of the dread of physical death is about the death of the ego-self, the death of the masks. But if we know that there is a bigger reality in which we live, we can become less afraid of our own authenticity.

When Milarepa went in search of help, he had no idea where he was headed. But he had something that we might call *faith,* some trust in his own capacity to find his way. Confidence cannot mature without the acceptance of uncertainty—a lesson that I was just beginning to learn. When I first came to Sherab Ling, I was one of many novices who adored Milarepa and aspired to honor his life and his lineage but did not know the best way to do so. As I had written in the letter that I had left behind for my students:

> . . . during my first three-year retreat, I had the good fortune to study with a great master, Saljay Rinpoche [1910–91]. In the middle of the third year, I and a few of my fellow retreatants approached Rinpoche to ask his advice. We had derived tremendous benefit from the retreat and asked him how we could help uphold this precious lineage. "Practice!" he told us. Milarepa's early life was filled with misery and hardship. Despite all the bad karma he created as a young man, he eventually overcame his dark past and attained complete enlightenment while living in isolated caves deep in the mountains. Once he was enlightened, Milarepa thought that there was no longer any need for him to stay in the mountains. He made up his mind to go down to more populated areas where he could directly help alleviate the suffering of others. One night, not too long after he decided to depart, Milarepa had a dream about his teacher Marpa. In the dream, Marpa encouraged him to stay in retreat, telling him that through his example he would touch the lives of countless people.
>
> . . . Marpa's prophecy came to pass. Even though Milarepa spent most of his life living in remote caves, millions of people have been inspired by his example over the

centuries. By demonstrating the importance of practicing in retreat, he influenced the entire tradition of Tibetan Buddhism. Thousands and thousands of meditators have manifested the qualities of enlightenment because of his dedication.

Rinpoche responded, "I've been in retreat almost half my life. This is a genuine way to help others. If you want to preserve the lineage, transform your minds. You won't find the true lineage anywhere else."

It was still dark out, with no sign of dawn. More people were sleeping than talking. I could not have been on this train for more than five hours, but it felt like a lifetime. I had traveled through bizarre landscapes, inhabiting the hell realm one minute and in the next, yearning for protection like a creature in the realm of the hungry ghosts who never know satisfaction. Then a return to meditation, and to gathering my mind to just *be*—minus the distortions. Fear, despair, glimmers of courage, and open awareness. *My first night. I am learning that I cannot inhabit the wandering-yogi-mind overnight.*

I first learned about the six realms of existence on a visit to my oldest brother, Chökyi Nyima Rinpoche, at his monastery in the Boudhanath section of Kathmandu. I must have been six or seven years old. An elderly monk had been assigned to show me around the temple and we stopped before a large Wheel of Life painting, where he started to patiently explain the entire wheel, an intricate diagram of concentric circles. The most prominent band is divided, pie-like, into the six realms, each one characterized by a prominent affliction; and each affliction has the capacity to be transformed into wisdom. The entire wheel is held in the grip of Yama, Lord of Death.

The old monk, like many old-school disciplinarians—as I

would come to discover—concentrated on the scariest lower realms: the hells, and then the hungry ghost realm, which is inhabited by skinny stick figures with narrow elongated throats and bloated bellies. He droned on and I became restless. I did not want his teachings on samsara—the suffering and confusion of this life. Besides, my father, who in my estimation knew more about everything in the whole world than anyone else, had already explained to me that hell was a state of mind, not a location. He had insisted that horrific descriptions of the hot and the cold hells did not point to the next life, but to this one. Their real intention, he explained, was to awaken us to the self-imposed punishment that anger inflicts. When we act out of anger we punish others *and* ourselves. Our equanimity evaporates. Our hearts shut down. The capacity to give and receive love freezes on the spot. From our own disgust, we tell others, *Go to hell.* My father had also explained that within the wheel of suffering, our neurotic spinning contains the seeds of liberation; and that the human realm provides the best opportunity for waking up. That meant I could get enlightened in this life. I just wanted to learn meditation and get off the wheel, and the old monk wasn't telling me how to do that. I broke away and ran off to find my brother.

On the wheel, the six realms move from lesser to greater anguish, although we do not experience them in any particular order, and they are not to be taken too literally. For example, we do not have to be wealthy to know the characteristics of the god realm; but the traits of this realm often set one apart, and wealth can be used to keep one separate—or above—others. My own sense of separation was partially a result of my privileged upbringing, and of my role and rank within monastic enclosures. These are themselves a form of separation, although those very circumstances had pushed me into risking the uncertainties of anonymous wandering. Then in the Gaya station and on the train, the shock of being alone felt like a hell realm. When I first left Tergar and the taxi did not show up, I had entered the ignorance of the animal realm, not using reason; I returned to my animal-mind later, by reacting to sounds before investigating their origins or impact. In the hungry ghost realm of insatiable greed, the craving for protection was like a thirst in my heart. The demi-god realm manifests jealousy, as its inhabitants never stop wishing to be in the god realm. As a child, my jealousy had been directed toward those with more social freedom than I had, especially when I was a boy and longed to escape the watchful eyes of my caretakers. Yet on this ride, I had felt a bit bruised by being totally ignored; and my mind jumped right back into the god realm, for I could smell the stink of pride.

We know about the damaging power of negative emotions. We study the realms in order to learn about the fluidity of the mind. Anything—including Milarepa's life story—that demonstrates the constancy of change helps dismantle our attachments to fixity. No one realm had yet claimed me as a long-term resident; I was a traveler, just passing through, and I hoped I could settle into the human realm, where we know enough about suffering to want to bring an end to it, and we know enough about happiness to aspire to more of it.

The wheel signifies circularity, perpetuation, and suffering. Yet every moment provides a chance to wake up. Without becoming conscious of why we behave the way we do, the patterns that keep us spinning in samsara are reinforced by recurrent behavior. Our activities today tend to conform to our ideas of who we think we were yesterday; and this perpetuates the very behavior that limits our capacity for change, and transforms our tendencies into patterns that feel immutable. This is the nature of karma. Aspects of our past are carried forth into each new moment. At the same time, each new moment also provides a chance to relate to old patterns in new ways. If we do not take advantage of these opportunities, then there is nothing to interrupt the inherited karma of negative mind states. We inherently have free will, yet this only arises from an examined mind. Our future is influenced, but not determined or destined, by past conditioning. Until we learn how to examine our minds and direct our behavior, our karmic tendencies will compel habits to reseed themselves.

Modern people often talk about themselves in static mental postures, such as *I am an angry person,* or *I am essentially jealous,* or *basically greedy.* Highlighting the dominant trait of one realm strengthens karmic tendencies. By funneling our immense complexity into a reductive profile, we become tricked into thinking that we know ourselves, while missing most of what there is to know. This keeps us spinning in repetitive loops, and narrows our options for finding out who we are. These realms are considered *afflictive* precisely because our attachment to them narrows our experience. We all spend more time in some states than in others, but when we prioritize one in order to identify *the real me,* we diminish access to the never-ending variations that influence how and what we perceive; and this induces our habits to repeat themselves.

Realms can help us identify emotions in terms of movement, not as static aspects of our personalities. Instead of saying, *This is who I am,* we might reconsider and think, *This is how I sometimes feel.* Taking a step back creates some room to maneuver in. Anger, greed, and ignorance can ensnare us—like alluring tourist traps—but they're not lifelong residences. The term *realm* signifies something vast, even though it's no bigger or smaller than the perception we bring to it. In this way, *realm* can expand the thin bandwidth of *me.* For example, to know freedom from hell, we must allow aggression to die. If we inhabit anger as if it's the skin of our body, then allowing it to transform feels like death itself. Yet the attempts to protect ourselves from this death only perpetuate the very afflictions that keep us imprisoned.

It's the mind's habit to experience the transition between realms—or between breaths or thoughts—as uninterrupted. Yet with examination we can learn that there's always a gap, a moment of space in-between those things that we assume are continuous, just as for breaths and for thoughts. Even though we speak of continual *nowness,* some moments offer heightened opportunities to recognize the gap and experience a glimpse of emptiness. Let's say that we take an in-breath; every moment along the spectrum of breathing is another *now* moment. Yet the moment that is closest to the end of the inhalation—the moment that exists at the very edge of a pronounced transition—intensifies our sensitivity to change. Therefore this moment holds greater potential for accessing awareness of the gaps that are always there. On the train, I was in the middle of a big interruption—an obvious, intentional interruption of my patterns. I was on the edge, between the inhale and the exhale. I had not quite left, and had certainly not arrived.

The sun had come up; I could not detect when it had risen but only acknowledged that this had happened. *I am in the bardo of becoming,* I thought, *traversing different realms.* With the advent of morning, more chai vendors rushed into the cars at each stop and crowded around the windows. More plastic wrappers from small packages of snacks littered the floor. The train was late, as usual, but it would be pulling into the Varanasi station soon. *And I am in the bardo of dying, trying to let go of my old life and not yet born into my new one. At least I am not stuck. I am moving.*

8

Varanasi
Rail Station

I HAD THOUGHT TO use the Varanasi station to initiate my new life, to spend a few days here and sleep on the station floor. It definitely seemed like a starting point. Yet this journey had roots that reached all the way back to my childhood, though its precise origin was hard to pinpoint: youthful fantasies inspired by Milarepa; the moment I left my room the evening before; or when I slipped past the front gate; or entered the taxi; or stepped onto the train at Gaya. Each event was a beginning, each leading to another beginning.

The train arrived around midmorning. Just surviving the first night had left me feeling light and energetic. Although I had not slept for more than ten minutes the entire night, I was eager to see what the day would bring. For the first time since I'd gotten past the Tergar gate, the thrill of new possibilities returned and I savored the scent of freedom. But as I walked from the platform into a station five times the size of Gaya's, my manner became more confident than I felt, as if to disguise a creeping intuition that at any second I might become overwhelmed by too much newness, or faint, or flee like a spooked horse.

I could see my mounting distress; I watched the anticipation as if watching lightning approach from across a valley. I acknowledged the discomfort in my body. I greeted these sensations with curiosity about what might happen next. I felt like one of those life-sized plastic dolls shaped like snowmen that are weighted on the bottom. They can be knocked from side to side but cannot get knocked down. Despite my anxiety, I felt ready to continue my adventure.

I had an idea of what it would mean to make the world my home. I had always imagined that internal mental ease could extend to *any* context, whether my body was in an international five-star hotel or hanging around Brazilian slums or walking through Times Square. To be at home everywhere meant not getting hooked by sights, sounds, and smells that attract and repel. It meant letting go of the impulse to pick and choose, and allowing the objects I saw and smelled and heard to just be, without going toward them, without withdrawing from them; just staying with the clarity of the awareness and allowing all the phenomena around me, whatever they might be, to drift by like clouds.

I had wished to enter the Varanasi station with the ease that many people reserve for coming home after a hard day's work. I thought of people my own age who had spent the previous decade trying to figure out long-term plans for employment, relationships, and lifestyles; to find their groove and establish personal identities. The groove might increase into a protective trench that offered insulation from an impersonal and uncaring world. Say you come home from a grueling day, or a long commute. You walk through the door, so grateful to find shelter from an uncontrollable world.

You walk into an Indian train station on a hot June morning . . .

So many rats and pigeons. This will certainly be a different type of home from any I have known before. Most of my friends do not live with rats and pigeons. And still I wonder how many of them actually feel at home in their homes. Isn't that what drives them to meditation, and to talking to me? Didn't Saljay Rinpoche try to tell me this when I was eleven years old in India and missing my family

*in Nepal, when he explained that we are all homesick, all longing
for our true home?*

When it came to friends my age, midthirties, who live in the
world, I already knew something of their discouragement. Too
often the protective trench transforms into a rut, a hamster-wheel
with no exits. The achievements that once promised purpose and
satisfaction have not really lived up to their expectations. The office with a view has conferred status but not real confidence; the
bank account may have grown in value but is never enough. So
much effort goes into creating a landing pad, but the wheels of
desire and dissatisfaction keep spinning. On the heels of expectation, disappointment follows. And more often than not, this is
accompanied by recrimination. The blame might target a spouse
or a boss, a city or a president; then changing partners or jobs or
houses looks like the perfect way to regenerate a life that has gotten stuck. The difficulty here is that this benign-looking repetition keeps the longing for freedom just below the surface. And
the so-called normalcy of hamster-wheel activity keeps people
running away from themselves. Isolated, but too scared to be
alone. *Running in circles* describes the world of confusion.

My routines had not become boring or unfulfilling. But this
station definitely did not feel like my clean, safe rooms in my
monastery, and I could only pray that this journey would last long
enough to discover why not, to find out what held me back, what
made me uptight and uneasy.

Throughout the day we ask, *Where are my kids? Where are my
keys? Where is my phone?* We tend not to ask, *Where is my mind?*
If we can train ourselves to slow down and watch our thoughts—
not to get carried away by them, but just to notice—we will be
amazed by the universes that we traverse moment after moment.
Generally, we do not watch our minds and do not know much

about how they work; all the while, the range and mobility of our normal mental meandering challenge ideas that we have about being stuck, or being incapable of change.

Where was my mind as I ventured into the immensity of the Varanasi station? Definitely looking outward. I circled the unfamiliar station on high alert for threats. People walked quickly in every direction. Some businessmen in Western clothing carried briefcases; teenage girls in tight jeans and T-shirts and long straight hair walked arm in arm; parents struggled with their belongings and their children; some travelers pulled suitcases behind them, or ran after porters, and everyone had to navigate near-collisions.

My awareness did not stick with any particular object but moved as I checked out the districts of my new habitat: where the homeless were permitted to sleep; the swarming area just outside the station where the beggars squatted; the tiny greasy food stalls; the newsstands; the doorways to the exclusive lounges, the toilets, and the police posts; the ticket booths and the entryways to the tracks.

This walking tour of the station typified an intermediate state of mind. I had made it through the Tergar gate and gotten out of town. I had not slept in a public place, and I had not begged for food. I had left home, but had not yet become homeless. I had wished to give up robes but still looked like a Tibetan lama. As I circled, at a slow, deliberate pace, I assumed that some spot would emerge as a safe place to stop; and that once I arrived there, the waves of discomfort would die down.

I had felt this way too when I had gotten into the taxi, and when I had finally found a seat on the train—as if that spot, an arbitrary location, would soothe my sense of dislocation. It did not, but we often get caught in the illusion that arriving at a predetermined destination will end the mental agitation of feeling in-between. This happens when we do not know the continuity of awareness—or when we know but still lose the connection.

Within this life, I am in the bardo of change, transition, imper-manence. I did not die en route to Varanasi, and the outer forms that defined Mingyur Rinpoche did not disintegrate. Nor was I exactly the same person who had left Tergar. I had spent a night like none other, but that had not turned me into a ghost or a transparent body or any other form that might manifest after my body dies. Between Bodh Gaya and the Gaya station, I was in-between. Between Gaya and Varanasi, I was in-between. For the past twelve hours, my composure had been challenged repeatedly. Yet I had been sustained by trusting that states of mind were as transitory as life itself, as breath itself. From the moment I left Tergar, I was *in-between* in a literal way. Even on entering the train and getting a seat, I was in-between—as I was still, now, circling the station. Yet the true meaning of *in-between* has nothing to do with physical references but is about the anxiety of dislocation, of having left behind a mental zone of comfort, and not yet having arrived anywhere that restores that ease.

In the literal description of the bardos, *in-between* describes an insubstantial, nonmaterial state of being that is in the process of seeking to return to substance. It seeks to resolidify, and to once again become some-body. From within our material forms, we already know that generally the experience of ourselves as *no-thing* and *no-body* is simply unbearable. We humans actually cannot stand this possibility—unless we wake up and realize that this transient and fluid state is our true home.

Yet we are always in a state of not-knowing and of uncertainty. That's the nature of existence. As a daily life experience, the bardo of becoming expresses a heightened state of displacement, of falling apart, of not knowing what's happening. These are the underlying conditions of those times when we experience certainty and when we do not ever really change. The shift comes from our perceptions. When I entered the taxi in Bodh Gaya, the anxiety of dislocation subsided, though hurtling through the night at a speed that far surpassed the limit was hardly safe. When I was standing on the train platform, I anticipated that getting onto the train would diminish some anxiety. But the time spent flattened against the door by a human wall instead provoked more anxiety. I assumed that things would be better when I found a place to sit on the floor, but the continuous contact with strangers falling against me made me feel isolated and agitated. I thought it would be more comfortable when I found a place on the bench, but shortly after, I had panicked at the sound of the train whistle.

For the sake of social sanity and discourse, we speak of beginnings and endings. We start and end a train ride, a phone call, a day. We begin an exercise program and end a vacation or a relationship. We speak of the bardo of this life and the bardo of dying, followed by the dreamlike passage called the bardo of dharmata, and then the bardo of becoming, yet when we move past the convenience of language and categories, every second manifests the bardo of becoming. Becoming and becoming. All phenomena always just become. That's how reality works. When we sensitize ourselves to the subtle transitions of emotions, or of bodily change, or shifts in social circumstances, or environmental transformations such as differences in landscape and light, or developments in language, art, or politics—we see that it's all always changing, dying, and becoming.

I had thought that overnight I could become a sadhu, a wandering yogi, and drop all the outer roles at once; but I had not properly assessed the ways that these identities had become embedded in my body. I still had faith in the plan to add wood to the fire, and to know rebirth through burning up the grasping self's influence on the senses. Without faith in the capacity to regenerate, we cannot make the most of dying every day. As I considered where to sit down, I did not even hold the illusion of locating a safe space to reassemble myself. I would find a place to sit, but it would not be a refuge. I continued to circle the station, all the while telling myself—while noting the paradox—that the cycle of samsara is not predetermined and that we are not fated to unhappy repetition.

I reflected on friends who had undergone life-changing shifts without turning their worlds upside down. *But I haven't turned my world upside down either,* I reasoned. In an obvious way, I had intentionally upended my world; but in essence I was honing a process that I had been steeped in all my life. *Yes, I am adding wood to the fire, but this fire has been burning for many years. I am not changing direction. I would burn up the outer identities, yet in every important, inner way, this retreat is an extension, a deepening, of the same aspirations that have defined my entire life.*

One friend around my age had moved from job to job, sometimes quitting, sometimes getting fired. I had not seen him for a few years, and then, before I left on retreat, he'd come to visit. This time he was running a successful helicopter business. First, he'd taken lessons for his pilot's license. Then he'd rented a helicopter and hired himself out for chartered services. Now he owned four helicopters and had ten employees. I asked him what had accounted for his success after so many misadventures. He explained that he had always been too proud to risk failure. *Until I was willing to fail, really fall on my face, I couldn't do anything.*

Now, as I circled the Varanasi station, I asked if I was ready to fail, to really fall on my face. But other than returning to my monastery, I could not quite imagine what that would look like. I also thought of a woman who had been married to an alcoholic. After many awful years, her husband went into a 12-step program and became sober. She was so optimistic about their new lives together. Then a year later they split up. She explained, *As long as he was a drunk, I was always better than he was; once he got sober, I could not blame him for everything and feel superior.* Then she told me that they were still close, and had talked about getting back together.

What would it take for that to happen? I asked.

She told me, *I would have to accept that I am worthy of being loved by someone other than a drunk.*

I asked, *And now?*

She said, *I'm working on it.*

I had liked her answer, and now thought, *Me too. I'm working on it.* Working on seeing all the ways that I had been treated as special; and letting that be within awareness. *Don't push. Don't pull.* And seeing too the need for the kind of protection that had been provided by attendants and caretakers—though I was just beginning to discover how dependent on it I had become.

My disorientation did not diminish by learning the station layout. I looked at my watch. It was almost eleven. Soon the letter would be discovered. In it, I had written,

> . . . In my early years, I trained in a number of different ways. The time I spent with my father involved rigorous meditation training, but I was not in strict retreat, in the sense that I met other people and could come and go freely. My three-year retreat at Sherab Ling Monastery, on the other hand, was held in complete isolation. A small group of us lived in an enclosed compound and didn't have any contact with the outside world until the retreat ended. These are two forms of practice, but they are not the only ways. As demonstrated by the great yogi Milarepa, there is also a tradition of wandering from place to place, staying in remote caves and sacred sites with no plans or fixed agenda, just an unswerving commitment to the path of awakening. This is the type of retreat that I will be practicing over the coming years.

Within minutes of my absence being discovered, my brother Tsoknyi Rinpoche and my only living teacher, Tai Situ Rinpoche, would be informed. I pictured my grandfather, who was now ninety-three, learning about my disappearance and grinning with toothless approval. I was not worried about him, as I knew that he was not worried about me. His view, vast as the heavens, could accommodate anything. Word would spread; people would express concern. Where did he go? How will he eat? *Who will tell my mother?*

I sat down on the stone floor in the area designated for people to spend the days and nights. The beggars had to remain outside the station. Some of these people had no other place to go, but others were passing through Varanasi and spending a night or two here to make their rail connections. Indian Rail is so inexpensive that entire families can travel a thousand miles to funerals and weddings where food might be abundant.

I crossed my legs and sat with my back erect, my pack in my lap, my hands on my thighs—perfecting the image of the disciplined monk. Except that now I could allow myself to notice my attachment to this role. Within minutes I also noticed that I was becoming quite agitated again. The police looked at me suspiciously. People around me stared. My maroon robes attracted curiosity. When I had studied the beggars in Bodh Gaya I had thought, *I can do this!* I spent hours picturing myself holding out my alms bowl, not washing, sleeping on stone floors or in the forests. But the grip of social nakedness that I had first encountered at the Gaya station had escaped my projections.

I had concentrated on the absence of things such as food, clean and comfortable mattresses, soap, and hot showers. Naturally I had imagined these austerities within my tidy rooms, eating favorite foods and surrounded by people I love and who love me. What caught me off guard was a sense of embarrassment, of having no place to hide, of being stared at, of feeling devoured by my inhibitions. I had known my place among people, and they knew it as well. When I traveled, I did so as an emissary from a select social sphere, and I was treated accordingly. I had never completely outgrown the self-consciousness of my childhood. I did not always have a relaxed public demeanor or an easygoing social style; but the intense embarrassment that I was feeling now matched the wave that had pressed into me when I first entered the train the previous night. The alienation from myself transferred to alienation from others. Within minutes, I was no longer among the meek and the indigent but someone being stared at by lunatics. As I had walked around the station, I had seen people jumping into the tracks to pee and defecate.

I now initiated the same type of scan that I had undertaken on the train, as a way to relax my body—or I tried to, going from the top of the head to the soles of the feet. After about five minutes, the effort shifted to feeling the changes within my body.

I brought my awareness to my forehead.

Sitting quietly, I tried to feel any sensation there, perhaps heat, tingling, or vibration.

Subtle sensation always exists, but I was too stressed out to detect it.

After a minute or two, I brought my hand up to my head and kept the palm side about a quarter of an inch from my forehead, not touching. Then my palm could feel the heat that was coming from the inside, and some tingling.

I brought my hand down and returned my awareness to my forehead. I kept it there until I could feel a shift in sensation from heat to pressure to relaxation.

I stayed aware of this sensation, which always changes. *Let it go. Let it be. However pleasant, don't hold on to it.* I tried to rest in the experience of steady awareness.

Then, maintaining steady awareness, I moved my attention to the top of my head. The intention was to connect with any sensation. I felt tightness in my nerves, in my muscles, in my skin. My mind hovered above my head, twitching between past and future. I brought my mind back into my head. Into my body. *Try to feel the sensations.* If I could not feel the sensation, then I tried to stay with that: the awareness of no sensation.

Notice whether the sensation registers as pleasant, unpleasant, or neutral. Then rest.

I moved down to the face, the jaw muscles, the mouth, the lips. *Stay with whatever is happening,* I told myself, *and see if you can notice changes, both in the sensation and in your reaction.*

I wanted to reaffirm that every atom of body surface, every iota of skin, each pore is a sensory receptor that changes continuously.

I needed to reexperience the continuity of change, to remember that every moment holds a chance to transcend the fixed mind—the breeding ground for anxiety and stress. Between every breath, and every thought, gaps exist utterly free of conception and memory, but our mental habits obscure this information.

Because the scan allowed me to register change, it affirmed that I was not destined to this intense discomfort; but I could not relax and continued to sit with rigid, willful determination. Pride, that curse of the god realm, prevented me from moving just because rats scurried among the floor dwellers.

In retrospect, it's easy to understand why I attracted so much attention. I was too well groomed to fit in. My robes still looked pressed, my face and scalp were newly shaved, my nails were clipped, and my glasses hadn't yet broken. My presence must have looked like a middle-class experiment in slumming. In a way, it was. *A lot of my young students wander with backpacks, without much money. They have homes to return to . . . but so do I. I suppose most of them have spent time alone, on trains and planes and driving down highways. They surely have bought train tickets and take-out coffees and figured out travel schedules and ordered meals and eaten alone in restaurants.*

I got up to use the public toilets, and when I returned, a family had settled in nearby. For the first time, someone spoke to me. The man asked, *Are you from China?*

I told him, *I am from Nepal.*

His curiosity flagged. Indians are inquisitive with foreigners, but Nepal is not foreign enough, and Nepali people are not worth knowing. Still, he was friendly and wanted to talk.

He wore a ragged dhoti and a ribbed, sleeveless undershirt. He had a mustache, but the rest of his face was shaved. No one in the family had shoes. The woman wore a rumpled light cotton sari, faded orange, with the end wrapped loosely over her head. The children's hair looked tousled, as if it hadn't been washed for a while, and their clothes were ill fitting. Set out among their sacks was a large bag of rice and a small cooking stove. The man said that they had stopped here on the way from their village to the east, and were traveling to visit relatives farther south. They spent a lot of time on the lowest-fare trains, and the man knew the station quite well. He began sharing with me the best stalls for tea, and for peanuts and biscuits. I enjoyed speaking with him, but I soon turned my body at an angle, and he got the message to let me sit in silence.

9

Emptiness,
Not Nothingness

A n English friend once gave me a souvenir from a different kind of railway station, the London Underground. It was
a bright-red cap with gold lettering that read MIND THE GAP. This
is a warning to passengers to be aware of the space between the
platform and the train. Otherwise, you might step into that in-
between space and break a leg.

Mind the gap, I told myself, for a gap also exists between
realms, and between thoughts and emotions. However, unlike
the gap between the train platform and the train, this kind of gap
is subtle: hard to notice, and easy to miss. On one visit to Singa-
pore, I was taken to a fancy restaurant on the top of a six-floor
department store. As we rode up the escalator, I had a funny daydream about these gaps. I imagined getting lost in the basement
of a big department store. Bewildered and scared, I wandered
among generators and sizzling boilers, steam pipes, chattering
pistons, and loud hydraulic engines. No windows. No air. No nice
things to buy. No EXIT signs. In contrast with this hellish atmosphere, the highest floor, number six—where I was being taken to
lunch—had pink marble floors, glass walls, and terraces with
flowering plants. Twenty-four hours a day, seven days a week, the
escalators go from the basement hell realm to the abode of the
gods and back down again, reflecting the continual fluidity of
mental transitions.

Riding on the escalator, I saw that we cannot take the moving stairs in one continuous ride from bottom to top, or in reverse. For on each floor we must step off and then get back onto the next set of moving stairs. In other words, there's a gap. With training, it's possible to become aware of *the space in-between*—the space in-between our thoughts, our moods, our perceptions, and our breaths.

What makes this gap so precious? Let's say we are looking at a cloudy sky. Some clouds are lighter or darker than others; they move fast or slow, disperse and change shape and dissolve into one another. Then suddenly there's an opening, and for an instant we glimpse the sun. That opening in the clouds is the gap. The clouds represent all the normal content of the undisciplined mind, the endless muttering about our days, our meals, schedules, ailments, our past problems, our projections. Furthermore, these thoughts arise informed by our psychological history and social conditioning, and pass through our minds shaped by emotional tones of desire, greed, anger, jealousy, pride, and so forth. One cloud after another, moving into the mind, moving out of the mind, slowly or turbulently, creating surprises and instilling fears. We can get so caught up in the stories we tell ourselves that we do not even try to look behind the clouds. Or we might mistake this stream of moving thought-clouds for the natural mind that lies beneath it. But if we pay attention, we can recognize the gap, the fleeting space in-between thoughts.

A student once said, *I just want to turn the faucet off.* That describes the common experience of our monkey minds: a cascading rush of thoughts without interruption. But through awareness, we can detect that although the muttering appears to be incessant, there are gaps, in-between moments, empty spaces that offer experiential opportunities to recognize the uncluttered mind. In these gaps, we experience pure perception. No time, no direction, no judgment. The clouds of muttering and memory clear, and the sun shines forth.

The gap between thoughts—like the gap between breaths or moods—allows us to glimpse the naked mind, the mind that is not obscured by preconceptions and patterns of memory. It's that fresh glimmer that startles us into wakefulness, and reminds us that clouds are temporary surface concerns and that the sun shines whether we see it or not. Noticing the gap introduces us to the mind that does not reach out to grasp a story of loss or love, or a label of fame or disgrace, or a house or a person or a pet. It's the mind liberated from those misperceptions that keep us stuck in repetitive cycles.

Gap is another word for "bardo." Making a distinction between the bardo of this life and the bardo of dying offers an approach to studying stages of being; but actually, these stages have no sharp edges or boundaries, no ends and no beginnings. Everything is in flux. Everything is continually emerging, changing, transforming, coming forth, and fading out. If our mind doesn't get stuck in a particular realm, or attached to a limited set of identities, and can initiate and respond to movement, and appreciate transience, then we create an internal atmosphere that is conducive to recognizing the gaps.

The clarity that can be accessed through the gap is the natural, uncontrived wakefulness that was with me in the hell realms of the Gaya station and in the god realms of my former life. It existed even when I was disgusted by overflowing toilets, when I craved protection, and when I was frightened by a train whistle. This wakefulness is not dependent on circumstance. It exists now. Right now. It does not increase or decrease with acts of kindness or cruelty. What we call *the gap* refers to a fleeting moment of naked awareness, a split-second opening that introduces us to our original mind and provides a taste of freedom from confusion.

The resistance of the grasping self to give itself up can be pretty fierce. Its job is to remain in control. The ego of this abbot had known a busy night. Even when I had been able to cut through the misperceptions, they reconnected like a cut mochi cake—those glutinous Japanese rice cakes: You can slice them in half and watch them ooze back together. This is the tyranny of the grasping ego. But even a taste of freedom can turn us in a new direction.

Unless we have developed some understanding of the many different aspects of the mind, glimpses of emptiness are not necessarily of benefit and can sometimes create perplexity. People just do not know what to make of them. An American friend described a day at the beach when she was a teenager. Summertime, relaxing with friends; suddenly she "disappeared." *Everything was there—the friends, the beach, the water—and everything was shimmering and brilliant. I could see, I could hear, but I was not there.* This lasted for two minutes at most, and she offered that she had never taken hallucinogenic drugs. She did not say a word about it to her friends. The experience became an inexplicable shame shared with no one. She thought that maybe she had literally *lost her mind,* that this event might indicate insanity. The association between psychosis and this break/gap haunted her for years—until she started to practice meditation. Only then was she able to use this spontaneous experience to access deeper states of wakefulness.

This woman also told me that decades later, when she recalled this episode to friends who had also found their way to meditation, many of them reported similar moments of spontaneous glimpses, as well as the fear of revealing them. I only became aware of these histories through people who went on to practice meditation. Yet they point to the universal and inherent nature of our original, nonfabricated mind.

Over the next eight hours, the station floor seemed to swallow me up. My sitting bones, butt, and knees ached from being pressed into the marble. I had not thought to practice these last months without a sitting cushion. I had become quite tired and took notice of fatigue mixed with annoyance. The people around me felt so unfriendly. Finally, I opted for the railway dormitory hostel on the upper floor of the station.

I could have willfully pushed through with my plan to sleep on the station floor. Despite the obstacles, and even more so because of them, I still had a lot of enthusiasm for meeting the challenges. On the deepest level, I had known the recognition of awareness for many years now, and even when I lost the connection, I trusted in the wisdom of emptiness. Even though the waves had been stronger than I had anticipated, and even when they had kept me struggling for air, I never completely lost sight of the big spacious mind and was sustained by that. I never really doubted my capacity to stay with the recognition of awareness, or to return to it after some real breaks. This is what would have allowed me to sleep on the floor if I'd chosen to. But I made another choice. I did not wish to play superman. I was not out to prove any heroics. And I knew that willful pushing would entangle the fixed mind. It would take a lot of effort, and I would go to war with myself. It wasn't worth it. I decided, *If I cannot change overnight, that's okay.* I paid one hundred rupees (approximately $1.50) for a twelve-hour stay and was assigned to a room with about twenty metal-framed cots. The room did not look friendly or clean; it was quite hot and did not smell nice. But after the station floor, I fell onto my cot as if into the lap of the gods.

To acknowledge the discomfort and sleep in the dormitory was more in line with my intentions—to stoke the flames so that I could better see what was going on inside. I wanted to know everything that I could about this embarrassment—and not shut it down for the sake of looking comfortable sleeping on the station floor when I would not be. I knew that for an emotion to transform, it needed to become bigger than usual, clearer, more visible. In the exercises that I had been doing during the journey, there was always a witness; for example, *I*, over here, am working with this sound that is over there. The witnessing *I* never disappeared. There was always a watcher. Now, in the dormitory, I had to ask: Who is experiencing the embarrassment? Who was the "me" that the monk Nagasena points to in one of my favorite teaching tales from my childhood?

Lying on my cot, I drifted toward the story about a king and a monk. About 150 years after the historical Buddha died, a king named Menander encountered the venerated Buddhist monk Nagasena. The king did not know this monk, and asked for his name. The monk provided his name, but added, *This is only a name, a denotation, a matter of conventional usage. There is no individual person to be found here,* he explains to the king. *Nagasena is only a designation.*

Mingyur Rinpoche too is only a designation. I am not my name. Not my title. Not my robes. I meditate with the same aspiration that led to lying on this cot in the railway hostel: to dis-identify with the name, the titles, the robes; and to thereby connect with the unconditioned mind. Only with immeasurable mind can I be of immeasurable service to others.

King Menander then asked, *Who is wearing robes, who enjoys them, who meditates, who practices?*

The monk answered, *The designation Nagasena.*

Who is lying here in this railway dormitory?

The designation Mingyur Rinpoche.

Pushing him further, the king asked Nagasena: *Could it be that the hairs on your head are Nagasena?*

The monk said, *No.*

The king asked if his true identity might be found in other body parts, such as *nails, teeth, skin, flesh, sinews, bones, marrow, kidneys, heart, liver, membranes, spleen, lungs, intestines, stomach, excrement, bile, phlegm, pus, blood, sweat, fat, tears, saliva, mucus, or urine? Your brain, perhaps?*

I scanned my body, as I had when I was a child, looking for myself. *I am definitely not my nails, teeth, skin.*

The monk told the king that his identity could not be found in any of those body parts.

The king then asked if the monk was . . . *a feeling of pleasure or pain, a perception, an impulse, or a state of consciousness?*

It was easier to be sure that I was not a body part than to be sure that I was not a perception or a state of consciousness, for several times over the past day my feelings had overwhelmed my mental composure. I would bet my life that I was not my embarrassment, not my failure or my pride or my panic. Nonetheless these *things,* wherever they hid, were pricking my feelings.

The king then accused the monk of lying to him: *You said that you are Nagasena, when no such person exists.*

At this point the questioning reversed course. The monk now asked the king how he had arrived at this spot. The king reported that he had arrived by chariot.

The monk asked about the chariot, *Is it the axel, the wheels, the yoke, the reins?*

Was the train to Varanasi the wheels, the car, the turbine, the metal frame, the engine?

The king said that the chariot was not one of those particular parts.

Then the monk asked if there was a chariot separate from these things. The king answered, *No.*

Then Nagasena suggested that the king was also lying: *You say you arrived by chariot, but you cannot say what a chariot is.*

To this, the king said, *I am not lying, for it is because of these parts that a chariot exists as a name, a denotation, a conventional usage.*

Exactly, agreed the monk. *Because of my body, feeling, perception, and so forth, does Nagasena exist as a denotation, a conventional usage, a name. But ultimately there is no person at all to be found.*

I came to the end of the dialogue as I remembered it. *Okay, so I was not my meditation, not my roles, not my special status. Who will get off this cot? Who was so stressed out in the waiting area? Where do paranoia and embarrassment reside? How do they arise? If they cannot be located, or perceived with the senses, if the shapes of them—their size and weight—move like clouds, then they will pass through. Pass through where? My hands cannot hold them. Oh, this mind of mine. What problems it can cause!*

Empty minds, empty bodies, empty emotions, but not nothingness. The waves that surface in the form of emotions, desires, and aversions are also empty, and their force is also empty. Yet the empty force of the empty wave has the empty power to knock over a mind that is also essentially empty but does not know it, and is stuffed with ideas. But if we do not create a story around the wave, then we have empty water dissolving into the empty ocean, like water being poured into water. No problem. Emotions themselves are not the problem. It's how we relate to them.

Even though our dreams cause us to wake up laughing, crying, or screaming, we say that they are *not real*—while insisting that fear, panic, pride, and embarrassment *are* real. We put ourselves into our dreams and say, That is not the *real me*. We put ourselves into our fears and confusion and insist that they are the *real me*.

Is this body real? Is there such a thing as a "real" self or a "false" self? Nagasena says that his name, rank, body parts, and so on, are not false. Likewise, my own name, body, fears, or afflictions are not false. The term *no-self* does not mean "false self." Yet it's not *real* in ways that we imagine. Neither we nor the world around us is made up of the solid, independent, lasting qualities that we project. Our perceptions are false. The objects of our perception are neither false nor true.

• • •

Millions of people die every year, yet if we, or someone close to us, is diagnosed with a terminal illness, we ask, *How did this happen?* A question of even greater astonishment is: How do we hold such obvious misperceptions in place? We cannot grasp them with our hands. We cannot tie them down with chains. The mind alone has the power to imprison utterly false claims about who we are. *There is only one obstacle to knowing my own essential emptiness—the mind-cloud that got stuck in the fixity of embarrassment, or in attachment to roles, and the inability or unwillingness to let these clouds pass.* The information was not enough to create ease, but it allowed me to regenerate enthusiasm for adding wood to the fire.

To realize that life itself is change we only have to look at ourselves and the people closest to us. This will provide more information than we need. But we don't wish to see this, and the denial causes dukkha—which translates as "suffering." Dukkha ranges from torment and agony to dissatisfaction, distress, agitation, and annoyance. Every variety reflects a mental disturbance that arises when we substitute reality as-it-is for what we wish it to be.

My own experience taught me that we learn this lesson—and then the old habits return and we have to learn it again. And again. The trickery of the habitual mind was brought home through a very specific incident from my childhood in Nubri. Our house sat on top of a hill, and boys my age lived below. Our secret way for getting together was that I would slip out of my house, cup my hands around my mouth, and make a kind of *ca-coo* bird call. *Ca-cooooooo.* If they heard me, they would *ca-coo* back and we would run to a hidden grove filled with high trees. The trunks and limbs had twisted with age; some formed arches, while others looped through one another or bent toward the ground.

In the grove, we competed to see who could climb the highest and the fastest. Like a monkey, I hung on to a branch with one hand, then swung myself up to the branch above it. One day when I was swinging from branch to branch, there was suddenly a loud snap. I landed flat on my back with my robes covering my face. I was still holding a broken branch. When I finally disentangled my head, I saw my grandmother staring down at me. I remained motionless, waiting for her to scold me for sneaking out. Instead, she gently said, *Give me that stick. I want to show you something.* I sat up and handed it to her. She told me, *You believed that this was strong and hard, but look.* Beneath the bark, the wood was rotten and soft as dirt.

In the following days, I spent hours thinking about that tree, trying to comprehend that things were not as they appeared to be. My eyes had deceived me. The tree had betrayed me. If I could not trust appearances, then what was there to count on? I wanted certainty. I wanted the branch to promise me that it would not break, that I would not fall. *How can we live in a world with no certainty, where not one single entity remains dependable for even one second?* What an intolerable idea that was.

After that, when I competed with the other boys, I tested each upper branch before letting go of the one below. But mostly, the experience introduced a lesson that I would need to learn again and again. What would it take to perceive a tree as a process rather than as an object, as a living–dying form that grows, ages, dies, and transforms? What about the person we most love, or . . . what about ourselves?

Lessons on impermanence are not absorbed overnight. Our habits are too entrenched. We learn, have insights, but we do not apply them, or are too threatened by them. The Buddha identified mistaking impermanence for permanence as one of the primary causes of suffering. Known as the Supreme Physician, he offered a cure for the sickness of samsara. But until we identify this sickness for ourselves, we will not accept the cure.

10

If You See
Something,
Say Something

THE NEXT MORNING, I returned to the stone floor, intending to sleep there. After spending the night in the dormitory, walking down the stairs felt like a descent back into hell, though a less dense version of the previous day's—hell with more air, more light. The people looked less angry, they were not scowling as much, the police seemed less menacing, and the noise was not as loud.

I had drunk water but eaten no food since leaving Tergar. I headed for a snack stall where I bought a packet of biscuits and a cup of masala tea—delicious strong black tea made with boiled milk and sugar. Normally, I drink tea without sugar, but that morning, I thought, *Everything is changing, there is no normal.*

I carried my breakfast to a bench in the main waiting area. The biscuits were made with peanuts and yellow lentils and tasted delicious, but were salty, and soon I went back to the shop for another cup of tea. And then another. Initially, I had put aside some biscuits for later, but I quickly devoured those too.

I returned to the same area of the stone floor, but I was so thirsty from eating the salty biscuits that after a while I got up and walked out of the station to buy water from a street vendor. I also bought some roasted nuts that came in a cone of rolled-up dirty newspaper. Then I walked back into the station. *What kind of*

beggar buys bottled water? So what if this monk looks like an impos-
ter? Maybe someone will report me as a suspicious character.

On a visit to New York City, I had seen notices in train stations
that said: IF YOU SEE SOMETHING, SAY SOMETHING. This is intended to alert the public to suspicious activities, like the kind of
loitering that I was doing, though in Varanasi I was one of many.
Still, from New York City to Varanasi, certain things I saw looked
pretty similar: that we embody moment by moment physical
changes, traverse various realms of affliction each day, and live
through continuous, never-ending changes in our daily lives and
in the environment. The weather changes, our minds change, our
bodies change. We change jobs, houses, locations. Accepting impermanence intellectually is the easy part. But we seem to lack a
good understanding of how to use this information, how to put it
into service for the enrichment of our lives and others. Leaving
home, telling no one where I was going, and planning to live on
the streets affirmed the truth of impermanence and also took advantage of it. I did not have to stay stuck in my Mingyur Rinpoche
identity. I would not. *This is what I do not see: what is holding me*
back right now. How confusing that our habits promise so much
comfort, even when they work against us. Based on what I see, I say
that resistance to change puts us at odds with reality, and this creates
never-ceasing dissatisfaction.

I had expected the shrines and buddha images and sacred texts
of temple life to be replaced by forests and village squares; that
the other passengers would be my sangha—my companions—on
the path; that this station would be my shrine room; that travelers rushing to their destinations would be the living expressions
of the stone bodhisattvas at the Mahabodhi Temple. But at that
moment, I would have liked to have looked through a kaleido-
scope and jiggled the composition of this dream, for I could not
see it as a buddha realm. I could not see that each person here
had buddha nature—meaning the innate capacity for wisdom

and compassion—and to exactly the same degree that I did, no more, no less.

By about noon, I was famished. Food meant rice and dal. No matter what else I ate, if I did not eat rice and dal, I had not eaten. It was now one and a half days since I had eaten rice and dal. I looked around and located the man I had talked with the previous day. I asked him to recommend a good place to eat rice and dal. He directed me to a food stall outside the station. I asked him where he would take his lunch. He explained that he had no money and that he and his family would cook their own rice for dinner. I told him, *Today I will sponsor lunch for you and your family.* They gathered their belongings, and all five of us went to the stall and we ate a lot and enjoyed ourselves. Then we all returned to the stone floor.

States of mind continued to move through a revolving door. In ways similar to the train ride, moments of tranquility were followed by aversion, dislike, and judgment. Then slowly sounds took over as the dominant agent of distress, and in particular, the public announcements that screamed track numbers.

I recalled a student from Eastern Europe, a big guy who towered over me. He was a bit gruff, but never rude. He explained that the intellectual rigor of Tibetan Buddhism appealed to him, but he found the tradition too culture-bound and *religious*— a word he uttered with particular disdain. What vexed him most was the chanting that initiated every practice session. *I just want to sit down and meditate,* he complained.

Fine. I told him. *No problem. Do that.*

He tried this during our group retreat but found it impossible because the room was too noisy.

I suggested that he spend that time practicing sound meditation.

He tried this but he could not practice sound meditation because he was too irritated by the sound of chanting.

I suggested that he use that time to ask himself, *When does the irritation start?*

He recognized that long before he entered the meditation hall, he became so attached to his aversion that his mind had no room for inquiry.

Where had my own irritation started?

Every hour spent planning this retreat had filled me with joy. I had felt deeply confident. In the months before leaving, there were moments when I feared that in my excitement I would blurt out my secret—especially when I was around my brother Tsoknyi Rinpoche. Of all my brothers, he is closest to me in age, and I shared more of my life with him than with anyone else.

Stepping through the Tergar gate had had such momentous impact—like a shock, like lightning that strikes the monkey mind—that for a minute all muttering, all conceptual commentary had abruptly stopped. Was interrupted. And the feeling was wonderful. Mind beyond words, beyond concepts. Illuminating, vivid. But then the taxi had not come, and I'd slipped in the mud, and I was afraid of being seen, and I had no attendant. *That is not how the irritation started. That explanation is too simple.* I knew that I was not the rinpoche label, or any title. But I had thought that these illusory realities could be discarded more easily than they could be—after all, they were nothing but ideas. They were just empty concepts. They did not really exist. They were not part of my true self. I had even suspected that these identities might be living more deeply within me than I could recognize within the routine of my days, but I had not known the extent to which they had taken up residence in my body. Because they are fabricated, constructed, not inherent, yes, they could be transformed—but with more work and more time and more patience than I had foreseen. They could not just be made to stop functioning by volition, like taking off a sun hat in the shade. That would be like saying: *I am emptiness, food is emptiness, hunger is emptiness,* and then dying of starvation, benefiting no one.

Sitting on the station floor, I knew that for these sensations to be so intensely disturbing meant that I had to be misperceiving myself. That's the way suffering always works—our misperceptions turn us into targets. I recalled watching people in parks throughout Southeast Asia practicing the martial art tai chi. I'd watched from the side, amazed to discover that defense was based on fluidity rather than resistance. In tai chi, for a martial arts master, the opponent's blow has no place to land. The same is true with a master of the mind. The more rigid our sense of self, the more surface we provide for the arrows to hit. *Who is receiving these arrows? Who is offended by these loud noises? Who else but the high lama with impeccable good manners, disgusted by the smell of foul toilets and body odor. I wish I could see these vagrants with the same love and appreciation that I have for my students . . . but these people are not adoring me, they are not bowing to me, and they are not respecting me.*

You asked for this! Yes, yes. I know . . . but . . . I am still wearing my superior hats on my superior head but no one can see them. These people around me, blind to Mingyur Rinpoche, are not acting appropriately, and this is confusing, and I do not know what to do.

I sat quietly as my breath returned to its regular rhythm. For several years I had been noticing a growing attachment to my role as teacher—growing like barnacles. Imperceptibly one bit of shell at a time had been added. Sharing the dharma was deeply gratifying. It was what I wished to do more than anything in the world. But I had slowly intuited that I had started to puff out like a peacock with the attention that came from traveling around the world and always being treated as special and important. I could almost catch myself—but not quite—bending in the direction of adulation like a flower bends toward the sun. Doing so felt warm and nourishing, until slowly the hidden dangers would come into focus and I would feel myself veering off course. My father had told me many times to make sure to cut my attachments as soon as I could. Cutting my attachment to being a teacher had been part of the motivation for going on this retreat, although I had never before experienced this feeling with such precision. My silent outburst toward the people around me felt as if a toxic boil had burst, and now the healing could begin.

I needed to move and got up to buy another bottle of water. I hung around the stall. I walked around the station for a few minutes and then returned to the same area. The family whose lunch I had sponsored was serenely napping, the children using their parents for pillows. I missed my family. I missed being cared for—not just the protection it provided, but the affection as well, and I fought back tears.

11

A Visit
from Panic,
My Old Friend

AFTER ABOUT AN hour of sitting with relative calm, discomfort again grew like thorns piercing the skin. Soon I concluded that this bad dream surpassed the panic attacks I'd suffered from as a child. For about five years, starting when I was nine years old, these attacks would be set off by wild weather such as hailstorms, thunder, and lightning, and also by being around strangers. I would become dizzy and nauseous, then freeze like a deer in the headlights. My throat would close. I would start gagging and sweating. Access to reason vanished. I could not be comforted, or hear logical explanations from trusted adults. I could not properly discern my circumstances. My mind would seize with fear, and as the winds raged, I would tremble in a corner like a sick puppy.

I had hoped that when I began the traditional three-year retreat at age thirteen and lived full-time at the monastery, I would magically outgrow these attacks. But they continued and were often precipitated by the group sessions. Twice a day the community gathered in a hall for prayers and ceremonies. The chanting was accompanied by long and very loud brass Tibetan horns, clanging large cymbals, and large and small drums. There were about twenty monks, all in one room, engulfed in thick, smoky incense. This surely manifested a buddha realm of peace and prayer—but not for me. On some days, as the noise built to a deafening crescendo, my throat tightened and I would flee from this claustrophobic enclosure to the solitude of my room. Panic could capture my mind like an invading army, and I had come to hate it.

In a private meeting with Tai Situ Rinpoche, the abbot of the monastery, I told him about these attacks and the fear and anxiety that surrounded them. I told him that the group prayer sessions were driving me crazy. He said, *When the affliction of negative emotions is blazing like fire, then wisdom is also blazing like fire.* This sounded encouraging, but I misunderstood him. I thought that *wisdom* meant a more skillful or effortful approach to getting rid of panic, not the wisdom that can be accessed when our afflictions are blown up as if on a big screen in the sky. I could not accommodate the possibility that panic and wisdom might co-exist.

The worst and last attack took place when I was almost fourteen. The first year of the retreat was drawing to a close. I could not become bigger than the sound, or the fear, and felt humiliated to perceive myself, and be perceived by others, as weak and fragile. But as anyone in the hell of hatred knows, nothing binds you to the object of hatred more than your own aversion. Yet I was determined not to spend the next two years in retreat like this. I would use the teachings and practices and apply them to this panic. After all, I reasoned, if the tree with the broken branch was not permanent, then surely my panic could not be permanent. Could it really be that thunder and hailstorms and strangers were not the problem? That this intense suffering inside my body—and not a toy or a branch out there—was also a product of mental distortions? Was it true then, as the Buddha taught, that ultimately suffering is self-created?

I spent three days alone in my room, watching my mind. Just watching; no control, no manipulation. Just watching in order to ascertain for sure that nothing lasted, that everything was in motion—perceptions, feelings, sensations. I came to accept that I had contributed to fixing these attacks in place with the two aspects of craving: *pushing* the problem away to get rid of it, which only fueled the fear of panic as well as the fear of fear itself; and *pulling,* as in wanting to pull into my life what I considered the opposite: *If only I could be free of panic, my life would be wonderful.* I was still dividing the world into opposites: good–bad, light–dark, positive–negative. I hadn't yet figured out that happiness did not reside in a problem-free life. I was beginning to understand something about how I was contributing to my own anguish, but this was not enough to let go of my patterns. I was stuck in a dark panic cloud and could not separate from it. Panic attacks felt like iron rocks rolling over me, crushing my ability to experience anything but their bruising pressure. But once the worst of an attack passed, and I tried to examine what had happened, that same rock fragmented, and transformed into matter as soft and full of air as shaving cream. In this way, I could actually see the shift in my own perceptions. But to convince myself in a lasting way, I would have to reaffirm impermanence in every way that I could.

To do this, every object and event became an opportunity to affirm that my panic was impermanent: every breath, every sound, every sensation. *The tree outside my window will grow old and die. Saljay Rinpoche is old and will die. The paintings of deities in the shrine room will disintegrate, the neighboring puppies will grow up. My voice is changing. The seasons are changing. The monsoon rains will stop.* The more I examined the transitory nature of all phenomena, the more confident I was that my panic was just another temporary cloud; and after a while, I could no longer identify it as the one thing in the world incapable of change. *Okay, so this too can change. This cloud has no anchor. Now what? Just because it can change does not mean that it will.*

By now I was learning something about resting in awareness, and becoming more trustful of the knowing quality of mind beyond concepts. Bringing the mind back from getting lost in sense objects or with problems did not mean that the mind disappeared or died. Quite the opposite. Taking the mind off its preoccupation with an endless series of specific objects, thoughts, or problems made the mind bigger: vast, clear, and beyond imagination.

I came to understand that if I allowed the panic to remain, and stayed within the recognition of awareness, I would see that panic is just the display of my mind. In this way, panic would self-liberate, meaning that panic, as well as our thoughts, emotions, and perceptions, is already free in and of itself. Liberation comes with a change in perception. Our problems do not need to be liberated by some outside force. I saw that liberation would not— would never—come by focusing on the panic, or on any problem, and trying to get rid of it. We let it be, and then—the next cloud will roll in, and out, and calm waves will come, and turbulent waves will come. Life's problems would never end, and people that I loved would not live forever, and I would encounter new fears and anxieties. But if I stayed with the recognition of awareness, I would be okay. I would be able to deal with the clouds and the waves, ride them, play with them, get knocked over but not submerged. I would not get trapped. I finally discovered the only reliable liberation from suffering: not trying to get rid of the problem. Then the wave stopped trying to get rid of me. It was there, but it was not damaging. The critical insight came from contemplations on impermanence. *My thoughts do not last, this body is changing, this breath is changing. My panic is changing, the life I wish to pull in will change. All that we experience is like waves on the surface of the ocean, rising up and dissolving.* Slowly, instead of relating to panic as an immovable block of iron, I was able to locate a larger, impersonal view of perpetual movement: clouds, plants, airplanes, people—coming and going, arising and disappearing, belly expanding then contracting.

I saw that instead of needing to get rid of my panic, I had to become familiar with the rigid sense of self that kept trying to hold things in place. I could let the panic lead a life of its own. It would dissolve forever or maybe rise again, and yet again, but either way, I could live with it; and I saw that even if I got rid of my panic, other waves would arise and there would always be difficult circumstances, sorrow, sickness, anxiety, and strong emotions. But without a fixed mind, these daily life problems could return to the larger, more spacious ocean-mind. Trying to stop the waves would be like trying to stop the mind, or grasp air in our hands. It's not possible.

Since that last panic attack, no greater suffering had arisen, and I had not imagined that it ever would. I had wished to do a wandering retreat precisely for its difficulties; yet after overcoming panic attacks, I had assumed that no obstacle would defeat my efforts. I had slayed a dragon by seeing its true nature, and for more than twenty years all such demons had stayed away—until I came up against excruciating embarrassment, and the fear of rejection that I had first experienced in the Gaya station and that had intensified here in Varanasi.

As a child, I had come to accept that fear of panic itself could provoke an attack, as if the power of projection compelled the event to materialize. Therefore, in addition to panic, fear too became the enemy, another torment to reject and despise. All I wanted to do with the parts of myself that I disliked was get rid of them, discard them as garbage. I did not understand their value as compost for my sanity.

Now on the station floor, I could see fear rising like steam in the opening between me and others. Relating to others as *other* turned them into omens of calamity. For the fear to be eliminated, I would have to *become* the other—which was no different from dying as Mingyur Rinpoche. Yet at this moment, not yet forty-eight hours away from home, and alone for the first time, and despite my naïve expectations of instantly releasing my identities, they had become more solidified. *But I had let go of the panic attacks and had allowed that boy I was to die. I had once thought that panic would plague me for the rest of my life, but it turned out that it too was essentially empty. My roles were essentially empty, but my experience of them meant that they were not nothing.* They had slumbered contentedly for a long time. I had not anticipated activating sleeping dragons at the very start of my journey, but now that I had ushered them to the surface, I welcomed the chance to see them in the daylight. I noted all this, and then decided that I had done the best that I could for the day. Rather than spend the night in the main hall, I returned to the station dormitory, again paying one hundred rupees for another twelve hours.

I am not my embarrassment, I told myself, *not my confusion or paranoia*—even as these feelings felt solid enough to get slapped. The monk Nagasena had agreed, stating that *because of my body, feeling, perception, and so forth, does Nagasena exist as a denotation, a conventional usage, a name. But ultimately there is no person at all to be found.*

But, but . . .

My second night in Varanasi found me again on a cot in the railway dormitory, this time with the mental posture of a little boxer. Fists raised, I was fighting with Nagasena, like I'd done when I was a kid, the way I used to argue with my tutor, Saljay Rinpoche, insisting, *I am here. I exist. How can I not be here?* Again and again, Saljay Rinpoche had told me: *You are here and you are not here. Both. Like the grass rope and the ash rope. Same and different.*

Coils of grass rope, found throughout India and Nepal, are sometimes used for cooking fuel. As the coarse material burns up, the rope transforms into ash. The shape stays exactly the same, but it's empty of mass. Saljay Rinpoche was comparing the grass rope to the self, and the ash version to the *mere* self. This mere self is the fully functioning *I* cleansed of selfish concerns. It is the awakened self, freed from the grasping self—and therefore liberated from attachment to the labels that make up our identity. This is the healthy self, taking direction from its own sanity, and not tyrannized by the habits of grasping. *Mere* undercuts the misperception of an immutable self, and *mere-ness* becomes more like a hologram, a visible form that is not weighted down by habitual patterns of grasping, and by the tendency to merge our identities with external phenomena.

We all have the body parts, emotions, and perceptions that Nagasena listed—but Nagasena's point is that they do not add up to a cohesive, inherent *me*. Therefore, it's possible to function as the *mere* I, as one devoid of misconceptions about the self and liberated from erroneous views—especially from the misunderstanding that the compilation of parts adds up to something real and independent in its own right, not contingent on narratives and circumstances. We are all the self-inflicted victims of mistaken identity. When we confuse all the pieces for an essential, immutable *me*, then we surrender control to the ego. But we can learn how to make the ego work on our behalf in a healthy, constructive way. The *mere I* functions without attachment; it's not always engaged in manipulating the world for its own satisfaction.

We seek the liberation that comes from recognizing the self that is not defined by grasping, and is therefore capable of recognizing its original state. *Then why am I on this journey, and what am I seeking? Right now, I am seeking to let go of the illusory hats that I am wearing on this illusory head, and that live inside this mind that is falsified by confusion and muddled by misperception, hats that have never existed, all of them fake identities, created by a fake-identity mind, sustained by a fabricated constructed self, affirmed by warped perceptions, held in place by habit . . . and because they are not real, they can pass through and I am not stuck with them, and I will not be stuck with them. I will add them to the fire. I will toss the coiled grass rope of these hat identities onto the flames. And then? Will I turn to ash, become "merely" Mingyur*

Rinpoche? Or will I just become a corpse—a living corpse or a dead corpse? Being alive without waking up to the truth of emptiness is like joining the waking dead.

I lay on my cot, neither rope nor ash but somewhere in-between.

12
·

A Day
at the
Ghats

O N MY THIRD day in Varanasi, I came down from the dormitory and walked out through the main entrance, avoiding the station floor, and kept going toward the ghats, some five miles away. Each ghat is a set of high cut-stone steps that descends toward the Ganges, and in Varanasi the stretch of more than eighty in a row makes up the sacred heart of Hinduism.

I took a road along the river. My pace was neither slow nor fast, but soon the motion of walking melded into the relaxed sensation of walking meditation. I expanded my awareness to take in the experience of movement. I noticed the sensations in my legs and feet as they moved, the shuffling sound of my feet on the dusty road, and the colors and strong smells that surrounded me. For some time, I took note of these sensations and let my awareness move with them. After a few minutes, my awareness expanded further to take in the thoughts and impressions that were moving through my mind. Thoughts aren't necessarily an obstacle to meditation; with awareness, they can be used to support meditation, like the breath. I opened my mind and let all the experiences flow through like clouds of different shapes and sizes moving across the sky.

My thoughts turned to my last visit to the ghats, and the movement of my body—lifting, moving, placing one foot in front of the other—accompanied the movement of my thoughts. A few years earlier I had come here with a retinue of monks and about fifteen or twenty students. We'd stayed at a four-star hotel on the old cantonment behind the ghats. (*Lifting, moving, placing.*) For the first morning of our visit, a boat ride on the Ganges had been arranged for dawn. I walked into the lobby and was greeted by monks and students with smiles and hands together with a bow from the waist, some offering the white ceremonial scarf. (*Lifting, moving, placing.*) I had stepped into a limo and been driven to the river, where a large boat was waiting for us. An embroidered cloth and cushion covered the wooden seat reserved for me. (*Lifting, moving, placing.*) The oarsmen rowed us away from the shore as the sun rose to turn the limestone steps pink, and people began gathering at the river's edge to do their morning ablutions. (*Lifting, moving, placing.*) We had bought garlands of marigolds and placed these into the river, some as offerings for those who had just died, and we also offered lit candles on floating palm leaves.

Pilgrims travel great distances to bathe in this stretch of the Ganges. They come to purify their souls (*lifting, moving, placing*) and to be liberated from the cycles of samsara. Those who die in Varanasi are considered blessed, and guesthouses cater specifically to devout Hindus who come here to die and be burned at the edge of the river. Families, if they can arrange it, bring their dead to be placed on wood pyres and have their ashes carried into the consecrated waters. The smell of incense and charred flesh hangs in the air. We returned to our hotel and sat at long tables in a lush garden, where turbaned waiters served bowls of fresh fruits, curd, croissants, and lattes. (*Lifting, moving, placing.*) I now reflected that I had been away from Tergar for only a few days, and already that memory seemed to belong to a different lifetime. Then I thought of one of my beloved teachers, Nyoshul Khen Rinpoche. No one ever walked this earth with greater ease than he did. He moved across a room with the grace of a figure skater. His feet did not seem to go up and down, but to glide. Among my principal teachers, only he had lived on the streets as a sadhu. He came from humble origins and had barely survived his escape from Tibet; begging for alms would not have been his first experience of hunger. The title *khen* signifies an advanced practitioner who is also a scholar of traditional texts. Since he had not been identified as a tulku, a reincarnated adept, he had not inherited responsibilities from the past; and he had fewer formal obligations to maintain the monasteries than many other venerated lamas.

I knew how special Khen Rinpoche was from my father. This had nothing to do with things my father said. Just referring to Khen Rinpoche so obviously filled him with happiness, and his name was always accompanied by the most joyful smiles. I did not meet Khen Rinpoche until I was seventeen years old, in 1991. I was taking a break between the first three-year retreat and the subsequent one, when I would have the role of retreat master, and I had been invited to Bhutan to attend the cremation ceremonies for the great master of Tibetan Buddhism, Dilgo Khyentse Rinpoche. As Bhutan was Khen Rinpoche's resident country, I arranged to meet with him. At the time, I mentioned the possibility of studying with him, but that did not happen until much later. He had lived on the streets many years before my training with him began, although I had grown up hearing the story of how he had decided to become a beggar.

Sometime in the late 1960s, both the Sixteenth Karmapa, the revered head of the Karma Kagyu school of Tibetan Buddhism, and Khen Rinpoche had joined other high-ranking lamas and monastery officials at a conference in Delhi. The gathering had been organized to discuss the fate of Tibet and the exile community. When they ran into each other, the Karmapa looked at Khen Rinpoche with great affection and said, in a somewhat teasing tone, *You are a khenpo. You should not engage in politics.* Khen Rinpoche took this to heart. Soon afterward a monastery asked him to become the personal tutor to one of their tulkus. Khen Rinpoche took the job. The tulku, then around twenty years old, needed to go to Calcutta and asked Nyoshul Khen to accompany him. The tulku booked them into a five-star hotel. After two or three days, the tulku said he had business in the city. *You stay here,* he told Khen Rinpoche, *and I will be back in a few hours.* But he never came back. Khen Rinpoche had no money and the bill was already huge; after another day or two he explained the situation to the hotel manager. The manager fumed but finally said, *You can work off your debt by washing dishes.*

Nyoshul Khen did not speak Hindi, but he enjoyed the work and slept contentedly in the servant quarters. Meanwhile people became worried about his disappearance. After about three weeks they traced him to the hotel, paid the bills, and brought him to a monastery. At that point, he decided to see the Sixteenth Karmapa again, so he went to Rumtek, the Karmapa's seat in Sikkim.

The Karmapa said: *Khenpo, you are so lucky. Do you know why you are so lucky?*

Khenpo said, *No I don't. Why am I so lucky?*

Because, the Karmapa told him, *you got fired by that tulku, so now you're free.*

Khenpo went back to his room still pondering, *Why am I lucky?* He reviewed his encounters with the Karmapa. *First, he told me that I am not a political person. Now he says I am lucky.* Suddenly he thought, *I have trained all my life to transform obstacles into opportunities. Today, I finally get it. I will take advantage of having no job, and no money, and no responsibilities.*

At that moment, he made the decision to wander. For three years he alternated between monasteries and living as a sadhu on the streets. Everything about Nyoshul Khen inspired me: the graceful way he walked, consistently maintaining his awareness, how he taught, that he'd lived as a beggar. He had died twelve years earlier, and I missed him more than ever. I wished I had asked him questions about how he had lived on the streets.

I cut away from the river so that I could amble through the narrow lanes that led to the top of the ghats. Many shops in this area sell cloth, and I stopped to purchase sadhu clothes. I bought two swaths of saffron-dyed cotton, one to wrap around my waist for dhoti-type pants, and the other to wrap around my shoulders. I did not wear my sadhu shawls out of the shop but placed them in my backpack. While I might have boldly claimed to King Menander that *I am not my robes,* it now became evident that part of my identity lived in six by nine feet of maroon cotton. Though giving up my monastic robes might have signaled the death that I had yearned for, I just wasn't ready. I wondered if Khen Rinpoche had changed into sadhu clothes or kept his Tibetan robes. I wish I had asked. I wondered if he'd worn sandals or gone barefoot.

I went about halfway down one set of steps and found an outdoor tea shop in the shade. I ordered sweet masala chai and sat looking onto the promenade that runs the length of the ghats. It was too hot for many tourists, but the monkeys, as usual, were on the watch for handouts. A few sadhus and naked, ash-smeared Shaivites—Hindus who revere Shiva as a supreme god—moved slowly in the broiling heat with their jangling tridents.

Sitting in the tea shop, I was no less in-between than I had been at any time the past two days, especially as I was still wearing my Tibetan robes. But I had been at the ghats many times before, and the familiarity made this tea time a particularly relaxing interval before I returned to the tumultuous station and got on with my retreat—or continued the retreat I had started, and was doing right now. I was still uneasy with being alone, ordering tea, and handling money, but I was enjoying this quiet moment.

In the Tibetan tradition, we pay attention to three aspects of retreat: outer, inner, and secret. *Outer* refers to the physical environment. Some atmospheres are more conducive than others to disrupting our repetitive habits and supporting an exploration of

the inner mindscape. Yet the dharma path encourages us to cultivate inherent, lasting qualities that are not dependent on external
situations. If we have access to supportive circumstances, wonderful; this is very helpful, especially for beginners. But it's a trap
to mistake atmosphere and accoutrements for necessities. What's
necessary is a willingness to know the depths of your own mind.

My understanding had been that with the correct intention,
the Varanasi train station was as perfectly suited for meditation as
a shrine room or a flower garden. After all, I reasoned, I was not a
beginner, and perception defines the context, not the other way
around. However, the Gaya station and then the train ride and
then sitting with the homeless had pressed on my mental composure. For now, I needed to bring my body to places that soothed
my mind. Once again there was no point in pretending that I
could handle more than I could.

Inner retreat refers to the physical body. Because we create or
diminish suffering through physical actions and speech, inner retreat means creating an environment that protects us from the
ordinary patterns of gossip and slander, or from substances that
obscure the mind, or from household situations in which patterns
of indolence or impatience have formed.

Since boyhood, I had been steeped in the precepts that guide
behavior and speech, and I did not seriously question my discipline. I also knew that I would need to make distinctions between breaking cultural conventions and breaking true vows. For
example, for a tulku to sit on the floor broke a Tibetan custom. In
some monastic traditions, food is not served after the midday
meal; in others, swallowing is allowed in the evening—as in
drinking juice or slurping soup—but not chewing. I had given up
eating meat, but for my retreat, I would accept whatever I was
given, and I could not control the hours of receiving food. The
main precepts that relate to not harming or stealing or lying and
so forth were not just rules for specific behavior but functioned to
promote vigilance, and to become sensitized to those tendencies

that lead to grasping rather than to letting go. Confessing, or acknowledging, when a precept is broken can help purify the mind and reset the karmic balance. But without purifying the mind of attachment itself, negative behavior tends toward repetition.

When I was little and still living at Nagi Gompa, my father had a German student who owned the most expensive mountain bike that money could buy. He used to ride this bike from Kathmandu up to Nagi Gompa, not on the narrow dirt path but through the woods. He could make the bike leap across ditches and streams, and sometimes he would shoot straight to the top of Shivapuri, the mountain behind the nunnery, and appear to be flying through air rather than keeping the wheels on the ground. This man was such an excellent biker that he occasionally made money by racing with Nepalis down in the valley.

One day he told my father, *I have listened to you teach on the importance of letting go, and I do not know what to do about my mountain bike.*

My father said, *I know you love your mountain bike. But getting rid of it will not help break your attachment. Actually, it might strengthen it.*

The man was both relieved and confused. My father explained that the wish *to get rid of* also arises from the fixed mind. *If you are attached to the bike and you give it away, your mind will stick to the bike, whether you own it or not, and you might become proud of your action. If you do not work with the mind of attachment, the mind will stick to one thing or another. You have to liberate the attachment and then you can choose to keep the bike or not. Do not push away, do not invite. Work from the middle, and slowly you will transform attachment into an open mind that allows you to make appropriate choices.*

With regard to inner retreat, I knew that being alone in the world would present different options than I had ever known, and that to some degree my monastic vows had been safeguarded by my Buddhist robes. Exchanging them for the new yogi clothes meant giving up the protection that the robes provided. At this point, I still felt too vulnerable to do that. Even though no one around me was here to mirror the meaning of the robes, or to reflect their status, in the privacy of my mind the robes played the role of bearing witness. I would continue wearing them for now.

Secret retreat refers to intention. I have taken vows my entire life to help liberate sentient beings from self-created suffering, and to introduce them to their own wisdom. The intention for this retreat did not waver from the intention set for any other retreat, or for any practice that I had ever done.

I had been surprised when some Westerners asked me to explain the benefit of a wandering retreat. It appeared somewhat selfish to them—an idea that would never occur to a Tibetan. *Why not stay around and continue to teach dharma—to help others wake up? You could support the efforts in Bodh Gaya to clean up the groundwater; or advocate for the education of girls. So many worthwhile causes; why go off on retreat by yourself?*

People everywhere try so hard to make the world better. Their intentions are admirable, yet they seek to change everything but themselves. To make yourself a better person is to make the world a better place. Who develops industries that fill the air and water with toxic waste? How did we humans become immune to the plight of refugees, or hardened to the suffering of animals raised to be slaughtered? Until we transform ourselves, we are like mobs of angry people screaming for peace. In order to move the world, we must be able to stand still in it. Now more than ever, I place my faith in Gandhi's approach: *Be the change you wish to see in the world.* Nothing is more essential for the twenty-first century and beyond than personal transformation. It's our only hope. Transforming ourselves *is* transforming the world. This is why I was on retreat, to more fully develop my capacities to introduce others to knowing their own wisdom, and their own capacities for a peaceful life.

I thought about a man I knew who had visited the ghats on his first visit from America to India. He had gone to India as a college student on a study-abroad program and was taken out into the Ganges River in a small boat. He was shocked and appalled to see people bathing, even washing their mouths, just a short distance from where bodies were being burned and their ashes scattered into the river. A human torso floated by in the water, and he was overwhelmed by the intensity of the experience. Until that point, he had assumed that the spiritual path was one of orderliness—that it was clean, pleasant, and quiet, and he associated it with immaculate Zen monasteries and silent meditations. That day he learned that there is no spiritual reality separate from daily life, and that in order to know anything of value about himself, and about living in the world, he would have to travel deep inside himself.

To return to the station, I circled back on a road farther from the river. I stopped to buy a package of dried instant noodles and ate them out of the plastic bag. The road wended through a pastoral area, green stretches with fewer people and cars. It was now blistering hot, and I missed the shade of a parasol. In a field off the road, I saw two small horses and stopped to look. A field of lush grass stretched behind them. As if to prove that the grass is always greener *over there,* their necks reached out between the boards of the pasture fence as they strained to eat the grass on the other side. *Just like us! Continuously longing for what we don't have. That grass is better than this grass—all day long.*

Our continuous agitation reveals a low-level dissatisfaction that never entirely ceases except for a few peak moments here and there. We are restless with this scent of something better close by, but out of reach. It's like a subnormal fever. Not worrisome enough to see the doctor, but not quite right either. We remain convinced that the perfect temperature or perfect partner, or job, is just around the corner, or over the fence; we imagine that our compulsions will weaken; we will outgrow our immature cravings, some new friendship or job will rescue us from crippling self-hatred, or loneliness, or from feeling that we are always making mistakes. Illogically, these fantasies of change for the good persist—even for decades—while often few of them, or none, ever come to fruition. But the orientation of our fantasies and desires stays with contentment, and away from dissatisfaction.

Although our aspirations may go unfulfilled, this orientation toward happiness and away from dissatisfaction points to an innate quality. Even behavior that is misguided or destructive, such as stealing money, or inappropriate sexual relations, or using addictive substances, is motivated by the wish for happiness. The universal constancy of this orientation toward happiness is a reflection of our basic goodness. However misguided the expression of happiness might be, the yearning draws on an inherent desire for care, comfort, and a sense of well-being, and indicates that the wish for happiness arises from the core of our being. It could not arise from a belief in goodness, or an imposition of religious dogma, or of social values. Beliefs and values are concepts and therefore subject to change and whim. This orientation to be kind to ourselves—or to what we call *basic goodness*—is with us just as awareness is, recognized or not. We never live without it.

The more we recognize awareness, the more access we have to our own loving qualities. Loving-kindness and compassion are the natural expressions of awareness because genuine expressions of an open heart transcend conceptual ideas and attitudes, and exist beyond duality, beyond words and logic. The same qualities apply to awareness, and the more we rest within the boundless state of awareness, the more our love and compassion become boundless.

I knew the teachings. I trusted them. I had experienced them to varying degrees. But the difference between never having been alone and finding myself utterly alone caused a surprisingly harsh break. I had become fearful and uptight in ways that I had not experienced for decades. At such times, whatever illusions we may have just entertained about our feet being firmly planted on a station platform, or on anything that seems reliable, vanish. What do we do? Can we seize the unbidden opportunity to explore this new mental territory of nondefined spaciousness that is actually always there? More often we scramble as fast as we can back to the circumscribed limits of the mental or physical components of our known world.

The Gaya station provided a heightened chance to slip through the gap that was created by disruption, and to experience the unconditioned self—to explore reality once the grasping mind had been demolished by shock, and before it put itself back together. An hour prior to the Gaya station, the thrill of tiptoeing down the stairs of my house and eluding the notice of the watchman, and making my escape through the Tergar gate, had also shattered my conceptual mind. However, at that moment I was able to recognize the state of mind free from preconception. This had allowed the luminous, knowing qualities of the naked mind to prevail, and this had contributed to an exalted send-off. But then I slipped in the mud . . . and the taxi did not come . . . and . . . this glimpse of emptiness faded out like a disappearing rainbow.

I could not take advantage of this gap. I could not allow myself to be in that formless space, and instead struggled to regain my sense of *self;* which meant, at that moment, reconstructing my idea of Mingyur Rinpoche as rapidly as I could.

These breaks in the mental loop cannot be willed into being recognized. However, we can train to become more sensitive to their presence, especially with regard to common occurrences—for example, sneezing. In many societies, responses to sneezes offer protection against the invasion of an evil spirit; or it's believed that sneezing can eject the soul from the body, and that saying *bless you* helps the soul return to its internal place. In all of these responses a sneeze is identified—as it is in Tibetan training—as an interruption of habitual mind chatter, a gap. *Aah choo!* For a split second, the mind stream is cut. The muttering mind is silenced. It cannot coexist with a sneeze. This is the real blessing.

To suddenly be startled, or see a wild animal, or trip and fall, or learn of a life-threatening diagnosis, or see a natural phenomenon or an exquisite work of art, or anything that makes our heart skip a beat functions the same way. Yet we tend to place the mind over there—on the projected source of our reaction—and not on the mind itself. Without looking directly at the mind, we cannot recognize its clear, empty nature at that moment. Still, it's important to know that we all share these ordinary moments of naked mind. And we can learn to recognize them.

Once we begin to examine these moments, and to gain some acceptance of their common occurrence, we might be amazed to discover how frequently moments in daily life stop our minds. Then we can take advantage of these natural events to access remarkable information about the true nature of who we are. With these flashes of naked mind, a mini-death occurs. For an instant, the self that we identify as our very existence ceases. The *me* that defines our identity and directs our functioning temporarily dies. But we do not die into nothingness; we die into deathless awareness.

Yawning functions in ways similar to sneezing. Stretching to the limit can function this way. To suddenly stop after jogging or other exertions can have this effect. Once we acquire some familiarity with physical events that stop the mind, we might explore similar mental states that arise in more ambiguous situations, such as feeling elated on leaving the office on a Friday afternoon after an intense workweek.

Many people fear that the annihilation of the conceptual mind leads to nothingness. In reality, it reveals the luminous emptiness of mind that is always with us, and therefore accompanies our journey at the time of physical death. What we learn by becoming aware of dying before we die is that dying *is* rebirth. Recognizing luminous emptiness *is* a recognition of death. Becoming familiar now with emptiness diminishes our fear of losing our bodies, because when we lose our bodies, it is all that continues. What is this based on? On the fact that it has never been constructed. All conditioned things sooner or later disappear. Confidence in unconditional reality can only come with experience. Yet when we start paying attention to our everyday minds, the constructed version of ourselves falls apart—but we do not die, and we might want to investigate what is left.

A big question that exists in the West is whether or not something of us continues when we physically die. If we can connect with any aspect of reality that is beyond the normal limits of the thinking mind, then we must ask where this reality comes from, and how it came into existence. If we can prove to ourselves through investigation that it has no beginning, then perhaps we can accept that it has no ending. We do not need dramatic, life-shattering experiences of luminosity to pursue this question. We can start with sneezes, or yawns, or meditation exercises, or noticing the details of breathing in and out—anything that automatically contains a gap. But to get anywhere in our investigations, we have to be willing to relax our fixed minds and to let go of our ideas of what is real. Letting go itself is an example of dying. But recognition of this dying is what allows us to inhabit the continuous cycle of dying and being reborn with ease.

In addition to mini-deaths that come with glimpses of emptiness, sleep offers a deeper experience of dying before we die, and this can be understood as a kind of medium death, bringing us a step closer to the final big death that occurs when our bodies give out. Again, the only real benefit comes with recognition, not with the physical event alone. Training the mind to stay aware of the entire process of falling asleep is not easy. But even making conceptual adjustments to how we relate to this daily occurrence shifts our relationship with death. For example, Tibetans have a custom of turning over their cup before going to sleep, signifying not just the end of the day, but the end of one's life. In the morning, we first think, *I am alive, I can see, I can hear, I can feel.* Then we turn the cup right-side up. *My new life begins, and I am ready to receive.* In the morning, the mind is very fresh, and just one moment of appreciation for being alive can orient our whole day, and remind us of the continual cycle of living and dying.

After completing my long, hot walk, I reentered the station, grateful to be out of the sun, and to have purchased the sadhu shawls. But I was also a little apprehensive, because the station hostel imposed a rule of no more than three consecutive nights, and this would be my last. Back in the dorm room I lay down on a cot, both tired and restless. As always, I prepared to engage in sleep meditation, the last mind-training exercise of each day. I was ready to die to the day, and eager to see what rebirth tomorrow might bring.

13

•

Of Sleep
and Dreams

I STARTED THE SLEEP meditation with a head-to-toe body scan, bringing awareness into the body and noticing how knots of tension dissolved by doing this. Then I placed my mind lightly on the dissolution of the senses as they began to fade: seeing, hearing, smelling, feeling . . .

We tend to think of sleep as a necessary biological break from life. We take the dissolution of the senses for granted and usually pay no attention to what's happening. We just black out as if drugged or drunk. Yet this dissolution process parallels physical dying; night after night we actually undergo a mini-death. We get into bed each night with a solid sense of self. As our consciousness diminishes, the bonds that hold the conventional mind in place become unglued. The physical shutting down of the body's foundational grid absorbs into this process the fixed parameters of the small self—thus automatically releasing us into universes far beyond the limits of our waking lives. The content of dreams is nothing other than projections of our own mind, but without the controls or manipulations that we impose during the day.

Most of us cannot track the dissolution of the senses as we fall asleep; partway through the process our awareness submits to sleep, just as the sense organs do. To be able to maintain recognition of awareness throughout the process takes a lot of practice and an extraordinarily sensitive mind, one as evolved as that of

His Holiness, the Sixteenth Karmapa (Rangjung Rigpe Dorje, 1924–81). When he spoke of awareness, he meant pure, non-dualistic awareness, awareness without an observer.

I never met the Sixteenth Karmapa, but one of my older brothers was his attendant and shared a remarkable story. The Karmapa had arranged for a meeting between himself and a great nonsectarian scholar-monk who had tutored His Holiness the Dalai Lama. The Karmapa wanted to discuss a problem he was having with his meditation. My mischievous brother served refreshments, then hid behind the door to listen.

The Karmapa reported that he could maintain his awareness throughout the entire day, and track the dissolutions right up to *almost* falling asleep. Once he was asleep, he would again recognize his awareness. But there were a few moments each night, just before slipping into sleep, when he lost his recognition of awareness, and he sought advice on how to eliminate this interruption.

The revered guest listened, awestruck. He had never encountered such a stunning report of continuous recognition, and immediately made prostrations to the embodied wisdom before him. He then told the Karmapa that he could not advise him, but they did discuss texts that spoke of the mind that made no distinction between day and night.

As inspiring as this story was, I had never gotten anywhere close to that degree of steady recognition. My efforts to practice sleep meditation during my first three-year retreat proved difficult. In the formal curriculum, we had three months to learn this practice. As we approached the ninety-day mark, I was still dropping dead into sleep every night. Then one day, we had a prayer gathering in the main hall that started at five A.M. We were instructed to wake up at two A.M. and do our meditation and recitation practices in our rooms until gathering in the main hall. That night I did not sleep well. Once inside the main hall, I kept falling asleep. I tried all the tricks for staying awake—rolling my eyes up and digging my nails into my thighs—but I kept nodding off. Then I thought, *Okay, let's try to practice sleep meditation.* At first, I felt a bit like I was falling; then my mind quieted down, and I was able to rest in meditative awareness for about five minutes before losing this state and falling asleep as I usually did. After a few minutes, I woke up, and for the first time I was able to follow my awareness as I fell asleep again.

When I woke up I felt very rested, very light, and my mind was in meditation. Peaceful, relaxed. Open with clarity. That was the first time. For me, the best time to practice sleep meditation is still during a meditation session when I get very sleepy and allow myself to fall asleep—or during one of those indescribably long, boring ceremonies.

On my last night in the station dormitory, it took a while to fall asleep, and at some point I lost my awareness. I then had a dream that brought no solace: I was en route to my hometown in Nubri, a trip that I had made many times. On foot this trip takes about eight days, climbing dangerously narrow paths in view of glistening Himalayan peaks. On some stretches the path winds precariously along a sheer drop of more than a thousand feet to a raging river. Ominous boulders jut out from the side of the cliff. If anyone were to fall off the path, their body would never be found.

In my dream I was on the path when suddenly harsh, crashing sounds filled the air, and the boulders above started tumbling down and crushing me. I woke up startled. I sat at the edge of my cot with my heart thumping and my mouth dry. I looked around at the rows of dormitory beds filled with sleeping men, some snoring loudly. I had not woken up and become lucid in my dream of being crushed by boulders—as I had been trained to do. I had reacted as if I were a hapless victim. I felt relieved to be out of the bad dream but was still almost in tears trying to convince myself that this dream represented irrational fears and did not portend my journey.

When we practice dream meditation, we train to wake up within the dream and know that we are dreaming. We often speak of enlightenment in terms of *waking up*—which means directly seeing things as they are. Daytime or nighttime, the message is the same: Wake up! If rocks are crashing down on us, and we recognize *this is a dream,* then we can jump out of the way—or jump off the cliff into the river and not get hurt. We already know that anything can happen in dreams: falling, flying, meeting the dead, changing shapes, and so forth. We know that dream reality is without limits and inhibitions. Yet even when we acknowledge that our dream-body arises from our own minds, we insist that our dreams are *illusory,* not *real.*

Dreams can reveal useful psychological information that cannot always be accessed with our daytime minds; but when we use dreams to investigate reality, we do not try to interpret or understand their meaning or look for signs and symbols. We work with the direct experience that dreaming offers us to challenge our assumptions and expand our perceptions. A rigid mind demands that everything conforms to its expectations, including our dreams. For this reason, when we dream about dead loved ones, or drowning, or flying, we immediately conclude that the dream is not real. Dream reality is dismissed, and our static and confused perceptions remain the touchstone of reality. Yet this view shifts once we initiate our explorations of no-self, and the recognition of impermanence begins to dislodge our attachments to fixation. Then we can take a fresh look at dreams, for they present the very opposite of a closed, rigid mind. Dream images tend to be insubstantial, filmy, translucent, mirage-like, and out of our control—but not outside of our minds. We may be stunned by our dreams, or try to shake ourselves awake from nightmares, or repress taboo information that surfaces. Yet our dreams are us, for these images can only arise from our projections.

Nothing appears too stable in dreams; more often, everything is fleeting, or shifting. In daytime, we presume an individuated and controlling *self,* whereas in dreams this same self liquefies into every conceivable—and inconceivable—type of phenomenon.

The transitional period between dreaming and reentering conventional daytime existence offers another example of the bardo of becoming. We may wake up feeling scared or disoriented, as I did when I dreamed of the crashing boulders; then instead of staying with these feelings in order to find out more about what they offer, we generally scramble to reconstitute ourselves in terms of yesterday's reality: *This is my bed, my room, my body.* Once again, the anxiety of dislocation pushes us away from what is transitory, unknown, and insubstantial and toward familiar images that appear as solid and lasting. We wish to return to what best fits our expectations. *Thank goodness that dream was not real. My partner did not leave me. My child is not in the burning house. I am not drowning. I am once again who I am, who I really am.* We run away from the fear, and seek comfort in what is familiar. Yet since what we are running away from comes from our own minds, we are running away from ourselves, and as a strategy for happiness, this never works.

I was not crushed by boulders. That does not make me solid. I am alive. And I am dying day after day. I am still asking my father's question: Are you Mingyur Rinpoche? Are you the same or different from the Mingyur Rinpoche in the dream? I can touch my arm, my face. If I reach out now to touch the dream-me, I will feel nothing. The boulders did not hurt me. If the ceiling overhead were to fall down right now, I might be crushed. I might bleed. Same or different? Nagasena said that he only exists as a label, a denotation, a conventional usage, a name, that he is not his blood. But he could still bleed. Who then was bleeding?

Dreams are like every other aspect of our existence: They happen, we experience them, but they are not real; their appearance is deceptive, and we easily recognize this non-real aspect of our dreams. This is why dreams are so valuable for understanding the emptiness aspect of reality. Everything is infused with emptiness, and that includes our bodies and our blood, our boulders, our names, and our dreams. During the daytime, phenomena *appear* to be denser. This makes daytime a tougher schoolroom for learning about emptiness. It's much easier to recognize emptiness in dreams. To say that *life is a dream* acknowledges the ceaseless, boundless quality of emptiness in ourselves, in our loved ones, in our iPhones, airplanes, food, anger, lust, wealth—in everything. Phenomena have no inherent existence; everything arises from emptiness and never separates from emptiness. Yet it's a lot easier to perceive this with nighttime dreams than to acknowledge our own emptiness by looking in the mirror.

I woke knowing that I had just spent my last night in the Varanasi Station. I wondered where I would be tonight, where I would sleep. The uncertainty was a little frightening, but also a little thrilling.

14

Learning
to Swim

O N LEAVING THE dormitory hostel for the last time, I returned
to the stone floor of the train station. Soon I became agitated knowing that I could not return to the dormitory. I did not
want to stay in the town of Varanasi, as it was too popular a site
for pilgrims and tourists, even in the summer heat. I was not
ready to sleep in the area designated for the homeless. I had
longed to live with no plans and without checking my watch all
day. Now this open-ended horizon felt baffling. I had to make
decisions—just as before.

I reflected on the past three days and tried to take a hard look
at my resistance, my vulnerability, and at my aversion toward
those around me. I had not only been disgusted but had been
ashamed by my disgust. I did not want to experience those sensations again. I did not want to return to confusion. This station
was still not my home, but I no longer felt the intense alienation
from myself and others that I had earlier. I was beginning to let
down my guard a little, at least enough to edge toward the people
on the floor around me with an attitude of curiosity and kindness.

I was able to see that every move I made, from a blink to a
breath, to buying tea, even to making negative projections—all
stemmed from a wish for a change, and that this desire was always oriented toward happiness. Judging someone for looking
unclean or smelling bad, or being loud, or *anything,* is a pretty

neurotic way to seek happiness—but it provides a toehold to climb up from and allows you to temporarily enjoy the illusion that you are better than someone else. It's never just: *They are bad.* It is also: *Therefore, I am good.* I saw that even at my most walled-off, I was still longing to connect to my own true self and to others. Even the distortions and projections were tied to wanting to be free inside by pushing the negativity out of myself, away from me—all unskillful means for happiness, but the intentions were basically sane.

On the train, my body had been rigid and closed, making the waves big and strong, but I did not know how to play in such strong surf. I could not in any heartfelt, empathetic way connect to others. I could not know—completely know, in my body and mind—their own longing for happiness until I could acknowledge my own.

In Nubri, I used to love to watch the seasons change—the green summer grasses turning brown, the trees in full foliage dropping their leaves in fall, the deep blue skies turning into the gray, snow-filled skies of winter, and the arrival of new buds at the onset of spring. Our house had a stone courtyard with a border of flowers that my grandfather lovingly tended. I would wait with great excitement for those flowers to bloom, particularly the lush dahlias prized by my grandfather. Once the buds appeared, I would examine the plants daily. One spring two dahlias blossomed, and for several days they became the center of everyone's attention. I waited impatiently for the other buds to catch up. Then we had an unexpected late-spring storm and the temperatures plunged. The next morning every plant in the garden was dead. I burst into tears. My grandfather tried to explain that everything was impermanent and my grandmother gave me candy, but I sobbed inconsolably. Then my grandfather reminded me of how much I loved watching the seasons change. *That pleasure,* he told me, *comes from impermanence; the summer berries that you love come from impermanence. Everything arises from imperma-*

nence. Next spring, we will have new growth and new plants— because of impermanence.

If we see that the seeds for regeneration exist within change, then we can become more comfortable with dying every day— with dying before we die, with being delighted with the sand castles as they wash away. We can become comfortable with the process of dissolution and reassembling now. We can reshape the way we think about sleeping and dreaming and waking up. All this present moment possibility rests with impermanence.

This is not an overnight project. Old habits die hard, but they do die. On the train, I had continuously returned to seeing that this journey was about change and transformation, and that the seeds of regeneration were already growing. *And no, they will not die in the bud like my grandfather's dahlias,* I told myself.

May I have happiness. May I be free.

I repeated this refrain until I could feel the meaning slide down my throat like a thick syrup that takes its time, slowly encompassing my heart, my lungs, seeping into my stomach, inhabiting my legs, oozing into my feet. *May I have happiness. May I be free.*

I repeated this until the meaning of the words thoroughly soaked my being, until I softened, and my heart opened—not as fully as I had known at other times, but so much further than it had in previous days that I started to cry with appreciation. *May I have happiness. May I be free.*

After about thirty minutes I felt stabilized enough in relationship to myself to extend this aspiration to others. Unlike repeating the reminders on the train, I would not look upon a mass of *others* but direct my awareness to a particular person. I chose the wife of the man whom I had chatted with, who had come to lunch with us the day before. She had been shy, keeping her eyes lowered and not talking much, but her manner had been warm and gentle. I glanced at her long enough to hold her face in my mind, then lowered my eyes and repeated, *May she be happy, may she be free.* I thought about her life, her hardships. *May she have food, may she have shelter. May her children be healthy. May she be happy, may she be free.*

I repeated this until I felt her sweetness, her lovable qualities, her worthiness to be loved and respected as much as I was. We shared the same wisdom, the same fundamental luminous emptiness. Beyond dualities, we lived in the mutual boundless environment of unconditional love and awareness. Compassion that arises with empathy acknowledges that ignorance causes suffering. Not the suffering of poverty and homelessness, but the suffering of misperception, of taking phenomena to be real in ways that are not true. *The woman is as precious as I am, but there are no signs that she knows how to free her mind from misperception.*

I stayed with this woman's image until I knew that I loved her unconditionally. I loved her husband and their children. I wished for them the same happiness and freedom from suffering as for the children in my own family, and for the little monks at Tergar. I expanded my heart to all the people in the station—the people on the floor, the people rushing by, the vendors who had sold me rice and dal and tea, the dormitory manager. I expanded my love to include all of those on the train from Gaya, those who had stepped on me and had fallen into me, and I knew without doubt that they too wanted happiness. It was the same for everyone in this entire world, the same for every pet, every wild animal, every insect, every rat that scurried by seeking happiness in a crumb.

I rested. Quiet and calm. I entertained no delusions that this respite would bring an end to my difficulties, but it lessened my anxieties about having no place to go. Images of myself as a beginning swimmer kept emerging. The strong currents, especially the vulnerability that swelled from being alone, had carried me away from my own internal protection. I had kept my head above water but had struggled. Now the tide had turned and was coming in. I imagined a good swimmer feeling fearless in the water. No, not just fearless; it was not good enough to only negate fear. A good swimmer would welcome rough waters as a challenge. In this dirtiest train station in all of India, I would learn how to swim. *Yes, I can do this!*

I had left home and followed through with my plan to go to Varanasi. Now I had no more plans. But I could direct my future. I had many options. I could return to Bodh Gaya, or to Kathmandu, maybe even head north to my monastery in Tibet. *No. I am not attracted to that kind of shelter, despite the difficulties of the last days. I want to take rebirth as a wandering yogi. I am making this decision voluntarily, consciously. The chance to do this retreat is a gift from previous practices. These are my karmic seeds and I will not squander them. The joy and excitement about this retreat grew out of my practice. My confidence and courage are the fruition of my studies—awareness and insight practices, and sleep and dream meditations, emptiness practices, compassion practices, everything.*

I am not giving up. The embarrassment is still here. The shock in my body is with me. But I can still direct my future—not to continue without these unbidden companions but to continue with them. Unchangeable awareness in the midst of turbulence. I am directing this body to continue with the embarrassment and the shock of being alone, sun and clouds together. Naked and clothed. Learning to swim with the waves.

15
·

Memento
Mori

As the station rules prohibited me from returning to the dormitory, it was time to stop sitting on the stone floor. I had to figure out my next move. I noticed a group of Westerners standing nearby, glancing at me, and I quickly lowered my head and sat very still, examining them through squinty eyes. Men and women, maybe a little younger than I was, white, speaking English, maybe American. Dressed casually but neatly. They had maps and guidebooks and were making plans to visit Varanasi and then Sarnath, where the Buddha had first taught. Unlike the family next to me, they took up a lot of space, gesturing with hands and arms that flew away from their bodies, standing with hands on hips, elbows away from their torsos. They were uncontained, confident, maybe arrogant. I watched one young man walk to a tea stall, so sure of himself even though he was a foreigner. Yet they were here because they clearly wanted something from this sacred corner of the ancient world that they could not find in their modern lives. Maybe they were seeking inner transformation. *I hope they find something of benefit, some way of understanding the world and their place in it that can have a positive influence on their direction, and that they can share with their friends back home. I hope they do not get seduced into the modern machine of greed and money and power that is destroying our planet. They are certain to go to the ghats, where the public rituals for the dying create an intense spiritual*

*experience for the living. Visitors come here to go to the ghats. I
wonder what they will make of the place.*

I once heard a story about a man who had been skiing in the
French Alps. With no warning, a blinding snowstorm enveloped
the region, and he became separated from his friends. He wandered in fierce blizzard winds for many hours until he happened
upon a remote Catholic monastery. It was quite late and dark,
and he could see no sign of life. He banged loudly on the wooden
entry doors until finally an elderly monk arrived to let him in. He
was given a bowl of hot soup and shown to a cell with a single
bed. Hanging above his head was an image of Jesus Christ. He
had just fallen into a deep sleep when he heard a loud knock. He
opened the door and faced a monk carrying a lantern. The monk
said, *Memento mori.* Then he moved down the hall, knocking on
each cell door. *Remember death.* The exhausted skier looked at
his watch. He determined that this was a midnight ritual and fell
soundly back to sleep. An hour later the same knock arrived, and
the same monk, and the same message: *Memento mori.* Every
hour all night long. These monks were never allowed to forget.

The young Westerners were getting ready to move off. Being
reminded of death every hour could not be more different from
the prevalent view—especially among people who looked like
them—that contemplating death is morbid, and speaking about it
in public is impolite. *Perhaps they will head to the ghats right away.
If their timing is fortunate they will see a body burning by the river's
edge, and breathe in the smell of burnt flesh, and know without
doubt that they will die.*

Once they moved on, I stood up and began to meander
through the station, trying to figure out where to go. I stopped at
a newsstand and picked up a guidebook about India that had excellent maps with routes and distances from one city to another,
and a special tour of the four primary Buddhist pilgrimage sites.
Following the linear convention, the tour started with the birth-
place of prince Siddhartha Gautama, the Buddha-to-be, in Lum-

bini, which today lies in southern Nepal. Not knowing what else to do, I immersed myself in the Buddha's life story as if stumbling upon it for the first time.

The book described the prediction made at the Buddha's birth, that he would grow into either an influential political or spiritual leader. The thought of his being a spiritual leader alarmed his father, who was head of the Shakya clan. Determined that his son would continue his political legacy, the father constructed a pleasure palace of sensory indulgences and amusements intended to intoxicate Siddhartha and to curb his curiosity for anything else. Sights deemed unpleasant, stressful, or frightening were banned from the premises. Not only did the scheme fail, but it backfired in a big way. Siddhartha found his way to a nearby village, where he witnessed one person diminished by age, another ravaged by illness, a corpse, and in their midst a calm and contained ascetic. The blinders came off, and he soon fled into the forest seeking the truth.

Once, when I was visiting Mumbai, I was taken to see a Bollywood movie set that was built to look like a suburban neighborhood. Now I thought, *What if a modern Buddha-to-be escaped the artificially perfected life, a kind of one-dimensional cinema version of a suburban idyll, a palace-prison, and came to Varanasi?* Maybe the Westerners I had just seen came from towns like that, with every house the same, every plot of garden the same—manicured but not alive. Varanasi was the best place to learn about sickness, old age, and death. But what about the fourth encounter that Siddhartha had in the village, with the contained and centered ascetic in robes, someone who might have resembled me? *What could I inspire, biding my time with my nose in the pages of this guidebook because I do not know what to do, where to go?*

When the prince ran away from his father's estate, he died as Gautama. He gave up his life of luxury to follow the ascetic principles of the forest yogis. He barely ate, he never washed, he slept on the ground—practices that denied comfort to the body as a means for awakening the mind. But after six years, extreme austerities had not led to a liberated mind. In order to pursue his path, he needed to renounce asceticism.

The guidebook moved on to Bodh Gaya, where Gautama sat down under the bodhi tree at what today is the Mahabodhi Temple. Here is where Siddhartha was reborn as the Buddha, the "awakened one." No matter that I knew Bodh Gaya more intimately than the travel writer. I would keep reading with furious fascination. I would read the story of my heritage for as long as I needed to—for the next step required leaving the station.

The text spoke of the Buddha *attaining* enlightenment under the bodhi tree. I began making corrections. Too often enlightenment is understood as some new state of consciousness that is achieved, as though it is an object to be obtained, or something to strive for, outside of ourselves. Yet the Buddha saw that his grasping mind was the problem. He had gotten reality upside down. After years of trying to control the mind and deny the most basic needs of his body, he made a decision to stop trying to *get* enlightened, and to simply sit down and look into his own mind in order to see what he could learn from directly observing his experience in the present moment. That is what he did under the bodhi tree. What he discovered is that our true nature is already awake, already perfect as-it-is; and that what he initially sought to attain was already within him.

The insight that the Buddha discovered is so simple, and yet so difficult to accept. His teachings introduce us to a dormant, hidden, unrealized part of ourselves. This is the great paradox of the Buddhist path: that we practice in order to know what we already are, therefore *attaining* nothing, *getting* nothing, *going* nowhere. We seek to uncover what has always been there.

In Sarnath, only seven miles from Varanasi, the Buddha taught for the first time. The guidebook explained that his first teaching expounds the truth of suffering. Fair enough, I thought, but left unexplained, this single statement has led people throughout the non-Buddhist world to mistakenly consider this tradition to be nihilistic, even morbid, and preoccupied with mental anguish.

Where does the suffering arise from? To function as if our own lives and those of our loved ones will last forever is clearly a misperception. To think that we will never be parted from family or companions is a misconception. To think that our relationships, our health, finances, reputations, and so forth are stable is an inestimable mistake—as many of us have already learned through loss and abrupt change. Even now, after the World Trade Towers have fallen, and the *Titanic* has sunk to the ocean floor, and the Bamiyan Buddhas have been blown off the earth, we still get fooled into perceiving structures as lasting—the bigger the more durable.

The Buddha's truth is that yes, life is suffering, and the nature of our life as we now know it is one of discontent, frustration, and dis-ease of all kinds, as long as we remain stuck in our misperceptions; but these misperceptions are not fixed—they are not bound to anything. Therefore, we have a choice. The avoidance of our inner demons—our fears of change and death, our rage and jealousy—only imbues these adversaries with greater power. The more we run away, the less chance we have of escaping. We must face suffering, move into it; only then can we become free from it. This is the first noble truth.

I suddenly saw that I could spend a long time here, for I had reverted to my role as teacher. I was in my old skin, which was as familiar as the robe I was wearing. *Where was my pilgrim mind— the mind that goes forth with head bowed in humility, the heart in supplication to whatever arises? I cannot stay here forever.*

The last major site is Kushinagar, where the Buddha died, in around 487 BCE. There the tour came to an end. Two thousand six hundred years later, inspired by the Buddha, my own tour was just beginning. *Or had already began. Or will begin when I remove my monk's robes. Or when . . . I am not nailed to this floor. Even as I am standing still, my blood, heart, and lungs circulate, beat, and breathe, my cells are dying and regenerating, my organs are aging. If I knew where to go, I might move.*

Kushinagar turned out to be only fifty miles to the northwest. I had only been there once, many years earlier with my brother Tsoknyi Rinpoche. In general, Kushinagar does not receive the same pilgrim traffic as the other Buddhist sites—all of which I had visited many times. With June temperatures climbing to 120 degrees, even the devout stay away—especially Tibetans, who are still adjusting to the southern climates of their exile. That was a useful detail, since I didn't want to be recognized. I bought a ticket for the next train to Gorakhpur; from there I would catch a bus to Kushinagar.

About five hundred years after the dialogue between the monk Nagasena and the king, the same deconstruction of self was re-phrased by the eighth-century Indian master Shantideva—only he took it a step further:

> The teeth, the hair, the nails are not the "I,"
> And "I" is not the bones or blood;
> The mucus from the nose, and phlegm, are not the "I,"
> And neither is it made from lymph or pus.
>
> The "I" is not the body's grease or sweat,
> The lungs and liver likewise do not constitute it.
> Neither are the inner organs "I."
> Nor yet the body's excrement and waste.

To demonstrate how the deluded self creates its own suffering, Shantideva asks:

> If such a thing as "I" exists indeed,
> Then terrors, granted, will torment it.
> But since no self or "I" exists at all,
> What is there left for fears to terrify?

This *I* named Mingyur Rinpoche had been stressed out in the Varanasi station. And this *I* was being asked by Shantideva—as each one of us is being asked: *What is there left for fears to terrify?* Or, put another way: *Who am I?*

If we play along with Nagasena and Shantideva—even as intellectual wordplay—it's easy to conclude that this *I*—this recipient of terrors—does not exist, not in any essentialized form. *And yet . . . this I that cannot be found, that is as essentially transparent and fluid as water, can still get so hurt.*

Without any training, I might have concluded that the railway station was the problem, not my mind. True, that station could have used some rat control, and had more efficient services for cleaning litter and poop. That would have been nice. But when we look at our middle-class lives, or at the lives of those who live vermin-free, with sufficient food and soft chairs, we do not encounter much contentment. The Buddha taught that the mind is the source of suffering and the source of liberation. When I started traveling to modern, industrialized countries, nothing in the world affirmed this foundational truth more than firsthand encounters with the tormented anguish that coexists with god-realm splendor. Without personal transformation, and without some sense of humility—even with regard to the universe itself—greed and anger are pushing us over the cliff. It seems that without acknowledging the way each of us sets ourself up to receive the arrows, we just keep slinging them at each other, misperceiving the source of our anguish to be outside ourselves.

. . .

This time when I boarded the train I felt like an old hand at third-class rail, less intimidated by the shoving and pushing. Instead of fighting my discomfort, I became more accommodating. *So I feel uptight, so what? I don't like people looking at me suspiciously, that's okay. Notice it, don't pretend, let it be.* Even though Varanasi had been unexpectedly difficult, I departed feeling less disoriented than when I had arrived. Without some basic trust in the truth of change, I might have returned to Bodh Gaya.

With a more relaxed mind than on my first train excursion, I found that my companions looked as destitute as on the previous trip, but they no longer represented a foreign brigade, and displayed none of the hostility I had first encountered in Varanasi. I noticed how often they smiled, how they shared their meager supplies of food, how gently they held their children. Once again, I concluded that modern urban people seem more stressed and agitated than poor rural people. Having material comforts seems to make people grasp excessively, as they are more afraid of losing their possessions. They are always wanting more and more and are never satisfied. Disadvantaged people in Nepal and India, with much lower expectations, seemed more satisfied with what little they had. I had begun to recognize that the problems that beset modern people at the peak of their family and work lives closely parallel issues that arise for people everywhere at the end of life: an inability to accept impermanence, grasping at what is not available, and not being able to let go.

Underlying so much anxiety in the modern world is the fear of death: of what will happen and how it will happen. Will it be painful? Will it be difficult? Will there be guilt, remorse, redemption? People everywhere are afraid of dying, but the *fear* of death, and the denial of death, seem to be reinforced by material values, by our tendency to grasp at the life we know.

I wondered how dying as Mingyur Rinpoche would affect my

own relationship to future changes, to working with impermanence and physical death—assuming that I could pull this off. I
wondered how my father's generation of masters had added wood
to the fire. Many of the older generation of teachers, including
my father, had wanted to do a wandering retreat. Yet after the
Chinese invasion of Tibet in the 1950s, there was a tremendous
sense of responsibility on the part of lamas, especially tulkus and
lineage holders, to maintain the tradition. The rebuilding of the
monasteries in exile and the training of young monks took precedence over personal retreats. I was very fortunate to have been
born in Nepal, and never had to endure the dangerous escape
from Tibet. I was also fortunate that by the time I wanted to go
on an extended retreat, Tibetan Buddhism had stabilized enough
in Nepal and India to allow for my absence from responsibilities
to my lineage, and to the monasteries that I had inherited from
my incarnation. The work of rebuilding the monasteries that had
been accomplished by the older generation of Tibetan masters
had made this retreat possible. Now that I was on my way, I recalled their sacrifices with renewed appreciation.

In the weeks leading up to my departure, everything that was
being left behind loomed like a golden mountain that reflected all
that I trusted and treasured. For weeks, my mind had swiveled
from excitedly looking forward to looking backward with a touch
of sadness. I had endured many moments of doubting if I could
go through with this plan. Even on the train to Gorakhpur I was
wavering between firm resolve and questioning whether I had the
courage to exchange the radiant warmth of this mountainous love
for the questionable hospitality of the streets. When I felt the
balance tipping too far into darkness, I recalled stories to boost
my confidence. So much of my introduction to dharma—as with
all Tibetan kids—had taken the form of unforgettable stories.
One in particular was about a relative of my father's.

As a young monk in his twenties, this man wished to see Patrul Rinpoche (1808–87), one of the greatest of all Tibetan mas-

ters. Patrul Rinpoche generally preferred traveling alone and often tried to sidestep monastic responsibilities. He wished for nothing more than to live in the mountains, unrecognized. He looked so destitute, with such tattered and shabby robes, that he was frequently mistaken for a beggar; he had even been turned away at the gates of the very monasteries that had invited him to teach. Patrul Rinpoche might teach from the abbot's seat or he might be shunned; served the best food, or given a handful of barley flour and told to keep moving. Either way was fine with him. I wondered if I could train my mind to be that steady in all circumstances, accepting whatever arose.

According to my father, this young monk caught up with Patrul Rinpoche during a journey that the venerated master was making in the company of several other lamas. One night they slept in a field at the base of a high pass. During the night word spread that Patrul Rinpoche was nearby, and the pilgrims woke to shouts of excited devotees scrambling down mountain footpaths from their villages to make prostrations and present offerings. One man stepped forward with an exceptionally large, heavy gold coin. He told Patrul Rinpoche that a family member had just died. He held out the coin and asked for prayers. Patrul Rinpoche said he would happily offer prayers but had no need of the coin. The man insisted, explaining that he could not accept the prayers if Patrul Rinpoche did not accept the coin. This went back and forth until Patrul Rinpoche said, *Okay. I will accept the coin. And after the prayers, I will give it back to you.* The man agreed but after Patrul Rinpoche offered prayers, the man refused to take back the coin.

While the disagreement continued, the rest of the party packed up the bedrolls and cooking gear. Patrul Rinpoche finally said, *Let's put the coin down on this rock and leave it here.* Everybody agreed that this was a good solution and began moving off. Only the young monk stayed behind. He could not take his eyes off the big gold coin, and he could not believe that everybody else had walked away from it. He calculated that if he didn't take it, a villager would sneak back and grab it. He tried to rationalize stealing by imagining all the altruistic things he could pursue with so much wealth. He stayed near the coin for such a long time that Patrul Rinpoche and the others had almost reached the top of the pass, and still no villagers had returned. He started running toward the pass but stopped and turned backward. The morning sun had risen above the mountains, and now the rays of light hit the coin, making it radiate like the sun itself. Again he fastened his eyes on the coin. He did this once more, and then ran to catch up with the others.

However many times my father told me this story, he always made sure that I understood the main points: *You will have a thousand chances to choose between a negative and a positive direction*—meaning increasing or decreasing suffering for yourself and others; and, *If you really aspire to cut your attachments, you can do it no matter what the circumstances*—but there will always be something pulling you back in the other direction. It will never be easy, but it can be done.

I understood that feeling the pull of what I valued and loved and what is familiar is a necessary part of cutting attachments. I also started to see that dying to the old self, and being reborn as something new, would not happen overnight. I was not in the familiar setting of a monastery, but I was still too much myself, my Mingyur Rinpoche self, to sit comfortably on the floor among strangers. *But it will change. I am sure of it.*

I stared out the train window. I had just been picturing Patrul Rinpoche in the cool crisp mountain area of Tibet. Now I saw flat fields under a blistering sun. If I could have talked to my father at that moment, what would he have said?

Ami . . . listen to me . . .

And then what . . . What was the next line?

Lulled by the motion of the train, I dozed off.

PART TWO

RETURNING
HOME

16

Where
the Buddha
Died

THE BUS RIDE from the Gorakhpur rail station to Kushinagar
takes about an hour and a half. Handling money was becoming easier, but I still had to examine each rupee note for the correct denomination. I took a seat on a wooden bench by an open
window. The highway passes through landscape that becomes
increasingly remote and rural—fewer and smaller villages between longer stretches of green fields. Teams of yoked oxen prod-
ded from the rear by old men in skimpy white dhotis made their
way through the fields slowly, their tails swatting flies off their
flanks. I saw entire families working together. The bus shared the
highway lane with cars and trucks as well as with small horses
hitched to carts that carried people, along with caged birds or
plastic sacks of grain; others contained mounds of fresh-cut cau-
liflower, or stacks of long wooden poles that looked like building
supplies.

I felt relieved to be away from Varanasi. The last few days had
been difficult. Still, I had enthusiasm for this retreat. I had stayed
aware of the turbulence in my mind, which remained at the surface. Deeper down I feel alert, confident, even content. *I know
that the turbulence is not the real problem. I still wish to be reborn
as a carefree wandering yogi. I don't want to live like a prince,
trapped in a sanitized environment. If the point of meditation were*

*to simply get rid of negative emotions, I would not be interested in
practicing it at all.*

Mongrels roamed freely; cows, chickens, pigs kept their heads
to the ground, either eating or looking for food. Crows chattered
from branches, and white cranes sat still as pillars on the ground
or perched on the backs of cows. The farther into this peaceful
countryside we traveled, the lighter I felt. *These views of fields and
animals must look similar to what the Buddha saw.* During the
Buddha's time, Kushinagar was the capital of a small dynasty
called Malla. *There would have been more forests, with dangerous
snakes and leopards and tigers. I suppose the Buddha walked barefoot on dirt paths. I wonder if he was ever afraid.*

Pilgrims come to Kushinagar to visit the Parinirvana Park, the
site that commemorates the Buddha's death. According to the
guidebook I had read in the Varanasi station, this consists of an
extensive area of manicured lawns that surround a stupa, and an
adjacent nineteenth-century building that houses an ancient
twenty-foot sandstone statue of the dying Buddha reclining on
his right side, his head facing north. A mile away is the Ramabhar
Stupa, known as the Cremation Stupa, built to hold the relics
from the Buddha's cremation pyre. There isn't too much else to
see. Since my last visit, several temples from different Buddhist
countries such as Tibet, Burma, and Thailand had been built
near the Buddha-sites. Mostly Kushinagar remains an indistinct
Indian village.

The park entrance is just off the highway, and from the direction of Gorakhpur, it's located before the bus depot. The driver
kindly agreed to drop me near the gate. I bounded off the bus and
headed for the park, happy to have arrived and to be away from
Varanasi. It had just stopped raining, and the air smelled clean
and the grass still glistened.

Two uniformed guards sat at the entryway. They examined my
Nepalese citizenship papers and waved me on. I went directly to
pay my respects to the reclining Buddha. Setting my knapsack

aside, I did three full prostrations, and then sat in a kneeling position on the floor. I prayed to stay connected to the timeless awareness that is the very essence of all turbulent emotions. I prayed to allow feelings of discomfort, and especially of embarrassment, to self-liberate, to let the feelings be, and to hold them within awareness. I prayed for the courage to welcome negative emotions and to try to work with them. I prayed to see the waves not as monsters or other threatening obstacles but as displays of enlightened activity that reflected the true nature of my own mind. I prayed to deepen my understanding so that I could be of more benefit to sentient beings.

I picked up my pack and backed away from the reclining Buddha, not turning away until I stepped through the doorway. Then I circled the park a few times, enjoying the quiet and checking out places where I might wish to sit the following morning. I passed the guards on the way out and walked slowly toward an area of guesthouses that were five minutes from the park. On the way, I bought an ear of roasted corn for five rupees from a street vendor, and five bananas from another vendor for only one rupee each, astonished that bananas were so inexpensive.

I checked in to a one-story guesthouse. Its name, Dharamsala, means "pilgrimage house," indicating the simplest and cheapest accommodation. The proprietor, a friendly middle-aged man, showed me to a room, about eight by eight feet. It had a small bed, a ceiling fan, an attached bathroom with a shower, and no meals, for two hundred rupees a day (about three US dollars).

This would be my home, from which I would venture out in the morning to tentatively test the homeless life, and return in the evening. *Don't be in a rush,* I told myself. *I will stay on this bridge for as long as I need to, becoming homeless, becoming a beggar and a sadhu, becoming familiar with this new way.*

The dormitory at the Varanasi station had been my safe ground. This guesthouse in Kushinagar would function the same way. This retreat was supposed to expand my edges so far beyond the boundaries of what I knew about myself that there would be no *me* left to feel self-conscious. There would be no roles to play, no expectations to be fulfilled, no titles that needed to be honored. But I had gotten ahead of myself. My father was always telling me not to be so impatient. For all my efforts to please him, I had not learned that lesson. I mistook adding wood to the fire for an event, instead of understanding it as a process. Somewhere in my imaginings, adding one skinny stick of kindling at a time got mixed up with igniting a bonfire.

17

•

What
Is Your
Happy Dream?

THAT FIRST NIGHT at the guesthouse, I had another disturbing dream. I was outside, in no place that I can name. It was dusk. Images unfolded in grainy black and white. Suddenly a commotion erupted. Police officers surrounded me, pushed me into a car, and took me back to a monastery. That's all I remember. On first waking, I was not clear whether returning to a monastery expressed desire or dread. The monastery represented protection for my body, and liberation for my mind. But as the dreamscape came into focus, it definitely resembled films in which bad guys get carted off to prisons, and inmates live in cells.

Less than a week had passed since I'd acted like a jailbird leaving Tergar. Now the police had picked up an escapee, a dangerous most-wanted Buddhist abbot, armed with emptiness, aspiring to move deeper into emptiness. Just as with the bad dream that I'd had in the Varanasi station, it registered that I had not woken up within the dream. In taking the dream imagery as real, I had allowed fear to once more gain the upper hand. Now that I was awake, I thought, *That was a strange dream. I do not have negative associations with monasteries. I love my monasteries and my monks and nuns, but I do not want my retreat to be interrupted, and do not want to return. In either case, it was just a dream—good, bad, let it be. Anyway, I am more interested in how dreams affirm emptiness, how their translucent appearance reflects our own essential emptiness.* Even though I had felt the police pushing my body into the car, I had no sense of mass within my own body, or in theirs. I had woken up with the threat of menace, but it had no shape and was no more or less reliably real than the intense embarrassment I had experienced in the train stations. Still, both the embarrassment in the stations and the fear in the dreams were embodied experiences. Real, but not true.

What is your happy dream?

I asked this question of a man I once met in California. Several years earlier he had quit an excellent job at a high-tech company in Silicon Valley. He had been reading books about emptiness and had come to the conclusion that his job was empty—empty of meaning, of value—and that the workplace, the status, the money, these things too were essentially empty. He decided that his life had no meaning, and he quit to do something that he had always wanted to do: become a painter.

He spoke in an earnest manner, often bringing his hand to his mouth, as if checking on the accuracy of his words. His hair and beard were turning from black to gray, and he was dressed casually, but carefully. For several years he had worked in his studio making art and had led a rewarding life. Then he had attended teachings that I was giving on emptiness. After one session, he asked to speak with me. *I like these emptiness teachings,* he told me, *but there is one problem. Before, I read books about emptiness, and I saw that my job was emptiness so I let go of it. I really like making art, but after listening to you today, I see that even my art is emptiness. Now maybe I need to let go of my artwork, but if I do that, I will have no money.*

I told him, *Emptiness doesn't mean nothing.*

He was quite shocked. I told him, *Everything comes from emptiness. It is full of alive potential, full of possibility.*

Then I asked him, *What is your happy dream?*

He said, *To have a house on the beach.*

Okay, let's say that one day you have a nice dream in which you have the house on the beach. And you are so happy, right?

Yes, of course.

Then suddenly, a fire burns your house down, without dream insurance. How do you feel?

It will break my heart.

I asked, *Is that house real or not?*

He said, *Of course it's not real. It's a dream!*

I said, *If you have a big problem like your beach house burning down, what would be the best solution?*

He thought very carefully, and then said, *Maybe wake up in the dream.*

Yes. If you know you are dreaming, then the tiger cannot catch you, and fire cannot burn you. If your house burns down, you can build another one. In our daytime life, we do not deny wanting the house or the career. But if we recognize the essential emptiness of phenomena then we can enjoy our desires without getting attached to the misperceptions that cause suffering.

You and I right now, we are the same as the dream beach house. Not real. But we are not nothing. Many people think that emptiness is nothing. But everything comes from emptiness. If you recognize the dream house in the dream, and look at your dream house, you know that it is not real. But the dream house is still there. Real and not real together.

When people hear about emptiness, they often think it means something negative, like the tech executive who did not find meaning in his job anymore. This is a common misunderstanding. Emptiness is not an idea or a story. It is an embodied experience that occurs when we explore experience itself, and discover that the seeming solidity and permanence of phenomena do not really exist.

Dreams are a perfect example. The dream house appears in

the dream. We see it and feel it. Yet it doesn't exist. We easily accept that dreams arise from our minds. The executive acknowledges that the dream house is empty of substance and does not really exist. But that does not mean that he does not experience it. If it burns down in the dream, it will still break the man's heart.

This is how life works. Our minds are creating our experiences moment by moment, and we experience these creations as real—so real that we mistakenly assume that we are seeing reality out there, independent of our own mind. But the object of perception cannot be separated from the mind that perceives it. We cannot feel our dreams. We cannot feel, taste, or touch emptiness. We cannot know its origin. We cannot actually say emptiness exists. But saying this doesn't negate it. It's as real as a dream. Everything arises from this unknowable ground of emptiness. Things appear, but they do not exist in the ways that we assume that they do. What we are pointing to is beyond words and language and cannot be known by the conceptual mind. We have learned to think in dualities: real versus not real; daydreams versus night dreams; good–bad, living–dying. When we encounter experiences that do not fit into these dualities, we tend to dismiss them. They make us nervous. We cannot accommodate them into our dualistic logic. When the conventional world agrees that what the mind knows with its ordinary perception sums up all that can be known, then it becomes more difficult to pursue the truth.

As we gain more insight into daytime and nighttime qualities of mind, we gain more confidence in accepting the limits of consensus-reality. With investigation, we can see that the social fabric is pasted together by consensus. The more people who share the consensus, the more real it becomes, and the harder it is to change or dismantle it.

This lesson was learned the hard way by a maharaja in ancient India. The India of today used to consist of separate principalities, each with its own king, or maharaja. Animosity often plagued

neighboring regions. One time, after a particularly heavy monsoon rain, when all the wells were filled to their brims, members
of one principality crossed into their enemies' territory and poured
poison into every village well. Only the king's well was exempt, as
it was protected by guards.

The poison induced delirious happiness. Everyone stopped
working. The fields and livestock went untended. The villagers
danced in the streets all night, sang songs, and flirted outra-
geously. The maharaja knew that his rival foe had plotted this in-
toxication to destroy his kingdom. He went into the streets and
explained to the people that they had been tricked by the enemy.
But the people all agreed that the maharaja had gone mad. For
several days, the maharaja tried to make sense among people who
had gone senseless. Finally, isolated from the people he loved,
and alone in his misery, he drank from their wells and joined the
revelry.

The maharaja suffered in isolation. We do not need to do that.
We can swim against the stream with the help of masters and
wisdom texts—and our own intelligence. Traders and hunters
who encountered Milarepa wandering through snowy mountains
in winter with no boots or clothes thought him a total madman.
In turn Milarepa thought they were insane, for they kept themselves locked in prisons of their own making, even while holding
the key to their own liberation.

I tucked a few rupees and my identification papers into the
pocket of my shirt, left my backpack at the guesthouse, and set
off in the dawn light to pursue my own happy dream. My first day
meditating outside! My menacing nighttime dream was swept
away by my enthusiasm. The early air was refreshing and not too
hot. During the summer, the Parinirvana Park opens to the public
from six in the morning until six at night. I arrived just as the
guards were opening the gate. They examined my Nepalese citi-

zenship papers again and waved me on. I continued to the far side of the gate. In the shade of a grove, I removed the upper robe and spread it on the ground to use as a sitting mat. I began by contemplating my motivation.

My motivation was the same as it had been on the Varanasi station floor, the same as sitting before any shrine: to become free of self-created suffering in order to help liberate others. That morning I began with a reflection on why the Buddhist tradition places so much emphasis on motivation. Over the previous few days my motivation had never faltered, even though my meditations had known more distraction than usual. Meditation experience will go up and down. If we get attached to what we deem *good* meditations, we will surely be disappointed. Commitment to working with the mind means sticking with the intention, the aspiration. We keep trying. Continuous effort has more long-term value than fleeting results, no matter how positive they may be.

For the next several hours, I did a simple practice of resting the mind in awareness. And then I ended the session by dedicating the merit. This is the final step of any formal practice period. We do not want to keep any virtue that we may have accumulated for ourselves. For that reason, we give it away to others. I dedicated the merit to family members, to teachers, to the world, to all sentient beings. Dedication is a way of sharing, a function of what we call *spiritual generosity.*

After the first few hours in the grove, the freshness of early morning gave way to oppressive heat. Few visitors entered the park, and I enjoyed the relative isolation. Yet being alone in new surroundings kept my senses on high alert, even though I was once again within a gated enclosure protected by guards. I welcomed this sanctuary while noting the irony. It was the perfect place for me to experiment with my new life. Not in the wild, not subject to predatory animals; secluded, but not isolated. The park was midway between new and familiar, an expression of the Buddhist religion in a Hindu town . . . *just like me* . . .

I got up and replaced the upper robe. Despite the heat, I would continue the custom of wearing a robe that covered my left shoulder, leaving my right shoulder bare. This ritual would not change—yet. I had already had several cups of tea with sugar, totally contradicting my regular diet, but the robes were in another category. They were my only precious possession, and I would take my time giving them up.

I circumambulated the park a few times, stopped at the public toilets, and then at the public well, where I pumped water for drinking. Another first. After that, I left in search of something to eat.

I stopped at a makeshift outdoor food stall with a few metal benches and a tarp overhead. I ordered the cheapest and most desirable item on the menu: rice and dal. To my delight the lentils were the large yellow variety that I knew from Nubri, and prepared very close to the way my grandmother had cooked them. For a few minutes, the taste carried me back to my childhood, and I got lost in memory.

After lunch, I returned to the guesthouse to avoid being out in the hottest hours and continued to practice sitting on my bed under the ceiling fan. *Still picking and choosing, but it's okay. I am learning.* At around three o'clock I returned to the park, again showing my identification papers. I did not eat after lunch, and when the park closed I returned to the guesthouse by the most direct route, not venturing into the village. I sat on my bed and repeated the same sequence of practices that I had done in the morning and the afternoon, and then reflected on my day.

On the surface, I was still getting pushed around by how new and unfamiliar it felt to be in the world, and to be by myself: meditating outside, staying in the guesthouse, handling money, ordering a meal, eating alone in public. On another level, every first-time event induced excitement and wonder and optimism. *The journey has really started. Now I am moving. Where am I going? I don't know. How wonderful.*

• • •

That night I concentrated on the intention to recognize the dream within the dream. The basic preparation involves setting the intention, just as we might say, *Tomorrow I want to wake up at five* A.M. To remember our dreams on waking up, we make a similar wish. If we determine to wake up within the dream, we can repeat over and over—a few dozen times—*tonight I want to recognize that I am dreaming while I am dreaming.*

I dreamed that I was in Tibet. Expanses of emerald fields uninterrupted by rocks or trees spread in all directions under a brilliant sun and dazzling skies. Large colorful flowers dotted the fields as in a Technicolor version of extra vividness. Black yaks grazed in the distance. In one direction, the field ended with a steep drop to a river. I was walking on the grass when I recognized that I was in a dream: *I can do whatever I want!* With my hands stretched out from the sides of my body I held my robe behind me and ran, at first hopping, then jumping, until the wind caught the robe like a kite and carried me up and away into the mountains, and then back down to the river. It was so pleasurable to fly through space. Free as a bird, carried by the wind.

I like this dream more than the dream of getting picked up by the police. I like the dream of Kushinagar more than the dream of Varanasi. I like the dream of these trees, and this fresh air. Buddha became Buddha because he recognized that everything is a dream, including himself.

The next morning, on the way to the park, I stopped to buy roasted corn. I tried to pay, but the vendor refused, making this the first offering prompted by my monk's robes. This made me really happy. The day was especially clear and fresh, no clouds, no sign of rain, just like the perfected weather of my dream the night before. I returned to the Parinirvana Stupa, showed my papers, and walked to the far side. My circumstances were beginning to feel very friendly.

I had enjoyed flying. I had enjoyed the encounter with the vendor, and the corn was nearly the best thing I had ever eaten. Thoughts of home mixed with the sweet recollections of the morning. Yet here in the park, images of home, corn, vendor, flying through space all existed equally distant from where I sat. One image was not closer or farther than the other. Nor could I say that one thought was more *real* than the other. These thoughts, images, concepts just drifted through like clouds. Memories of home might snag on emotional knots, but the thought of home itself had no stronger roots in an object called *home* than the image of corn lived in a plant called *corn*. When we stop to investigate the quality of these thought-clouds, they emerge more like dreams than like what we normally label *real*. Neither nighttime dreams nor daytime thoughts have substance or durability. Yet until we wake up to reality, day and night perceptions have the capacity to disturb our lives.

I am not the same person as I was in Varanasi. In the past forty-eight hours, I have wandered in hell, taken refuge in a dormitory, spent time with my teachers, especially Nyoshul Khen Rinpoche, hung out with Nagasena to help affirm that my titles are only outer masks. I have felt sad and lonely, confident, optimistic, and despondent. But the mind that experienced so much agitation is gone. Finished. Dead. That doesn't mean it will not reappear—it may be reborn. Either way is okay.

I felt comfortable with my decision to slow down the transition to the street. I had not physically died as Mingyur Rinpoche, but I was in-between mind states. I had flown through space with no more substance than a rainbow. I had traversed mindscapes and had arrived newly reborn into this realm, with this human body—which was not exactly the same body as I had yesterday. If we can appreciate that the body has changed, we can cultivate a sense of renewal, and feel energized to fully live our best day—before going to sleep and dying all over again.

18

Coming
Through
Darkness

M Y FATHER HAD explained to me, *Without the capacity to die continuously, we end up living in a place where only fungus grows—life-forms that grow from dead matter and live in darkness.*

In the conventional view, life comes before death. In the wisdom view, ego-grasping death comes before life. Until we wake up to the pure perceptions that are not filtered and distorted by culture and compulsions, we are sleepwalking, fully alive during neither the day nor the night—*living in places where only fungus grows.* In the wisdom view, in order to wake up to reality in this life, first we must allow the limited, conditioned self to let go and die.

I once saw a cartoon of a hippie seeker who had climbed to the top of a mountain to ask a wise man, *Can you tell my future?*

And the wise man replied, *Sure. Easy. Unless you wake up, tomorrow will feel like today.*

Our rational minds know that if today is the same as yesterday, our bodies will never end. But they do. Yet today often *feels* like yesterday. Right in this example, we can see the difference between stories that we tell ourselves and what actually exists. We can see that our feelings are not in tune with reality. Our bodies are changing while our minds remain stuck. This is not a good prescription for living, especially as we grow into old age. However, we can start right now to cultivate more sensitivity to the subtle everyday transitions, the ways that they require letting go, and the lessons they offer.

Within the bardo of this life, there are three stages to every new endeavor, and these parallel the bardo of dying, the bardo of dharmata, and the bardo of becoming. It works something like this: A new relationship with a romantic or business partner, or a new boss or a new residence or pet—any new beginning—starts with a moment of death. To enter an unmapped domain of newness, and to be completely open and available to what it offers, we must let go of our cherished ideas of how things are supposed to work. We must allow these preconceptions to dissolve; only through dying will the past not dominate this moment. Then we can fully appreciate the sweetness of the fresh atmosphere that accompanies this stage.

So often we determine to stick to a new diet or exercise regime, or we make New Year's resolutions, only to see our old patterns firmly reestablish themselves. When habitual behavior dominates our new aspirations, we cannot move forward, despite our best intentions. When the present is weighted down by past issues, then we live in darkness and cannot benefit from the revitalizing effects of rebirth. We carry into the new realm old idealizations and perfectionist fantasies, which make it difficult to truly succeed in the new venture.

Naturally, we draw on the skills, talents, and creativity that we developed in our past; but to really flourish in our new situation, we must leave our attachments behind. This parallels the bardo of dying. With the end of our bodies, we have no choice but to leave the life we have known. But we can still *choose* whether to let go of our attachments or hold on to them.

At the very end of our flesh-and-blood bodies, we all have an amazing opportunity to recognize deathless awareness. The dualistic mind that has been tethered to the body is automatically released by the collapse of the foundational structure, creating an intensified gap. The process is a more exaggerated version of the dualistic mind becoming unglued and dissolving into dreams when we fall asleep. The point of making these parallels to the bardos within this life is to recognize the continual process of our own dying and rebirth. This can really help us live a joyful life right now. It can also attune our perceptions to the big death that happens when our bodies give out.

If we recognize luminous emptiness at the very end—which is death beyond death—then we do not continue to the next stage, or the next bardo. Becoming completely one with death, and recognizing this union, allows us to enter the deathless realm, which is the eternal present, unconditioned by past or future. It is beyond time, beyond beginnings and endings. In this state, there is no next stage. We know complete ease with the situation we are in—the new relationship, the new job, whatever—not comparing it with the past or anticipating the future, not imposing expectations, not exaggerating possibilities, not being sneaky or suspicious, not making mountains out of molehills or denying unpleasant moments.

Yet typically, as had happened with me, some of the clarity of intent in the first stage wears off. I was still clear about the intention, but with the effort of figuring out things like buying tickets and tea, intention no longer took precedence. Before leaving the monastery, I had expected to die to my old life overnight. This turned out to be naïve. But I did not feel that I was living in darkness like a mushroom; nor was I fully present to either my old life or my new one. *I am trying to let go. I feel that I am slowly, slowly inhabiting a new form. I understand this. I am working on it. But I am not trying to push my old self away. Things will change. Let it be. Let it pass.*

Stage two within the bardo of this life is marked by opportunity, which reflected my own outlook. The scaffolding of my identity as a wandering yogi was in process; nothing was fully formed, but this ambiguity allowed for creative incentives. The unsettled period that characterizes this stage—as it was for me at that point—might be rough or peaceful, up and down, but the enthusiasm holds steady, and optimism is not diminished by the many uncertainties. Everything is in motion, fluctuating; nothing has quite gelled, and the atmosphere feels dreamlike.

The first stage is like dying at the end of our lives; or at the end of our days when we fall asleep. The situation impels us to let go. And then in the next stage we enter a dreamscape, where we experience the insubstantial quality of form. This parallels the bardo of dharmata—the bardo that follows dying. But whether this stage comes before or after we die, it does not last forever either. Slowly, the transparency of dream forms becomes more opaque, and the fluid atmosphere becomes more stationary. The framework is evolving into compact walls, and the possibilities start to constrict. I felt I was still in a dream state, somewhat floating, not walking with my feet on the ground. My mind knew that I had left Tergar, that I was in Kushinagar, that I had started my wandering retreat. But my body still did not feel that this transitory state was my home.

In the third stage, translucent dream forms begin to resemble our previous flesh-and-blood bodies, and the old tendencies strengthen. We become resigned to repetition, even to activities that we neither like nor respect. We may normalize argumentation in our partnerships; small white lies may evolve into deceit and dishonesty. Here, we commonly feel really trapped. The weight of karmic propensities feels as impermeable as rock, and we lose access to the imaginative resolve that might liberate us from whatever realms we are stuck in. In reality, we are no more inherently stagnant than the man who was told that if he did not wake up, tomorrow would look like today. Yet we feel so helpless that we convince ourselves that nothing can be done, that the exits are sealed, and that we are doomed to spin in samsara. The important point is that although it's harder to effect change here than in the previous two stages, it's definitely possible.

Older people have an especially difficult time believing that decades of entrenched patterns are still mutable. Social norms used to confirm these assumptions. Then neurologists discovered what they call neuroplasticity—the ability of the brain to change and respond to new experiences at all stages of life. This information can be incredibly helpful, because if we do not believe that change is possible, of course we will not try.

In the years leading up to this retreat, I had felt somewhat stuck. I loved my monasteries and my students, and nothing brought me greater joy than sharing the dharma. Yet I began to feel stifled in my roles as tulku, teacher, rinpoche, and abbot. I had started to resist the limits of my cocooned life. Even though I spent half the year traveling around the world and visiting new places, people everywhere treated me with similar forms of respect and reverence. I came to feel a little restless, and eager to push beyond my routines.

My good fortune was to know, through my training, that change is *always* happening. Feeling trapped, stuck, immobile—these are self-fabricated stories. We have the innate capacity to liberate ourselves from these numbing descriptions. We really do change every second, like everything else in our visible and invisible worlds. Fifty to seventy billion cells in our bodies die every day, allowing for billions of new cells to take fleeting existence. Life occurs on an ocean of death. Without death there is no life.

If we wake up to this reality, we can actively direct what comes next, and not just passively accept false conclusions of what feels inevitable. This is similar to the bardo of becoming. If we wake up in this stage, we can direct our next day—or rebirth in our next life. In the Varanasi station, I accepted my attachment to my roles and former identities. I could not let go. But I did not give up, and even as I sat on the stone station floor I was still working on it. I did not imagine that my yogi life would become rigid and repetitive, but I knew that without vigilance, anything can.

I did not eat lunch that day and did not return to the guesthouse until evening. By midafternoon, the clear blue skies had turned bleak and moody, and the wind had picked up. I enjoyed the cool breeze, and then drops of rain came down as heavy as hail. At first the tree I sat beneath sheltered me, as the water was mostly held by the leaves, but soon the leaves could not sustain the weight and became like hundreds of spouts that tipped over, and the rain came down on me as if from a chute. I grabbed my shawl and ran into the public toilets. No one else was there and I stood still and continued to meditate.

My intention was to stay present in open awareness—to stay aware of whatever was happening—and to rest in the awareness. Within the recognition of awareness, I acknowledged the sound of heavy rain, the sound of wind, the sensation of wetness, of bad smells, and of standing. I was not reaching out toward any sensation. Not withdrawing. Not getting lost.

On the train to Varanasi the toilets had smelled really foul and I had wished to get away from them, to sit on the train holding my nose, or to get off and buy a first-class ticket. Now I could recognize: *I do not like this smell. That's okay. No problem. I do not have to like it. I just have to be with it. This smell is another cloud. Do not invite it in for tea*—meaning don't create a big story around it, like complaining about the people on the train; and do not push it away, for this just escalates mental agitation and blocks the capacity for awareness.

When the rain stopped, I stepped out of the toilet and left the park to return to the guesthouse. On the way, I vowed that in the coming days I would just be with the rain. I would not take refuge in the toilets again.

• • •

The next day the temperatures soared. The main effort that morning was not falling asleep. Sweat dripped from the top of my head, soaking my robes. My eyeglasses kept fogging up. The humidity seemed to have vacuumed the oxygen out of the air, taking me with it. Heat rose from the ground, creating what looked like a desert mirage. At noontime, I returned to the restaurant with the delicious dal, and then took refuge in my room with its ceiling fan. By three o'clock I was back in the park. I had just unfurled my upper robe when the rain started. This was the type of monsoon downpour that feels like all of heaven has lowered its weight onto the earth. I continued to sit in the grove. My head was getting pelted. Water gushed down my face. I could feel it in my ears and dripping from my eyelids, from my chin onto my chest and down under my shirt. Water dripped from the back of my head onto my shoulders and trickled down my spine. My back itched from the wet cloth sticking to my skin. Within minutes I was drenched. The rain poured from above me, while the ground's wetness enveloped my bottom. A puddle formed in the lap of my robe. *Nothing to run away from,* I told myself, *nothing to avoid, nothing to love or hate, nothing to celebrate or regret. Wet, dry; happy, sad; good smells, bad smells. If I stay with the awareness, I'll be fine.*

It was more than eighty degrees even at night, so getting soaked would cause no harm. It was not as if I were sitting resolutely in a snowstorm getting buried alive. This is the wisdom of discernment. And besides, since I had never washed my own clothes, my robes were getting a good cleaning.

After that I did not go inside when it rained, and I did not return to the guesthouse to avoid the heat. I would continue to pick and choose—between a banana or an ear of roasted corn, this food stall or that one, but I would diminish choices, especially those relating to avoidance.

Three nights later, I again dreamed that I was walking between Kathmandu and Nubri. This time the path led across a valley floor surrounded by high mountains. I was with my mother and other people I did not know. A wide river ran parallel to the path. Suddenly, just behind us, one side of a mountain crashed down into the river. Chunks of stone and dirt, as big as houses, blocked the current. As the water slammed into this impenetrable dam, the river began to rise. My mother and I moved to the side, farther away from the river, but the water continued to surge so rapidly that soon we would drown.

Instead of forcing myself to wake up in order to escape the terror, I recognized, *This is a dream.* I grabbed my mother and we walked on top of the water to get across the river, and then continued our journey through a green field, free from danger.

If I could free myself from fear in a dream state, I could free myself now, on the street, with my eyes open. Why not? Ultimately the waking form is no firmer than the dream form, no more lasting, no more *real*. There is only one big obstacle: It's much easier to recognize the emptiness of a dream when we are sleeping with our eyes closed than to recognize the emptiness of all phenomena when we have our eyes open. The point is not to convince ourselves that we really can walk on water, but to understand that the solidity we normally ascribe to our bodies is not real; and that bringing a more realistic perspective to who and what we are has lasting benefits. Acceptance of our own essential emptiness, and the emptiness of all phenomena, diminishes our impulses to hold tight to things that cannot really be held.

Every day I increased the length of my meditation sessions in the park. Each time I entered, the guards examined my citizenship papers. How quickly I took comfort in this routine, returning to *my* spot in the park, and returning to *my* room. Being outside and alone was getting easier, but I still noticed that it provoked feelings of self-consciousness that decreased on returning to *my* spot and *my* room. Yet at the same time that my mind became more peaceful with the perception of safety, it also became smaller. It's as if it shrank to become compatible with the size of the room. While the confinement brought a certain degree of comfort, it also revitalized my curiosity about the world outside, and I became eager to expand my adventures.

I began exploring different restaurants within the area near the guesthouse, always ordering rice and dal. I also began increasing the number of hours between meals, and experimenting with fasting for entire days. Then the hunger in my stomach transported me to Nubri, and to the honeycomb mushrooms that my grandmother roasted. Each spring she picked morels, dusted them with barley flour, added a little salt and butter, and placed them over embers. When they turned bubbly and soft, she brushed off the ash and we ate them standing at the fire. That dream was from some thirty years ago, and the memory-aroma filled my mouth with saliva.

The summer heat brought outdoor movement to a near halt. A stillness usually reserved for graveyards settled over the village. Until the temperatures cooled down in the evening, the villagers mostly slumbered indoors, venturing out as little as possible. After five or six days of just going to and from the Parinirvana Park, I began exploring the town—or more specifically, exploring my mind as I strolled through empty lanes, or stopped to sit and meditate. Occasionally I passed the Tibetan temple but never went in. One day a Tibetan in monk's robes came out onto the street and tried to get my attention. I pretended not to notice. I did, however, enjoy the Thai temple. It was silent, and the stone floors felt refreshingly cool. I never saw anyone there, and enjoyed hours meditating in the beautiful interior courtyard surrounded by sweet-smelling flowers.

Then I began exploring areas farther away, including a nearby site where Shakyamuni Buddha was served his last meal by

Cunda the blacksmith, a meal that has been in dispute ever since. Cunda the blacksmith was a devout adherent of the Buddha, but a man of modest means. His greatest blessing was to receive the Buddha and offer the midday meal to him and his followers. According to legend, one day the Buddha intuited that the meal contained poison. In order to protect his community members, and wishing not to offend his humble host, he asked that he alone be served. Following this meal, the Buddha became ill; soon afterward he died lying between two sal trees near the Hiranyavati River. The dispute has been over whether the Buddha ate poisonous mushrooms or contaminated pork. In the early texts, the words *pig* and *mushroom* both exist with regard to the Buddha's last meal. But because pigs are often used to locate mushrooms, the meaning of the text is ambiguous. The site of Cunda's house is marked by a small commemorative stupa, but the area functions more like a town square than a holy site. There are no gates or guards. In the early evening, children played on the grass, families enjoyed picnics, and young lovers strolled through the grounds. None of these activities looked unfamiliar, nor could I recall a previous occasion of sitting in a public park with no agenda other than to enjoy it.

One evening at dusk, I walked to the village with the intention of meditating on the street as late as possible. The minute I sat down a swarm of mosquitoes, thick as molasses, descended around my head. I wrapped my top robe around my face and head and then unfurled it to cover my feet and hands. I ended up back in the guesthouse before dark. *Did I anticipate mosquitoes? Do I have to accept everything that arises, make every little mosquito my friend? I know the theory. I get it. But . . . I could have contacted dengue fever from those mosquitoes.* That was possible, though actually dengue fever did not occur to me until later, when I was trying to make excuses for running away.

19

•

A
Chance
Encounter

A FTER ABOUT TEN days, an Asian man came into the park. He was quite tall with dark yellow skin, maybe in his forties, wearing a white cotton button-down shirt, khaki pants, and sandals. I had no idea of his nationality, but I noticed that he sat down, then stood up, sat down, stood up, again and again. He appeared the next day, again sitting, standing, sitting again. After a few days, he approached and asked, *Do you speak English?*

I said, *Yes.*

Are you a monk?

Yes.

Are you meditating?

Yes.

He said, *I came here to meditate, but I am finding it very hard and I cannot sit down for long. Do you mind if I ask your advice?*

He explained that he had been taught anapanisati. In Sanskrit, *sati* means "mindfulness," and *anapani* refers to breath: "mindfulness of breathing." He had been trying to place his mind on his breath, on the sensations of the stomach rising and falling, and on air passing through the nostrils. He had been taught this practice by a Buddhist teacher in the Theravada tradition of Southeast Asia. But his mind grew restless. He could not stop thoughts from flooding in, and his mind often chased after those thoughts. And he could not stay with the sensation of breathing.

I explained that there was no need to get rid of thoughts. *Do not make thoughts your enemy,* I told him. *The problem is not thoughts, it is following them. When you feel yourself moving toward an image, an idea, a past event, a plan for later or tomorrow, that is what you have to watch out for, not the thoughts themselves. When you get lost in thought, or hooked by the story, then bring the mind to the breath as a way of coming back to yourself.*

Then I explained to him, *If you forget awareness, then you are no longer meditating. The breath is like an anchor that helps you to stay connected to awareness. As long as you do not forget awareness, then you can allow thoughts to come in and out like a swinging door. No problem.*

He told me, *When I try to calm the mind, the thoughts multiply.*

This is a common experience. I explained that when we first become aware of thoughts, they seem to multiply; but there aren't really more thoughts than before, we are just more aware of them. Learning to meditate can express a yearning for freedom, a genuine aspiration to transcend the grasping ego; but we are also frightened by this, so our conventional mind has tricky ways of fending off this quest. I told the Asian man, *What you describe is exactly right.*

He looked perplexed, not sure if this was a joke at his expense. It was not. *The first thing that happens when we begin to meditate,* I told him, *is that we learn just how crazy our minds are. Many of us take that as a sign that we are not cut out for meditation. Actually, it is just the opposite; it's the first sign that we are becoming familiar with our own mind. It's a great insight. You will be fine.*

I meant that. This man had traveled to this sacred site and each day, in sweltering temperatures, he had come to the park to practice. To try. That's all any of us can do.

One piece of advice, I told him. *Don't conclude that your mind is significantly different from anyone else's. We all have this monkey mind. Once we put the monkey under the magnifying glass, the mind commonly appears crazier than ever. It's not. You are just allowing yourself to become acquainted with how crazy it has always been. This is great news.*

The fact is that the mind makes thoughts. The lungs breathe. The dynamic element of air—sometimes called wind—within the body keeps thoughts in motion. We can no more stop thoughts than we can stop the wind, or stop our breath.

The man described himself as a very busy guy who had taken time away from an important position in his company in order to meditate and find inner peace. He was staying at the only expensive hotel in the small town. This trip was using up all of his annual vacation time and he felt defeated. He was at war with his thoughts, fighting them and failing. I told him, *It's amazing that you chose to spend your vacation this way. And you are learning exactly the way everyone does—with misconceptions, and frustrations, and trying and trying again. There is no other way.* Then I explained that his frustrations demonstrated a positive sign. They indicated that thoughts had already been recognized as the cause of distress and dissatisfaction. *Just think of how common it is to never stop blaming circumstances, and never even consider looking at one's mind to resolve problems.* Then I said, *Everything that we want is already within us. We need to relax and allow our innate wisdom to come forth.*

Two days later, the Asian man approached me again. He had found the advice very helpful and wanted to thank me. It had been a big relief to learn that meditation did not require getting rid of thoughts. He was able to sit with less agitation. His mind still wandered away from the breath often, and although he was not trying to push thoughts away, he was still troubled by them, and by one in particular. He had difficulty accepting that wisdom was inherent; and that enlightened qualities needed to be revealed, not created. His business depended on bottom lines, goals, and productivity. Striving for gains had defined his life. *I have always feared that becoming more accepting would make me passive. I do not want to be a passive person,* he said.

Acceptance and passivity have nothing to do with each other, I explained. It's important to make this distinction, especially where associations with nonviolence, peace, passive resistance, and passivity have gotten all mixed up. Even some Buddhists think we are supposed to lie down on the train tracks in the face of danger. True acceptance requires an open mind, one willing to investigate whatever arises. It can never be programmed. Quite the opposite, for it necessitates meeting the world with freedom, and maintaining a fresh mind that shows up for all situations. It requires trusting in uncertainty. Acceptance allows for genuine discernment to arise from wisdom, rather than having our decisions limited by rote, unquestioning patterns.

The man explained that even though his work stressed him out, it provided purpose and accomplishment. Since first learning anapanisati, he had tried to figure out how to make meditation more active, more productive, more of an asset to his work.

This man's interest in using meditation to advance his career reminded me of an exchange that took place in Taiwan between a Chinese professor of economics and a close friend of mine, who had been trained in the traditional curriculum of a Tibetan scholar-monk. The professor had asked, *Is Buddhism productive or creative?* This question had left my friend dumbfounded. He barely understood the words, and had never related them to dharma. Still, he wished to place his tradition in the best light. Finally, he concluded that Buddhism was productive.

The professor said, *Actually, productivity will not help anyone. If you concern your efforts with productivity, you get stuck. Conditions change all the time. That's certain. If you get attached to the fixed goals of productivity, you cannot stay open and flexible. You cannot adapt and innovate. Rigidity sets in, and you cannot move the goalposts, even when they no longer serve your purpose. Soon enough, the next new thing—method, product, strategy—has arrived and your way of functioning is obsolete and ineffective. By the time you realize you are going down, it's too late.*

My friend had a lot of trouble sleeping that night. He continued thinking about the discussion, and a few days later he asked to meet with the professor again. This time he told the professor, *I am very sorry. I gave the wrong answer. Buddhism is much more concerned with creativity.* He explained that he had arrived at this conclusion by investigating uncertainty. You could never be certain of anything. *All things are impermanent; death comes without warning . . .* We can die at any moment, and even though we may relate to this information as an inconvenient fact, we never actually lose sight of it—however hard we might try. Impermanence is the bridge between birth and death, which makes every step uncertain. To remain open and responsive requires flexibility. *That flexibility,* explained the monk to the professor, *is creative. We are always taking a chance, whether we acknowledge it or not, precisely because there is no certainty. And to accept impermanence and uncertainty means risking failure. Preoccupation with certainty indicates a fixed idea of success. Creativity means staying open to change, and risking failure.*

I told the Asian man: *Do not worry about succeeding or failing. You do not know the size or the measurements of your mind, so you cannot measure its so-called progress. Taking the focus off the goal doesn't mean giving up. It means staying receptive to the present; it means allowing for a fresh response to what's happening, and becoming more comfortable with innovation than with repeating stale impersonations of your old self. Of course your mind will stray. It will get caught, hooked, you will be distracted by sights and sounds, your mental composure will fall apart and come together again. That's how it works. If you can accept whatever happens—good, bad, or indifferent—that is the best practice.*

We need to develop some confidence in order to know that dropping the masks is not an act of suicidal madness but of renewal. I once watched a video of children making plaster masks of their faces from strips of newspaper dipped in flour and water. When the masks dried, they took them off and painted them in colorful designs and then reattached them to their faces with strings. The children's delight was contagious. I recall thinking, *Just remember to remove the masks. You added them. You can subtract them. Don't forget.*

The same holds true for all of us. I have been told by psychologists that personality traits of young children between the ages of three and six develop into lifelong patterns. These patterns then get reinforced by interacting with an environment that reflects and reinforces these traits. Or we could say: You build a mask and then grow into that mask. In another ten to fifteen years, you fully inhabit the mask. With collaboration from friends and family, it becomes *the real you.* But not quite. On some gut level, below the thinking mind, we know there is more to our being than the masks that hide our true selves. In the middle of the night, a gnawing low-level disturbance leaves us doubting our own authenticity, but often we just do not know what to do, and end up doing nothing.

The process of training the mind peels off the masks. We are not robots programmed to imitate ourselves; but we do not know how to use our creative reserves to let go of rote behaviors, even those that drive us crazy. Being defensive and uptight, lazy, irritable, or self-conscious—these behaviors are not in our DNA and do not have to continue their destructive influence. They can die before we do. We will survive the death of impersonating ourselves, and of wearing masks. We will not just survive, but flourish.

The Asian man had sat quietly, nodding. He looked attentive, appreciative, and gradually sad—as if it was slowly dawning on him that he might soon be saying farewell to behaviors that he had once cherished. He thanked me, and we parted company, each returning to our own meditations.

After another two days, the man again approached me. He asked questions about where I had learned meditation. I explained that my father had been a Buddhist master, and I had gone through traditional monastic training. I did not ask him questions. I wanted to maintain the boundaries of a solitary retreat; although I wanted to help him in his practice, I did not wish to initiate a friendship. Yet he seemed genuinely interested in learning about Tibetan Buddhism and asked if I could introduce him to a practice from my own tradition.

It seemed that this man's main problem was still trying to control thoughts. And that he was stuck with the idea that meditation was about attaining joy and clarity through non-thinking— a common mistake. The essence of meditation is awareness. Joy, clarity, inner peace—these are the by-products, but they are not the essence of meditation itself, and the more we strive for them, the more the mind constricts around ideas of what *should* happen. These ideas about what *should* happen diminish the capacity to recognize our own awareness.

I decided to introduce him to thought meditation. I told him to start this meditation with the same instructions as for anapanisati. *Just as you have placed your mind on your breath, now place your mind on your thoughts. Whatever comes, just watch. In the same way that you could use the breath as support for meditation, now use thoughts. Breath never stays the same for an instant, but it can be a stable support. So try to practice this way, just staying aware of your thoughts, without chasing after them.*

Thoughts come and go. No problem. Register sounds, sensation, no problem. Take note of discomfort in your body, agitation, restlessness. Fine. Be with the clarity of mind, with the clarity of mere knowing. Knowing without concepts. Knowing without the grasping impulses of the ego-self, or knowing without fixation. This connects you to your own inner reality, your inner wisdom.

I suggested that he try this and then come back and tell me how it went. He left for another area of the park. About an hour later he came back and told me: *When I try to watch thoughts, I cannot find them. My mind goes blank.*

That is the secret of thought meditation, I told him. *What you are calling blank is actually open awareness. Here, there is no object of awareness, as with the breath, or with thought. Awareness is aware of itself; it recognizes the spacious, knowing qualities of mind that are always present. When one looks for a thought and suddenly can't find one, in that moment there is no object, just awareness, so it's a perfect opportunity to recognize awareness without getting hooked by an object. But you are not used to recognizing that—so you think it is blank, or nothing.*

Then I pointed out that after the experience of the blank, he had recognized that he could not find his thoughts. *This experience,* I explained, *is not true open awareness, but it's a little more spacious than cascading thoughts. This is awareness without too much thought. If this experience of blank is dismissed as being irrelevant or unimportant, that will not be helpful. The "blank" exists within awareness, but even when we do not recognize it, it means less thinking, less mental spinning. If you can recognize that the blank has less thinking, then you are connecting to the quality of empty-mind—and in that moment, there is clarity and luminosity. What is this luminous mind? It is the mind that experiences thoughts with awareness.*

In other words, when you recognize awareness, then this experience of blank—or of gap—becomes spaciousness. The Asian man saw the blank. For some people, when they watch thoughts, they can see thoughts.

If you can watch thoughts, I told him, *then it's like watching television. You are not in the television, you are watching it. It's like standing at the edge of the river without falling into the current. You are watching your inner television, but remaining on the outside. There is a big screen, and there are many free channels. There are only two problems: The programs are quite old and there are a lot of reruns.*

Again, we decided to part and continue to meditate separately.

Several hours later the guard came around to announce that the park was closing. We approached the main gate at the same time, and the man again thanked me and told me that he could really feel a change in his practice, and that our discussions had made his trip more valuable than anything he had anticipated. He looked very happy, and we wished each other well. I would not be seeing him again as I was almost out of money and had already decided to move to the cremation site once I left the guesthouse.

The man had struck me as sincere. My vows include giving anything I am asked for whenever possible; and to do this without picking and choosing. It is not about liking or approving whom you give to; rather, it's about just giving—when you can. Yet when I returned to my room, I saw how easily I had fallen into the role of teacher; how comforting it was to inhabit a familiar voice. I had wandered between lives for two weeks—and then reemerged as Mingyur Rinpoche, the Buddhist lama, the correct monk, the dedicated teacher. I vowed to be more watchful and hoped that wearing yogi clothes would help.

20

•

Naked
and
Clothed

Each evening in the guesthouse, I wrapped the sadhu shawls around my body, just to try them out. There was no mirror and little space to walk, and at first I wrapped the dhoti around my legs so tightly that I could barely move. Eventually I figured out how to bunch up the material in the front, which allows the legs to move easily. Then I took them off, folded them, and returned them to my backpack. Not wearing Buddhist robes was still disturbing.

I had received my first robes from the great master Dilgo Khyentse Rinpoche, when I was four or five years old, and have worn robes since that time. Monastic robes help shelter the mind from straying into wrong views or incorrect behavior. They offer a constant reminder to stay here, stay aware. They reinforce the discipline of the vinaya vows—the rules that govern Buddhist nuns and monks. I wasn't too concerned with behavior, but rather with the discipline of maintaining the recognition of awareness amid new chaotic environments. My discipline had been safeguarded by robes. I would lose my main public prop; and my suffocating discomfort in the Varanasi train station had left a dent in my confidence. The closer the time came to removing the robes, the more they felt like an infant's blanket. Without them I would be naked and vulnerable, a babe in the woods, abandoned to sink or swim on my own. *Then again . . .* I reminded myself . . . *this is what I signed up for. This is why I'm here—to abandon the robes, let go of the self who is attached to robes, to live without props, to be naked, to know naked awareness.*

I used the last of my money to pay for one more night at the guesthouse. The next morning, I folded my maroon robes and sleeveless yellow shirt with the mandarin collar and little gold buttons that look like bells, and placed these cherished items in my backpack. I wrapped the cotton orange dhoti around my lower body. The cold showers with no soap had been enough to leave my body feeling cleansed, but it had been more than two weeks since I had last shaved. My beard and hair had grown out quickly, creating sensations around my face and neck that I had never known before. I looked around the room, as I had in Bodh Gaya, in another farewell gesture. Goodbye to my life in Buddhist robes. Goodbye to sleeping where I belonged—even if *belonging* was a superficial transaction secured with two hundred rupees a night. *No more private dwellings—except maybe in a cave; mostly streets, and groves, and forest floors. No more paying for food or lodgings—the true beginning of making the whole world my home.*

I looked around the room one last time, and then I left, taking short steps and deep breaths. At the reception area, I told the proprietor that I would not be returning. I had anticipated that he would ask about my outfit, but all he said was, *Your robes are very nice.* I thanked him.

Finally. No Tibetan robes. I felt like a branch that had been cut from the trunk, still oozing sap from the fresh wound. The trunk of my lineage would be fine without me. I was not sure that I would be fine without it. Still, there was a pervasive pleasure, even a thrill, in finally doing this. One step outside, however, and embarrassment pinned me in place. I became a saffron statue. The cotton was so thin that I could hold both shawls in the clasp of one hand. It was practically nothing. I felt nude. Never had so much air touched my skin in public. Body and mind were covered in shyness. The workers in the nearby restaurants and food stalls and the corn vendor who had seen me come and go these past days began to stare. Once again, it was too much too soon. New clothes, no robes, no money, no lodgings.

I must move, I told myself, and the shackles tightened. No one said anything. No one smiled. They just stared. I tried to affect a look of chilled-out detachment, as I had on the Gaya platform. Once my breathing calmed down and my heart stopped racing, I turned and began walking.

The wave was not as crushing as riding flattened against the door when the train had first left Gaya, but it was strong enough to break my awareness. I noticed this, with no particular judgment. What a wonderful change from previous years, especially from when I was a young monk. In the old days, I berated myself quite regularly for any discrepancies between some ideal version of practice and what I was actually able to do.

If I can stay with awareness, great. If not, that's okay too. Don't create stories around good and bad, about how things should be. Remember: Shadows cannot be separated from light.

By now the guards at the Parinirvana Park and I knew each other and I was concerned that a saffron dhoti might arouse their suspicions, that they might wonder if I had committed some wrongful act that would make me want to hide behind a different identity. I walked to the Cremation Stupa. The casual tourist might remain unimpressed by this large irregular mound of dirt, completely unadorned, but for the pilgrim, enshrined objects can invoke the mind that we share with Shakyamuni Buddha; and both sites had brought comfort, no matter what I was wearing.

The Cremation Stupa is also within a guarded, gated park. As I planned to spend the night there, I did not enter, but walked between the outside wall and a small stream, which is where the Buddha supposedly took his last bath. Now plastic bottles, bags, and wrappers line the banks. About halfway around, a small Hindu temple sat in a clearing. I chose a grove to the side of the clearing, near a public water pump. In my sadhu persona, even if I was noticed by the temple caretaker, my presence would cause no concern. I placed the folded lower skirt of my maroon monk's robes on the ground for a sitting cushion. The area was still and quiet. By the time I arrived, a pack of mangy dogs had already settled in for a listless summer day of sleep, jerking awake only to scratch their fleas. Once I sat down in the shade and began my regular practice, the change in outfit had no impact.

At midday, I walked back to the restaurant that I had most often frequented, passing shops with large glass display windows. For the first time, I saw myself dressed as a sadhu. Who was this guy? He looked sort of familiar, and not. Now I could see how long and thick my beard had grown. I thought I could see some black insects near my shoulder, but it turned out to be wisps of hair. I had already lost some weight, but the greatest shock was to see myself out of Buddhist robes. Just as I had not known how reliant I had become on external forms of protection until I stepped into the world without them, I also had not imagined the degree to which I had identified with my robes until I experienced their absence.

21

No Picking,
No Choosing

ACCEPTING WHATEVER GOES into your alms bowl is a huge challenge to the ego's addiction to picking and choosing. The Buddha had accepted Cunda's offering knowing it was poisonous. *What was he teaching? No picking and choosing even at the risk to one's life? Or did he choose to protect Cunda over himself?* As I drew closer to the restaurant, my breathing became markedly erratic. This was my first time begging, and I started to inhale as if trying to inflate my vocal cords with self-assurance. Just to ask loomed as the critical test of this retreat, the defining moment that would complete the passage to the homeless life; the moment that would skewer my pride, test my humility, and measure my resolve.

I had thought this through. I knew the drill—so to speak. But it's not too hard to imagine eating whatever goes into your bowl when your attendant only serves your favorite foods. I had vowed to eat whatever I was given. I would not refuse an offering of meat if it was presented as alms; I would not starve to death to protect my own preferences. By now I was quite hungry. When I stepped into the restaurant wrapped in saffron, the waiters recognized me, and using a term of respect for an Indian holy man, called out, *Babaji, Babaji, you are Hindu now!*

Even with this jovial greeting, and my many rehearsals, my blood froze. For the second time that day I stood still as a statue, my palms sweaty, my voice stifled, my mouth quivering. I wanted to run away. An interior voice goaded me on: *Yes! You can do this! You must!* But my body said, *No! You can't.* The waiters began to stare. I had to force words from my mouth. *My, my . . . my . . . mon . . . ey . . . is finished,* I stammered; *can you please give me something to eat?* The manager displayed neither surprise nor disdain and matter-of-factly told me to return to the kitchen door in the evening, after they had served the paying customers. I had the impression that however momentous this request had been for me, he was an old hand at the begging business.

Just asking for food was a big step for me, even if the results were mixed. My request had not been totally refused. But it had not been granted either, leaving me feeling humiliated; and still hungry; and practically naked in a robe as sheer as mosquito netting. I navigated my way back to the stupa by way of the corn vendor. With my change of outfit, he showed no sign of friendliness and refused my request. More discouraging news, but still I had asked; I had put another puncture in the fabric of old customs.

I returned to the grove near the Hindu temple. As my stomach gurgled from hunger, various emotions again surged, for I had taken the refusal of food personally. *What craziness! I am working to take off the ego hats, to know that they are not real, to know that my monk's role is not real, that my sadhu persona is not real—and yet some version of me just felt stung by not getting what I asked for. Who is this? Spoiled baby Mingyur Rinpoche? Esteemed abbot? What difference would that make? None. It is all gone. It is all emptiness, all delusion, the endless misperception of mistaking this collection of labels for—as Nagasena put it—this designation, meaning that because the conventional composition of how we identify our-*

selves does not really exist, there is nothing "real" to receive the arrows. Because of our essentially empty nature, the hurt that we experience is self-inflicted.

I had been doing an open awareness meditation. Basically all meditations work with awareness. The essence of meditation is recognizing and staying with awareness. If we lose our awareness, we are not meditating. Awareness is like a crystal or mirror that reflects different colors and angles: forms, sounds, and feelings are different aspects of awareness and exist within awareness. Or you might view awareness as a guesthouse. Every type of traveler passes through—sensations, emotions, everything. Every type is welcome. No exceptions. But sometimes a traveler causes a little trouble, and that one needs some special help. With the hunger pangs fueling feelings of vulnerability, shyness, rejection, self-pity, the guest whose name was *embarrassment* was asking for attention. Embarrassment might be subtler than anger, but its impact on the body can be almost as great.

The intention when meditating with emotion is to stay steady with every sensation, just as we might do with sound meditation. Just listening. Just feeling. No commentary. Resting the mind on the breath can turn breath into support for maintaining recognition of awareness, the same as with anger, rejection, and embarrassment. At first, I just tried to connect with embarrassment, which was the dominant feeling.

Where is this embarrassment, and how is it manifesting in the body? I felt the pressure of shyness at the top of my chest. If I had a mirror, I thought, my chest might look caved in—I was pushing my shoulders forward, and making my body smaller than it was, as if trying to hide from public sight.

The embarrassment weighed on my eyelids like flat stones that kept them lowered.

I could feel it in the downward pull of the corners of my mouth.

I could feel the resignation of it in the limpness of my hands.

I could feel it behind my neck, pushing my head down.

Down, down. The feeling of going down. In Varanasi I had wished to crawl down a hole. I did not have that image now, but the sensations echoed being lowered, becoming smaller, taking up less room, not feeling worthy of being on this earth.

At first, I felt resistance to these feelings; and I had to make resistance itself the object of my awareness. Then I could work more directly with the sensations in the body. *I do not like these sensations. I started off feeling bad. And now, added to that, I feel bad about feeling bad.*

Slowly I brought each sensation into the guesthouse of awareness. I let go of the resistance, let go of the negativity, and tried to just rest with feeling small, unloved, and unworthy. I brought these feelings into my mind—to the big mind of awareness, where they became small. The guesthouse-mind of awareness encompassed the feelings, the dejection, the bleakness, and became bigger than all of them together, dwarfing their impact, changing the relationship.

I continued doing this for several hours. I was starving, but had become happy about feeling bad. Feeling bad was just another guest, another cloud. There was no reason to ask it to leave. But my mind could now accept it, and from the acceptance, a distinct physical feeling of contentment pervaded my body.

Not much happens in Kushinagar on hot summer nights, and the restaurants close early. I had only drunk water for the whole day. The handle for the pump was quite long and many feet from the spout. After pressing the handle down, I had to race around quickly to catch the water—my private exercise machine. At about seven o'clock, I walked back to the restaurant and stood at the kitchen door. The rice and dal that had been left on people's plates had been scraped off into a pot that sat on a counter. No more choices. A waiter scooped some leftovers into a bowl for me. The rest would be fed to the dogs. I ate standing at the door—a more delicious meal than any I had eaten at five-star hotels.

I returned to the same grove along the outer wall of the Cremation Stupa. As the evening light faded, I rolled out my shawl and lay on my back. I could not quite believe it, my first night outside. Spending the last of my money had taken a toll. The lifeline that could have reeled me back to safety, to food and shelter, had been broken. I was now adrift. I could no longer afford to reject anything. Not the food I was given nor the bed that I now had. I had begun this journey with preparations. I began again when I left Bodh Gaya, and again when I boarded the train, and again when I sat on the floor at the Varanasi station. Now I thought, *This is the true beginning. Sleeping outside, alone, the ground for my bed, begging for food. I could die here and no one would know.*

All my life I had been in the presence of others, but I had not recognized the cushioned depth of protection they provided. I had understood that it was the responsibility of certain individuals to take care of me. Now there was a more delicate sense of these bodies linked together—like a chain-link fence—to form an unbroken circular shield around me. I also saw that I had not fully appreciated how this protective shield had functioned until it was gone—there would be no more coat in wintertime, no parasol in summer.

Despite my yearning to be self-sufficient, my first days— especially in Varanasi—had showed me in a very primitive way that I had taken my life for granted. For the very first time ever, I had walked alone, talked only to myself, taken a train alone, ordered food and eaten alone, laughed alone. Feeling so isolated from my protectors had left me feeling flayed—stripped of my own skin, bereft of even a thin casing.

The absence of this shield had come into focus slowly. My

extreme discomfort in the train station had provided clues. Although my daytime excursions in Kushinagar had been increasingly relaxed, I had still felt the undercurrents of embarrassment and vulnerability. Now, my first night outside, the undercurrents became more like riptides. I was seized by the full weight of solitude, the feeling of being very far from safety and utterly undefended.

I had taken this invisible shield for granted so completely that I had not been able to see it. It's like taking air for granted—and then suddenly finding yourself in a room without oxygen. *Oh, I get it, that's the element that my life depends on.* I had entered a strange land, an alien territory with alternative requirements. I longed for this world to feel hospitable, but it did not, and I could not find my footing. I recalled my bed at the guesthouse with more longing than my more comfortable bed in Bodh Gaya. Stripped of my lifesaving element, without even knowing what that was, I had peered into darkness like a sailor trying to navigate his return home. I longed to leave behind this misfit, this fish out of water, who was not even suited to share this public park with rabid dogs. *The ground does not accept my body. My shape is not right, my smell not nice. Nonetheless, I have given up choices and here I am.*

It was the longest night of my life. The mosquitoes did not let me sleep for an instant. When I got up to pee, the dogs that had been indifferent during the day turned vicious. But between intense spells of disorientation, my mind continued to comment on the wondrous triumph of pulling off this plan, marveling at actually lying here, on my maroon sheet on the dirt ground near the public pump. Throughout the sleepless night I vacillated between distress and delight, and welcomed the first hint of dawn.

22

Working
with Pain

THE STOMACH CRAMPS started at about four in the morning. They were not severe, and digestive discomfort in India occurs too frequently to cause much concern. Besides, I had a long history of having a sensitive stomach, and so I assumed the cramps would go away as usual. I went to the pump to wash my face and drink water. Then I returned to my spot and began the same sequence of practices that I had been doing every day. Within a few hours, the cramps had become more painful, and each one lasted longer. I had been doing a very simple practice of resting the mind. As the pain grew more intense, I expanded my practice to include working with pain.

The good news about pain is the way it cries out for attention. If you place your mind on your pain, you know just where your mind is. The trick is to stay aware of the mind. Most of the time, when pain asks for attention, we respond by trying to get rid of it. Pain becomes an object outside the mind that needs to be ejected, thrown out. Here's the curious, counterintuitive aspect about pain: When we meet pain with resistance, the pain does not diminish. Instead we add suffering to the pain. The feeling sensation of pain arises in the body. The negative reaction to pain arises in the mind of the fixed self and transforms physical pain into an enemy. That's how the suffering arises. When we try to get rid of pain, we pit ourselves against ourselves, becoming private war zones—not environments best suited for healing. For many people, self-pity attaches to sickness like sticky glue, and the voice of the ego asks, *Why me?* Yet this voice does not reside with the pain in the body but with the mind that identifies with the pain.

As a young monk in the three-year retreat, I had learned pain meditation. Since it's hard to initiate this practice for the first time during intense pain, a more practical approach is to develop pain meditation prior to needing it. The idea is to work with pain during times of good health. This is a critical preparation for aging and dying, as the chances of knowing physical difficulties increase as we grow old.

Pain meditation comes under a category called reverse meditations. *Reverse* means that we deliberately invite whatever is unwanted and unwelcome. If we normally associate practicing breathing meditation in a peaceful, rural landscape, then we try the same meditation in a low-class car of an Indian train, or at a rock concert. If full-bloom roses are pleasing objects of form meditation, then we might try excrement.

In the monastery, we learned a few harmless methods for creating pain, such as digging our fingernails into our thighs or palms, or biting down on the lower lip. We were cautioned not to be extreme, not to draw blood, and to stop once we acknowledged an unpleasant sensation. Now, twenty years later, I understood that this wandering retreat was essentially a reverse meditation. I had intentionally invited trouble.

A common metaphor for the entire Buddhist path is *swimming against the stream*. This refers to the *reverse* aspect of all forms of mind training. To investigate consensus-reality reverses social norms. In a noisy and materialistic society, to sit down and remain still and quiet is a reverse activity. To devote even one hour a day to becoming nobody when we could be in the world becoming somebody reverses socially rewarding goals. To aspire that *all sentient beings have happiness and be free from suffering* runs counter to self-centered preoccupations. When we take a wide look at *reverse,* we can appreciate that the meaning runs much deeper than labeling a category of discrete exercises. It can become a foundational principle for guiding daily-life situations. It can be used to cut through mindless behavioral loops, and for using disruption to wake us up from our sleepwalking habits.

If the avoidance of death is the social standard, then contemplating death becomes a reverse activity. This does not mean that we reject the sadness of death. We will die and the people we love most will die and this is the precious heartbreak of our lives. But the fear and perplexity that surround this ordinary trauma are not inevitable. By facing our fear of the future, we transform the present.

I started to meditate on pain by directing my mind to the sensation of stomach cramps. Then letting it rest there. *Just be with the sensation of pain. No acceptance; no rejection. Just feeling. Explore the sensation. Don't get caught in a story about the cramps, just feel them.* After a few minutes, I started to investigate: What is the quality of this feeling? Where does it reside? I moved my mind from the surface area into my stomach, into the pain itself. Then I asked, Who is having this pain?

One of my esteemed roles?

They are only concepts.

Pain is a concept.

Cramp is a concept.

Stay in the awareness beyond concepts.

Let the self-beyond-self accommodate both concepts and no concepts: pain and no pain.

Pain is just a cloud, passing through the mind of awareness.

Cramps, stomach, pain are all intense forms of awareness.

Stay with the awareness and become bigger than the pain.
In awareness, like sky, there is no place for the concept to abide.
Let it come. Let it go.
Who holds the pain?
If you become one with your pain, there is no one to hurt.
There's just a concentrated sensation that we label pain.
No one holds the pain.
What happens when no one holds the pain?
Just pain. Actually, not even that, for pain is just a label.
Feel the sensation. Beyond concept, yet present. Nothing extra.
Experience it. Let it be.
Then I returned to just resting my mind in open awareness.

Whether we train the mind by using our breath or using pain, or by doing compassion exercises, every practice is about waking up and becoming conscious of a universal reality that transcends the contents of our individual minds. As with a crystal or mirror, awareness has an innate capacity to reflect, even if no object exists to be reflected. This is *mere* awareness—the capacity for knowing, regardless of objects or reflection. Through intense meditation, or other ways of liberating the conceptual mind, we can access mere awareness without perceiving its reflection—it is just knowingness itself. This is the luminosity aspect of mind, the knowing recognition of awareness.

One reason for having many different meditation exercises is that prolonged engagement with one reflective facet of the crystal can grow stale. The meditative mind can be refreshed by moving the dial to another facet. Sometimes we can become overwhelmed by practicing with pain, or with difficult emotions. Then it's best to take a break, have a cup of tea, walk around the block—or try another approach. It's important not to give up, not to stop trying. But we can shift the reflection to another facet—for example from sound to sight, or to breath. I now felt so appreciative for this awareness practice. More than ever, it was my trustworthy companion.

Normal pain—that is to say, the pain that we want to get rid of—is static and solid, and arises from a mind that is stuck in a negative attitude toward the pain. The recognition of awareness can hold the pain without taking a position, or adding a story. This makes it immeasurably easier for the pain to lessen or move on. We cannot change pain directly; but we can change our relationship to it, and this can reduce suffering.

A year earlier a friend had come to see me in my second-floor rooms in Bodh Gaya. I was surprised when he walked in on crutches. *What happened to you?* I asked. He had been going through an acrimonious divorce, and I already knew that his wife had kicked him out of the house. He explained that he had tried to get back into the house by climbing up a tree to an open window on the second floor. But he had slipped and broken his foot. Then he started laughing. *This pain,* he told me, *is so wonderful. I love this pain. It draws all the suffering right out of my head and stuffs it into one little area, like sticking my foot into a sock. I know where the pain is and how to treat it. Now I can think clearly again.*

By midday, bouts of diarrhea had started. I kept telling myself, *This is India*—another way of saying, *This is normal.* By evening I had been draining my stomach and drinking only water for the entire day. I had no appetite but decided that lentils might renew my energy, and that perhaps eating would help settle my stomach. I gathered my belongings and slowly walked to the same restaurant that had provided food the night before. I returned to the kitchen door and stood silently, waiting to be noticed.

Hello, Babaji!

I was again given a bowl of rice and dal from the pot of leftovers scraped off customers' plates.

The manager came over. He stared at me and then asked, *Babaji, are you okay?*

I'm fine, I told him, although obviously he could see that I wasn't. This turned out to be my last visit to the restaurant.

The walk from the restaurant to the outside area of the Cremation Stupa was exhausting. At times I became dizzy, my breathing shallow. It was still twilight when I reached the area near the temple, and I sat down with my back against the wall. I started vomiting during the night. Between squatting and retching, I dozed fitfully for a few minutes at a time. Although my condition did not change with the signs of a new day, I nonetheless felt cheered by the light.

23

The
Four Rivers of
Natural Suffering

D AY THREE OF my outdoor adventure found me circling among the bushes, the pump, and my little encampment. The scorching heat kept visitors away and I was thankful for the privacy. I remained optimistic, and my body was still able to sit in formal meditation posture.

By midday, I reluctantly acknowledged that I was losing strength. When I stood up, my legs shook, and it took increasing effort to lift one foot at a time. I started to worry. I had passed a small clinic in the town but had no money for medicine. Sadhus asking for free medicine are routinely sent away. I knew this from the ones who came to the clinics at the Buddhist monasteries, where they could receive treatment. It crossed my mind to try to return to Bodh Gaya, but I would not be so easily deterred. Each time I stood up, I concluded that I had no place to go. I began sitting with my back against the wall.

Although I still did not take my illness too seriously, I could not avoid the glaring presence of the cremation mound on the other side of the wall. I began thinking, *At least there's no place better to die than right here, where the Buddha died. What a fantas-*

tic coincidence. If these cramps get worse, I might die with pain, but with the blessings of place.

Given that I was now dependent on a wall for a semi-upright position, and with my energy dissipating, these ruminations seemed inevitable. Yet without taking the possibility of dying seriously, they provided little more than entertainment—until they suddenly transformed into a less cheerful option: Maybe being here was not coincidental. *Perhaps I have been drawn here to die. When I first woke up from my bad dream in the Varanasi rail dormitory, I feared that it foretold disaster. Maybe that dream is coming true, and the rocks that fell on me prophesied my death near this crumbling stupa.*

I recalled a story about a man who had almost suffered a terrible death in a perfect place. He was from the eastern Tibetan province of Kham and his greatest aspiration was to visit Lhasa, as it had been for many Tibetans. He traveled with a friend, and it took them several weeks to trek across Tibet. On arriving, they immediately set out to visit the Potala Palace, the seat of His Holiness the Dalai Lama. The man became so ecstatic on seeing this magnificent sacred site that before entering, he stood at the base looking up and cried. Once inside he began to explore different rooms. Some outer rooms had tiny windows set between wooden columns and barricaded by iron grids. The magnificent views of Lhasa from these windows are legendary, and to increase the sight lines he stuck his head through the grid. When he finished admiring the landscape, he could not pull his head back out. He twisted one way and then the other. *I will die here,* he told his friend. *Please tell my wife and family that I died in the Potala Palace, the best place in the world to die. Even though the way it happened was not so nice, I am very happy.* After accepting his situation, he relaxed; and once he relaxed, he was able to withdraw his head from between the bars.

If I could be more relaxed, I considered, perhaps my stomach would not remain squeezed between iron bars. Then again, *he had a friend and I have no friend. I am not even accepting that I might die,* I thought, even though I could no longer keep my head from lolling forward and my hands from slipping off my thighs.

When I returned to my sitting spot from frequent trips to the bushes, before sitting down I would begin to turn and face the stupa. I tried to concentrate on it, as if coaxing my eyes into X-ray vision. I wished to see what really remained and what had died. *The Buddha had died. But I am also buddha, and that guard is buddha, that dog is buddha, you are buddha, even the stupa is buddha. If we are buddhas, not separate from Buddha, who dies? Whatever happens to my body, I am dying; I have been dying from the day I was born. Something continued after the Buddha's body died. Will something continue if I die, here at the cremation site, alone, with no friend to help me?*

The coincidence of place was no longer amusing. I had enough discipline to return to resting with awareness when my mind drifted; but with more frequency it drifted into fear of dying. Yet in my bones I still rejected this outcome. It was like being on an airplane when the pilot comes on the PA system and orders the passengers to fasten their seat belts because they will soon hit extreme turbulence. You think, *Oh no, maybe I am going to die.* You don't really believe this; nonetheless your hands grip the arms of the seat, and you begin to pray, just in case. To God, to Buddha, to Allah. You pray not to die; and you try to connect with people that you love. Those dearest to you come to mind, and you passionately wish for them to know how much you love them before the plane goes down.

I thought of a woman whose husband had worked in construction. He was assigned to one of the highest floors of a new skyscraper. The outside walls were not in place and the wind ripped off a safety net. He was blown out of the interior and fell to his death. The couple had not been getting along well. The night before his death he had slept on the couch, and he had left the house early without saying goodbye to her or their children.

She had been raised Catholic and believed that each of us has our time here on earth, and accepted that for whatever mysterious reason, his time had come to an end. But she remained haunted by not having told him how much she loved him.

Many hospice workers hear similar regrets, that love had not been expressed, or not expressed enough, when the chance existed. A student told me that when her mother lay dying, her mother had told her, *Tell everyone you love that you love them. Don't wait until you are dying.*

I wondered if my mother and Tsoknyi Rinpoche and my grandpa and Tai Situ Rinpoche knew how much I loved them. Had I expressed that enough? I wondered about the khenpos who had trained under me, and everyone around the world who had helped me. I prayed for these people every day. I began reviewing the arrangements I had made for staying away: the video teachings that would be released over the coming years; the designs for new buildings at my monastery in Kathmandu. Many of the little monks in Bodh Gaya were orphans or came from impoverished families; I reviewed my efforts to secure their protection. I had said my farewells. I had prepared extensively. My mother and other family members and friends would feel so sad if I died. But then I thought, *Sooner or later we will all die. The man who fell from the building was not in control of when he would die and neither am I. But . . . why hadn't it occurred to me that I might die? How ignorant to have taken my life for granted. Adding wood to the fire was a kind of suicide, but the motivation was to be reborn in a form that could be of greater help to others. If I maintain the same motivation at the time of physical death, then the same will hold true. That means not getting distracted by pain, or by regret, or by self-pity.*

Shakyamuni Buddha spoke of four rivers of natural suffering: birth, aging, sickness, and death—the inevitable difficulties of life. But they can be experienced without extras, without compounding the suffering with story lines that solidify our misperceptions about reality. There's a teaching tale from the Buddha's time that makes this point. One day a distraught young woman arrives at the Buddha's encampment holding a dead child to her breast. She has come in search of a miracle cure to resuscitate her baby, and to ask of the Buddha, *Why me?* The Buddha tells her to return to her village, and to collect one mustard seed from each household that has never known death; then bring these seeds to him. The woman returns to her village and goes from one house to the next.

Before leaving for retreat, I returned to Nubri and went from one house to the next listening to stories of those who had died in the years since my last visit. An old grandfather, the father of one of my closest boyhood friends, the three-year-old daughter of a friend who had fallen over a cliff on a family outing, a woman I knew as a girl who had died of breast cancer. Every family told stories about births and deaths—and not even a few mustard seeds could have been collected.

The young mother returns to the Buddha empty-handed. *Is there another way?* And the Buddha says, *You cannot find a way to restore the life of your baby, but you can learn to live with death, to make yourself bigger than this loss. Then you can hold the sadness and not drown in sorrow.*

24

Recalling
the
Bardos

A T THE END of the third day of my outdoor experiment, I again decided that a little food would be helpful and prepared to return to the restaurant. Standing up took considerable effort, and after a few steps my legs began to cave in. I stumbled back to the wall, and sat leaning against it as my loud breaths became silent.

I recalled that at the time of dying, one of the first signs of irreversible decline is an experience of heaviness. I imagined that it must feel something like this, for when I returned to the wall and sat down, it seemed as if the weight of my body would continue to fall below the surface of the earth. This happens with the dissolution of the earth element.

We know about the retraction of the senses when falling to sleep. The five elements also dissolve night after night during sleep, but this happens so subtly that very few people can remain aware of the process. However, at the time of dying, the dissolution of the elements becomes as pronounced as the dissolution of the senses, and we can directly experience the dis-identification of form from consciousness.

The elements of our physical bodies have five qualities: solidity, fluidity, warmth, movement, and openness. In the Buddhist tradition, these qualities are referred to as the five elements: earth, water, fire, air (or wind), and space. These same elements make up all phenomena. At the end of our lives, the dissolution of the elements can be observed by bedside caregivers, and experienced by the dying. Even though so few people can track the dissolution of the elements as they fall asleep, many report experiences that relate to them, even when they cannot account for the cause. Some people feel as if they are falling when drifting off, as in *falling* to sleep—a sense of gravity pulling them down, which arises from the dissolution of the earth element. The sensation of floating suggests the dissolution of the water element.

The elements are not to be taken too literally. Earth suggests density and heaviness. It supports us, like foundational beams of a house, and when this support collapses, we experience the sensation of falling. When we speak of the element of fire, we do not picture flames arising from a combustion of fuel and oxygen but rather heat and radiating warmth, or a burning sensation. This dissolution of the elements as we fall asleep faintly parallels the same process when we die. In both sleep and dying, each element is absorbed into the next, so that at the end, space dissolves into itself—or, put another way, space dissolves into consciousness.

These five elements have existed from the beginning of time, and arise from the primordial ground of emptiness. They are the primary ingredients of all matter, including ourselves. Knowing about the elements provides a fundamental connection to every life-form throughout the universe. We live within the same interdependent field of natural forces that govern all matter, and it can be consoling to know that when we die, the sweep of our fleeting lives will bring us full circle, back to our most elemental beginnings.

The earth element relates to flesh and bones, the densest part of our bodies. When we die, the earth element dissolves into the water element. Our strength visibly weakens, and we often experience the sensation of falling or sinking.

The water element relates to our bodily fluids. When the water element dissolves into the fire element at the time of dying, the inner experience feels like floating, and we feel thirsty. The body dries out, the blood slows until it stops, the lips become noticeably parched, the skin feels dry, and the mucus congeals.

When the fire element dissolves into air at the time of dying, we cannot retain heat. The extremities turn cold, although the heart continues to stay warm and the mind feels like it's burning.

Inhaling air, or wind, keeps everything in motion. As the air element dissolves, breathing becomes labored.

Space is the foundational reality of all phenomena, including our bodies. Without space, we cannot have the other elements.

My mind drifted toward those bardo teachings that describe how to prepare for dying, and what happens to the body and the mind when we die. But my motivation was not strong enough to stay with specific teachings. The instructions came in and went out like a tide, forward and away. I continued to assume that the infection would run its course, rage like a fire until it extinguished itself, and that at any minute the cramps would seize with less severity. Like everyone I knew, I had experienced intestinal infections in India many times; they just do not kill you. Yet I had never eaten leftovers before. I had taken healthy food for granted. When I had studied the beggars in Bodh Gaya, I had assumed that they looked weak and weary from not getting enough to eat. I did not understand that their bodies must also have suffered from poisonous food. I had assumed that they had adapted their eating habits to their situation, like animals that live in the forests with limited options. I had not understood that their food source, however meager, might itself have contributed to debilitating their bodies. Now I saw that they too were fragile, and that the suffering of their bodies must be torturous. I still did not recognize that I was losing more water than I was taking in, and that severe dehydration was setting in.

I had a very close friend, a brother-monk from Sherab Ling whom I'd met when I was eleven years old. Two years later we entered the three-year retreat together. We were both very good students, and he was my assistant when I became the retreat master for the subsequent extended retreat. One day while I was traveling in Europe, he telephoned from India to tell me that he was very sick with stomach cancer. *I am in the last stage and cannot eat.*

I asked, *How are you feeling?*

I have no regrets, he told me. *All my life I have meditated on impermanence, and trained in bardo. I am ready, so do not worry about me. But please pray for my body.*

Even though he was not afraid to die physically, his attainment had not transcended his body. He had not yet died in the bardo of this life. As long as we use our conceptual mind to relate to our flesh-and-blood bodies, and use our sense organs to negotiate relative reality, then we will experience physical pain. With my father, it was quite different.

Several years before my father passed away, he became quite sick and word spread throughout his community that he was close to death. Among his students were both Tibetan and Western medical professionals, and they gathered in his small room at Nagi Gompa to direct his care. It was cold outside, with no heat inside, and the concrete walls made his room damp and frigid. In addition, the water was not very good, and was perhaps contributing to his deterioration. One of my older brothers came to visit and tried to talk my father into traveling to a warmer and healthier climate, maybe to Thailand or Malaysia. But my father refused. He said, *It looks like I am sick, but actually, there is no real conceptual body anymore. I feel fine. Whatever happens—whether it is my time to go or to stay—is okay. I am not suffering.*

The recognition of luminosity is the experience of dying before we die, dying within the bardo of this life. When this happens, the flesh-and-blood body no longer functions as the filter or anchor of the mind. Although the body will look ordinary to the ordinary observer, for an awakened mind, the body has become what we call an *illusory* body. It is no longer *real* in any conventional sense, but exists—to an awakened mind—more as a reflection, like a hologram. In this state, although other people will perceive a life that is ending, one who has woken up to their own deathless emptiness will not experience dying as a final ending—only as a transition.

To train in bardo means becoming familiar with the continuous process of dying. I had trained but I was not close to my father's attainment and had not gone beyond the understanding of my brother-monk. I assumed that my friend had meant that during this lifetime—in *the bardo of this life*—he had become familiar with recognizing the vast mind of awareness, the mind that is unborn and cannot die; and that he had developed confidence in the continuity of this mind after death. We were introduced to this view by our classic training. But his conceptual mind had still kept his body intact, and he had not yet known the illusory body, as my father had.

When we accept that we are dying every day, and that living cannot be separated from dying, then the bardos offer a map of the mind during this lifetime; and each stage offers invaluable guidance for how to live every day. Nothing in the bardo texts relates exclusively to physically dying. Every transformation at every stage has already happened again and again in this life; once we apply the bardo cycle to our daily lives, then we can see that all our efforts to wake up relate to change, impermanence, death, and rebirth—the essential markers of the bardo map.

When I learned meditation as part of the monastic curriculum, it was not presented as bardo training. Neither were the exercises on impermanence and dying, nor the meditations on loving-kindness and compassion. Yet once I studied the bardo texts, I understood that all my training was an immersion in bardo wisdom. For example, the basic instruction for the bardo of this life is to become familiar with our minds—and the most effective way to accomplish this is through meditation. Many people today pursue meditation with no reference to the bardos. But when we inhabit the bardo view, we instinctually understand meditation as another experience of dying every day. The transformation that occurs when we allow the conceptual mind to dissolve, and for awareness to be recognized, requires the death of the grasping mind. In the formal sequence of bardo teachings, the bardo of dying follows the bardo of this life; but in many ways, the bardo of dying *is* the bardo of this life—as is the bardo of becoming.

The bardo of this life includes sleep meditation, which means staying aware of what's happening as the eyes close, as the ears shut down, as the respiratory system slows. Advanced meditators, like the Sixteenth Karmapa, could rest in recognition of aware-ness during sleep. This is not easy. Yet even maintaining our rec-ognition to the point where we black out offers immeasurable benefits. Although falling asleep reflects a pale version of dying, the process follows the same course of sensory decline, with cor-responding effects: The sense antennae stop feeding the inter-pretive mind; consequently, this mind dies to its daytime role as the switchboard of our habitual misperceptions and contingent sensory reactions. We can never know for sure what will happen to us when we physically die. But we can learn a lot by paying attention to experiences of the mind that transcend the small, limited ego-mind—whether these moments happen on our med-itation cushions, or with unprompted glimpses of emptiness, or when falling asleep. In the mini-death of nighttime sleeping, the self cannot maintain the fiction by which it survives during the day, and we enter the unpredictable landscape of dreams.

Sleep is the most obvious of many daily deaths. Yet each micro-version of death can function as a portal through which we enter the realm of dying. Each experience of it allows us to learn about what we most dread; and to diminish our fears by befriending them.

With the darkening of the sky, and with some mixture of optimism and denial about how sick I was, I rallied my energies for sleep meditation.

I started with my eyes open.

I directed my mind to the sensation of opened eyes.

As the eyes started to shut, I kept the awareness on sleepiness.

Or dullness, tiredness, and the shift of these sensations.

I did not try to control the eyes, or control anything. I did not try to stay awake. I just tried to stay with the awareness of whatever happened.

When I was close to falling asleep, I did not worry about, or try to control, body posture.

I started to experience my body sinking, falling, weighted . . . falling into sleep.

My lids shut. I was aware of sensation.

Throughout the night, I woke up repeatedly with painful cramps. Each time I struggled to get to the bushes, I asked myself if the bardo of dying was really approaching. I could no longer hold the thought at a distance. I was in trouble. I did not maintain consciousness as I drifted into sleep in any of the subsequent times that I dozed off. I tried sleep meditation sitting up, as we might do in the daytime, placing my shawl over my head; and then lying down again. Dream images passed by, but I could not remember them. I could not recognize any of the gaps, not those in-between the moment between consciousness and unconsciousness as we fall asleep or between the breaths or between thoughts. My mind drifted. I drank water but wanted food.

25

Giving
Everything
Away

SOME PEOPLE LIVE with so much fear of dying, and even with denial that death will ever take place, that they cannot experience a common activity like falling asleep as a kind of death. I did not grow up like that. During my childhood, death was discussed frequently and openly. Imagining death was part of my practice. *Death and impermanence, death and impermanence* was the mantra of my training. And yet throughout my projections and preparations for this wandering retreat, it had never occurred to me that I might get sick, or that I might die. Only with this illness could I look back and acknowledge the limitations in my understanding. Only then did I think, *This is why the masters shake their heads in astonishment that death could ever come as a surprise to anyone, young or old, when the truth is all around us.*

Between stabbing stomach spasms, mosquitoes, vomiting, diarrhea, and the lethargy that must have come from severe dehydration, I did not experience the bright renewal that generally accompanies dawn. I had also developed a fever and could feel heat radiating off my forehead. I was now in the fourth day of my illness and decided that I had better start reviewing the instructions for dying.

If I am dying, then like many others, I will die with physical pain. I cannot change the natural suffering of sickness. That's why this kind of suffering is not the main subject of Buddha's teachings, nor of the bardo texts. In this bardo, *painful* refers more to the trauma of not wanting to leave what we know, and to the painful experience of separating from our deepest attachments. We ardently desire to remain in the bodies that have sustained and served us; with the people we have loved and who have loved us; in the home that has been our refuge. A person, or a situation, tugs at our heart, and it's intolerably painful to lose this connection. We may not be able to alleviate the pain in our bodies, but we can definitely work with the suffering that can beset our minds at the end.

With the final transition, if we do not want to die feeling burdened by things that bind us, there is no time to lose. Rather than fight the natural course, we can relax and let go. We can work with letting go of our attachments, and there is a particular practice for letting go that we call the mandala practice; but it's not necessary to learn the Tibetan context or ritual in order for this practice to be effective. What's important is to identify our attachments, and free ourselves from past conditioning in order to inhabit this moment as fully as possible, and continue our journey with less baggage, just as we try to do all the time.

Letting go doesn't mean throwing out things that we no longer value, like an old coat or a broken iPhone. Logically we understand the value of letting go, but it doesn't come easily. Letting go of what has meaning comes with a pinch; we give something away, but maybe with a tinge of regret. It's important to acknowledge the feelings, pushing away neither sadness, remorse, nor nostalgia; it's also important to acknowledge the feelings without getting wrapped up in the story, or replaying disturbing dramas— just as we do when we become familiar with our minds in the bardo of this life. Whatever we associate with *me,* or claim as *mine,* will indicate the most intense bonds.

In the bardo of dying, to free ourselves of our attachments, we combine letting go, letting be, giving away, and making offerings. We draw on activities that are familiar in ordinary life—such as *giving away*—with less material qualities. We identify people and objects, and even aspects of the universe itself, such as mountains or streams, that have personal meaning; then we offer these aspects of our lives to religious figures, or to the universe, or to the stars. We start with the most personal image of a reality bigger than any conventional models, both for the kinds of offerings we wish to make, and for the people we wish to offer them to. The form and shape of either the objects or the recipient of our giving is not important. The only truly important aspect is how personal, and sincere, one can be.

Very often giving something away combines genuine generosity *and* big ego. Both. We might give to a homeless person in order to feel better about ourselves. Or give to a hospital or university in order to have a building named after us. We give in order to get, which is better than not giving at all. But reinforcing pride counters what we are really trying to do. When we make offerings to the gods or to the universe, the confounding logic is that the effects cannot be known. For this reason it becomes a kind of pure giving, giving with no measurable rewards. This generosity arises from respect, gratitude, and devotion, with no self-reference. Making offerings always includes heartfelt giving. But giving does not always include offerings.

In the traditional practice, boundless generosity becomes commensurate with visualizing boundless realities. If we choose to make offerings to gods or deities, or to planet earth or the universe, we are letting go not just of objects, but of the grasping mind. We give away mountains and rivers—by giving away phenomena that are impersonal and inconceivable, we reconfigure our place in the universe. When we offer natural wonders, such as mountains or rivers, the shape of conventional reality changes. Working with immense scale loosens the tight grip of clinging to our small cherished self at the center of our small world. Universes that cannot be held, or owned, or that are barely imaginable help disrupt patterns of limitation.

On my fourth day at the Cremation Stupa, I accepted that I had entered the bardo of dying. I had set off wishing to build a blazing pyre, and had concentrated exclusively on the disintegration of my various identities; images of hunger had led to wondering about how to protect my mind from demented craving, but I had never imagined starving to death. I saw myself trudging up Himalayan goat paths hunched in against the wind but had not gone so far as to imagine a frozen corpse. It had just never occurred to me that I might physically die. And now I had no words to express the depth of this ignorance.

Even though a short version of the offering practice is part of my daily liturgy, I reviewed the expanded practice and began by imagining impersonal objects of pleasure that could be shared with others. The first image that came to mind was Mount Manaslu, the Himalayan peak above my village in Nubri. Its grandeur had always affirmed that it housed the gods, and I allowed my mind to rest with its visual majestic splendor. Then I registered the sensory pleasures that I had received from the mountain, how when I had feasted my eyes on it, I had felt my heart soar. I took note of the solace that it gave my sick body to remember the mountain of my childhood. Memories of playing against the backdrop of its sparkling peak surfaced, along with memories of my grandmother. I felt such fresh sadness that I had to remind myself that my grandmother had died long ago, and that this sadness was more about my death than hers, and that even if I regained perfect health, my boyhood in Nubri had died many years ago and this nostalgia could carry me far away from this moment. I also recognized the benefits of using nostalgia to see what hooks the heart. I took note of all these feelings and let them be. I did not have to travel with the nostalgia, or with any memory-clouds. *Just stay steady, and let them pass through.* I stayed with whatever objects came to mind long enough to allow the feelings to move on. With no stories attached to their associations they did not hang around for long.

I moved on to objects that were closer to home, such as wealth. This does not just mean money, stocks, houses, and so forth, but anything that we treasure regardless of its monetary value. Anything at all. I recalled an old friend who came from a very poor family. Many of their meals consisted of water and flour patties cooked on embers. For holidays his mother would make the same patties but fried in oil and sprinkled with sugar, and in his mind, this was the most delectable meal imaginable. He had hoped to earn enough money to repay his mother for her kindness. He became a wealthy man who dined in fancy restaurants all over the world; but his mother died when he was a teenager.

He told me that he had once played a game with friends: If your house catches fire, what would you rush to save? Others spoke of children, pets, important papers. He was embarrassed by his own answer: a piece of yellowed scrap paper given to him by his mother. On her deathbed, after she had stopped speaking, she had pressed this paper into his hand. It remains his most valuable possession: a hand-scribbled recipe for fried dough.

If we treasure specific philosophies or political views, and have experienced great attachment to those ideologies, we offer those. If we know ourselves to be angry or stingy, we offer that. Whatever arouses anger or pride, offer that. The deepest bonds of attachment will be found in both aversion and attraction. Every release of whatever we identify as *me* and *mine* deals a small death blow to the ego; and every decrease of ego-domination increases access to our own wisdom.

I do not have any conventional wealth. My monasteries must have monetary value but I have no idea what that might be, and no ownership exists in my name. My treasure is dharma. Its value is inestimable, immeasurable. If my room in Bodh Gaya burst into flames, I would try to collect the texts and the Buddha statues. Yet Buddha objects did not provoke in me the sting of ties being shredded, while the upper and lower robes of my Tibetan lineage told a different story. One was folded to serve as a seat, and the other was in my pack by my side.

Had removing my robes left my body too vulnerable for this adventure? Would spreading them over my body heal me, as they had Khyentse Rinpoche, the same guru who had given me my first robes? He had wanted to become ordained since his boyhood, but his family would not give their permission. Then he had a terrible accident with an enormous vat of boiling soup and almost died from the scalding burns over his entire body. He lay in bed close to death for many months until his father covered his body with Buddhist robes.

Maybe I should put my robes back on. But I am not a child, as he was. Dharma is the only protection, not robes . . . But are robes distinct from dharma? Did they really save Khyentse Rinpoche?

In the formal sequence, after our wealth we offer our bodies. I did not want to die. I had noble altruistic explanations. *I could teach the little monks, and disseminate the dharma, and train lineage holders, and help care for my family members . . .* all good reasons that barely disguised my attachment to this life, to this body. I recalled doing this exercise when I had been healthy. It was so much easier when I did not accept that I would die.

Living in ignorant denial of death is like eating poisoned candy. It tastes so delicious. But slowly, the poison of fear seeps into your bowels and saps the life out of you. It was like that with the rice and dal that I had eaten. It was my first experience of begging for food. I had intended to practice humility. But in order to beg, I'd had to let go of feeling uptight and self-conscious. Once I did, I regarded this as an accomplishment, and felt proud. The food had tasted delicious even as something in it was killing me. *But this was the lesson of the Buddha's last meal. Eat whatever you are served. Appreciate every meal as an offering, a blessing. A gift from the gods or the universe. And accept the consequences, whatever they are . . . But the Buddha was eighty years old, and at the end of his ministry, and the texts suggest that he had already been sick before accepting Cunda's meal. I am just starting out, only thirty-six . . . does that make a difference? Not really . . .*

Offer your pride. Offer your compassion. Offer your vow to help others. Offer the dharma. Can I offer the dharma? Of course. I offer the dharma to all the sentient beings in the whole universe.

I tried working with friends and family. Choosing an offering that is deeply personal—such as a family member, or our own bodies—brings forth the full weight of our bonds. Imagine letting go of a parent, a partner, or a child. What might encourage this? What holds us back? What about our own body?

What about this body? Ravaged by illness, starving; is there anything here to offer? My practice is still working. I offer my practice. Even as I am dying, my practice is working. I have gratitude for the teachings and for my teachers. I offer my gratitude. I offer my gratitude for this blazing fire—a different kind of pyre than what I expected—but it has illuminated the waves more clearly than ever, and this is inspiring. I offer this illness for allowing the mirror of wisdom to shine more brightly amid the confusion and difficulties. Suffering and liberation, blazing together. More wood, yes, more wood, hotter, higher. Dying is also wood. Vomit and diarrhea are also wood. Hope and fear are also wood.

I worked next with my own virtue, with those activities or qualities that had been of benefit to myself and others. All of us engage in positive activities, such as kindness, generosity, or patience. We may be responsible and loving parents, or children. We may take good care of our friends. Maybe we plant trees or feed stray cats or work for organizations that help others. This exercise is not meant to show off saintly magnanimity but to recognize our own ordinary instincts to help out, and to engage in acts—however anonymously and whatever the consequence—that draw on our intuitive understanding that we are all participants in this world system; and because of that, the distinctions disappear between helping ourselves and helping others.

I have always prayed for my family members, for my teachers, and for the monastic and lay communities under my care. I pray for world peace and pray that all sentient beings awaken to their own enlightened nature. What the results of doing this are, I cannot say. I cannot know. But still I pray.

Secret offerings come next. *Secret* refers to what's not obvious or observable. It's more like *self-secret*. Specifically, secret here refers to emptiness. The clearly defined objects of grasping—to one's body, loved ones, or wealth—will be easily identified. But to work with our attachments on the most subtle level of ego-clinging, we must work with the secret offering. This does not simply readjust values but challenges the very concept of *value*.

One approach is to review the content of the previous offerings, and then offer the emptiness of those forms, such as: I offer my house, and the emptiness of my house—in other words, I offer the form of my house, which appears to be substantial, but I also apply the wisdom that recognizes emptiness, and I understand that while my house appears substantial, it has no essential identity that makes it a "house." The same is true with my body. And the same with my robes. From the start of this retreat I had turned my Tibetan robes into a kind of talisman, imbuing them with magic powers to bless me, maybe heal me as they had Khyentse Rinpoche, and protect me. I had taken as personal slights displays of indifference toward the robes, or of disrespect—as if they had qualities independent from the projections of my own mind. I had searched for the source of blessings or protection in the weave of the cotton, even though I could no more have located them than found my true self by searching through the body parts that Nagasena had deconstructed. Nonetheless, because my robes were essentially empty, they were—like me—real; but real as *a label, a name, a denotation, a conventional usage.*

What I noticed now when I worked with offering the essential emptiness of Mingyur Rinpoche—of this human form, of this life, of this breath—was that it had been a little easier to offer the emptiness of this body when I had felt robust and healthy. Now, with my body so close to dying, imminent physical disappearance made it more difficult to recognize that the emptiness of my dying body was no different than it had been in my healthy body.

26

When Death
Is
Good News

THE SUN WAS high in the sky when these offerings had run their course. My outer circumstances were miserable, but the exercise had left me calm, and without fear. I felt more and more ready to deal with whatever happened. Many times during the morning, an image faded out as I nodded off again. Going to the bushes sometimes interrupted the recognition of awareness, and I could not always remember where I had left off. I no longer had enough strength to push down on the long handle of the pump, although I continued to vomit water, which left a rancid taste in my mouth. On and off I became disoriented, and opened my eyes not quite knowing where I was, or what was happening. Through the hottest part of the day, I drifted and slept and had dreams that I could not recall.

As it started to cool down, I was able to re-gather my mind with greater coherence. I wanted to continue the offering practice by working with motivation and dedication. *If I am about to die, what is my aspiration? Physical death offers the best opportunity for enlightenment; and enlightenment offers the best opportunity for helping others.* This is why my father used to say, *For the yogi, sickness is a pleasure and death is good news.*

My father was reiterating information known to wisdom masters through the ages: that the organic degeneration of the dying body offers an unparalleled opportunity for recognizing the true mind. As the flesh-and-blood home of the mind falls apart, the fabricated layers of mind also disintegrate. The mind that has been conditioned by misperceptions, and shaped by habitual tendencies, becomes unglued. The confusion that has obscured our original, innate clarity can no more maintain its vitality than the outer skin layers of our bodies. As confusion dissolves, wisdom shines forth, just as it does in the process of meditation.

When we commit ourselves to living consciously, we apply effort and diligence to diminishing our confusion. At the end of our lives, this same confusion dissolves without effort. In the same way that the normal processes of the body cease to function, the movements of the mind subside as well. This includes our sensory perceptions, but also the subtle beliefs and concepts that shape our experience and define our identity. When all these cycles of body and mind stop functioning, all that's left is awareness itself, the unconditioned open space of pure knowing, but this knowingness now has no object whatsoever. This is why the moment of death is held to be so special, for it provides the most precious opportunity. At the utmost critical juncture between life and death, with the body teetering at the very edge of existence, the absence of confusion allows for the experience of luminous emptiness. This is the same aspect of mind that is always revealed when we recognize a gap in the conditioned mind, when the clouds of confusion part and allow for an experience of nonconceptual awareness. Only now, at the time of dying, this pure awareness happens on its own, and the habits of past conditioning no longer have the force to rush in and obscure it.

This happens naturally to everyone. It's as certain to happen as death itself. I know this. But without training, we cannot recognize the clear light of luminous emptiness. It is there, always there. I have known it. It is with me now, hidden in this agitation, present with this pain. Like my brother-monk, I too have trained. He said he was ready. Am I ready?

If our bodies expire while our minds rest in recognition of emptiness, then we are forever liberated. We have nothing more to learn. In luminous emptiness—the deathless realm—recognition and acceptance are one. We cannot attain unborn deathless reality until we accept death. The bardo texts describe this as *mother and child union:* The air element inside our bodies dissolves into space; space dissolves into itself, into spacious awareness. Individuated spaciousness is like the contents of an empty cup. Space exists within the cup but does not belong to the cup. When the cup breaks, the contained space joins with the space that has no edges, that is not contained. In the bardo texts, this cup-space is called *child luminosity,* and boundless space is called *mother luminosity.* At the time of dying, with no shadow of conceptual mind left intact, child luminosity gravitates toward its mother, as if coming home, and nothing can prevent this reunion. If we can maintain the recognition of this spaciousness at the time of dying, then the samsaric mind that we have now will never again appear in any form that will be perceived as confused; and it will never be perceived by the fixed, confused mind. We become enlightened; and whatever form this unfettered mind might inhabit, it will be forever liberated from confusion and karmic propensities and will never involuntarily reenter the wheel of samsara. *This is what I have trained for. This is what my father and my teachers and the lineage masters have attained. I am sure of it. But they have also told us that in truth, most of us will miss this opportunity. At the moment when this once-in-a-lifetime opportunity presents itself, the pure mind will generally not recognize itself. Or we will not be able to sustain the recognition. Most of us will black out, as we do when falling asleep. What did my brother-monk mean when he said he was ready: that he could recognize mother luminosity? Perhaps he was referring to the bardo of becoming—which, we were taught, is where we will spend most of our time between this life and the next. I wish I had asked him.*

If luminosity is not recognized at the conclusion of physical death and we black out, then Western medical professionals will declare us dead. This differs from our view. Tibetans understand that this is an unconscious state that lasts on average from about fifteen minutes to three and a half days, occasionally much longer. We do not consider a person dead until this state has come to completion. There are various physical signs to indicate the very end of life within the body. Then, on completion of the dying process—as on completion of falling asleep—we wake up again, and continue our journey through a dreamlike reality called the bardo of dharmata. This is another state that most of us will pass through quickly, and most likely without recognition.

We enter the bardo of dharmata because we have not fully died in the bardo of dying. Our bodies are gone. All conditional phenomena that appear to exist will disappear. That is their nature and the nature of our bodies. But consciousness, awareness, luminous emptiness, clarity—these aspects of reality are unborn and therefore do not die. To become unified with these aspects is to enter the deathless realm.

With the body gone, only that which is unborn continues.

The home of the grasping mind will be gone. Our relative minds have never truly been more stable than a rainbow. We cannot pinpoint the origin of a rainbow, even if we know the causes and conditions that bring forth its appearance. We easily accept that these translucent arcs magically reflect impermanence, insubstantiality, and interdependence. Now what happens when we turn our attention to our own minds? Can we identify the origin of a thought? When it begins, where it goes, when it ends, when one thought dissolves and another arises? Can we identify the causes and conditions for each thought? Are our thoughts any different in quality from a rainbow? If the thinking, conceptual mind shares essential qualities with rainbows, then what's left if thoughts dissolve? What's left when our bodies dissolve? *Can I stay conscious enough to find out?*

When I asked myself that question directly, I could not bring myself to answer it. At the same time, my body continued to weaken and I struggled to resume the practice. In contemplating my motivation, I first identified myself as an aware, functioning sentient being, still capable of directing my aspirations to help liberate all beings and dedicating my activities to their well-being, and that included the activity of dying. Dying now loomed as both the best chance for an all-encompassing experience of wakefulness and the last chance. Motivation included purifying the mind of any past disturbances, anything that might cast a shadow on the pure perception of luminous emptiness. It's not helpful to simply say, *Everything is essentially empty, everything is essentially pure*. Although that happens to be *absolutely* true, in order to know this absolute truth from the inside out, we must work with those thorns that cannot be plucked through intellectual reasoning or dharma philosophy. To be effective, working with subtle knots of guilt and remorse must be embodied experiences. Furthermore, these knots prevent the full expression of our compassion. In subtle ways, they keep us stuck on ourselves and hold us back from giving everything we have to the welfare of others.

I recalled two episodes from my boyhood in Nubri. A friend and I had taken eggs from a nest and tossed them like balls until they dropped. Another time some tourist trekkers had given their leftover food supplies to my grandmother, which included individually wrapped sugar cubes, three to a package. I loved these, and to keep me from eating too many, my grandmother kept them in a jar on a high shelf. One day she found a wrapper in the pocket of my jacket and knew that I had raided the jar. She berated me, called me a thief, and said that this was bad behavior.

I figured that I would probably go to hell, even though my father had told me that *from the absolute view, hell is just another dream.* Now I had to ask if fear of hell was really what had kept me on the straight and narrow. I could recall no other deeds I had performed that could be considered destructive or immoral. Something was not right. That my most monstrous delinquencies were breaking birds' eggs and pocketing sugar when I was about seven years old did not sound credible, even to myself.

Only in the apparent twilight of my life could I see that my fidelity to virtue was fueled by being a goody-goody, always trying to please my father and my tutors, and competing to be the best student. Although introverted and timid in groups, I wanted to be noticed, and to receive approval. I had thought I was using fear as a tool for renunciation, a strategy to stay oriented toward positive activity. In retrospect, I was hiding behind conventions of goodness, and acting virtuous in order to receive praise.

Other than fantasizing about a homeless life full of risks, I hadn't known how to get away from being the good little boy. My father's approval for a wandering retreat had come as a surprise. The visit to Gorkha—the one during which my mother rebuked the attendant-monk for allowing me to walk one block in the street alone—had occurred because I had been invited to my monastery in Tibet and would legally have to enter through China. I needed government papers, but my father would only give permission if my brother Tsoknyi Rinpoche accompanied me. Now I was in Kushinagar, alone. Dying. With no family or attendants to take care of me. With no teachers to help guide me through this journey.

When I had told my father that I wanted to do a wandering retreat, he told me then that he would not live much longer. He had been diagnosed with diabetes several years earlier, but although I could see that he was aging, nothing indicated that his death would come soon. Then he continued: *Two things: Whether you do a wandering retreat or not, continue to meditate for the rest of your life. And try your best to help everyone who is interested in working with their mind, regardless of their role or rank, or whether they are female or male, monastic or lay. Teach each one at the appropriate level as best as you can.*

He paused and then asked, *What do you think?*

I told him, *This is my passion, my calling. I know this to be true.*

My response made him very happy. Then he told me, *I have been meditating since my childhood. I am sick. My body is weak. But my mind is bright. I have no fear of dying.*

I tried to hold back tears but could not. Seeing this, he added, *I have confidence that awareness never dies. Keep this in your mind and do not worry about me.*

He died two months later.

Someone had worried about me. I must have dozed off, for I had no recollection of anyone having approached. When I opened my eyes it was dusk, and two one-liter bottles of water had been placed before me. I fumbled to remove the plastic covering and the twist-off cap, eager to drink, and then held a bottle in both hands. But I did not have enough strength to lift it high enough for the water to get into my mouth, and it dribbled down my chest. I thought about the many beggars who die without anyone showing any care. Maybe many sadhus die like this, I thought. How extraordinary to suddenly feel the serenity of gratitude. *I am not dying alone. Someone has noticed. Someone has cared. I am ready to continue . . .*

27

Awareness
Never
Dies

D AY FIVE OF my illness. Still no food. Outside, intense heat from the sun. Inside, burning heat from the fever. I lay slumped against the wall. The water bottles empty. I barely had enough strength to get to the bushes. I had wanted to wrap myself in mist like Milarepa had; now the mist that enveloped me was the damp dread of dying alone in Kushinagar by the Cremation Stupa. *Do I know, like my father did, that awareness does not die? Is my understanding reliable enough to count on? Will I recognize my true mind at the moment of death, or get stunned by the light and pass out? If I continue to practice, what could go wrong? But I have only practiced within this body. My father explained to me that as long as we remain in our bodies, even the most intense experiences of luminous emptiness will be shaded—however slightly—by the conceptual mind.*

Within the dullness of a mind bound to a sick body, inquiries into bardo teachings sharpened. What came into focus very clearly was that while the experience of luminosity presents itself, most of us will miss it. That's why we train. Not for the experience, which is a gift of nature; but to *recognize* it. Training to recognize the nature of our minds familiarizes us with child luminosity, and this familiarity is what allows us to approach the end of our bodies without fear and dread. With no previous glimpses of emptiness, it would be very difficult for a mind that has been habituated to conceptual thought to suddenly embrace emptiness. It is only *recognition* that is of benefit, not the event itself. With recognition, we become deathless.

If I miss the opportunities to become fully awake in both the bardo of dying and the bardo of dharmata, I wonder if I will be all right in the bardo of becoming. I am almost certain that this is what my brother-monk was referring to when he said he was ready.

I could not have had a better preparation for this in-between state than the past few weeks. But all my experiences of being in-between one life and another—in-between mind states, in-between physical locations, in-between having a home and becoming homeless, in-between never having been alone and being so completely alone—all these immense transitions have taken place within this body. The mind of in-between has been tethered; in the bardo of becoming after death, it will not have the grounding of a gross physical body. The container will be gone. All that will be left is a mental body, a form made of light that will slowly experience itself more as it was before death.

The transitions of consciousness in the bardo of becoming are the same as for this life. But the texts explain that the mind released from the physical body is seven times more sensitive than the mind that is experienced from within the body. It can see farther, hear sounds from much greater distances, traverse space unimpeded by gravity or direction. Our clarity is seven times greater than in our ordinary lives—but so are our fearful responses. If my only response to loud noises and waves that look like monsters would be to recoil in terror, then I would be driven out of this bardo. At this stage, the body can no longer filter the unleashed contents of mind, and we will be returned to the wheel of samsara, where we will take rebirth in one of the realms; and the cycle of ignorance will begin anew—and at the same time, as always, so will the possibilities for waking up. But if we recognize that we are in the bardo of becoming, then we can direct our next birth. Karma is a heavy influence here, but it is still not destiny. We are like feathers in the wind, getting tossed about, and our perceptions shift rapidly. At the same time, we are looking for our next body, a safe home to take refuge in. And waking up to our situation allows us to direct our choice.

What is my own situation, slumped up against the outer wall of the Cremation Stupa? *I do know that awareness does not die. And yes, my training is strong enough to recognize and stay with the mind of clarity and awareness. I trust my training. I will be okay.* And then the fear would return, seeping into every thought, directing every image, foretelling my fate. There was no longer any confusion about my condition. I was dying, fluctuating between fear and confidence. Images of my mother and other family members, friends, and students streamed before me—jumbled and disordered like a shredded photo album. Bodh Gaya, and Nagi Gompa, and Nubri with its summer flowers, and my grandmother and dead father and my beloved masters. I wanted these people with me now, to guide and comfort me. I wanted to hold them, to cry out, *Please stay with me . . .* but they drifted by like ghosts.

This is what it's like after you die, in the bardo of becoming, I thought. *You hover around friends and family and try to speak with them, relate to them, but they cannot see you. You do not know why your loved ones do not respond to you, because you haven't figured out yet that you are dead. What state of body do I have now, in this sickness that has left me already half gone? Maybe that is why they cannot hear me. Maybe I am more dead than they are. Who is dead and who is alive . . . and what should I do?*

In a startling pause, this bewilderment gathered into one point. I suddenly remembered that I knew by heart the telephone numbers for one monastery in Nepal and another in India. With a collect call, a rescue mission would set out. I could ask one of the caretakers at the Hindu temple on the other side of the stupa to place the call. Everyone carried a cellphone.

How wonderful to have this one decision to make. Immediately the frenetic scramble of memories and visions, fear and longing, fused into a single concern. To place the call or not. It would be so simple. Soon enough, I began to ask myself if a call would indicate defeat or acceptance; *yet who would be defeated, and who would accept what? Who might—or might not—die?* The spinning went into high gear once again, thoughts racing from here to there, going nowhere, once again flailing in uncertainty. The initial relief gave way to tumultuous competition between the two options.

Perhaps I would fasten my eyes on the past, like the young monk had with the gold coin. But my attachments were positive: teaching meditation and caring for the little monks. The young monk had struggled with greed and wealth on seeing the gold coin. *What difference does that make? To aspire to a mind like Patrul Rinpoche's, both positive and negative attachments must be abandoned.* I went over the story, wondering if my father could have meant for me to cut attachment to my actual life—to this body.

I could not decide what to do and the indecision started to brew like a storm, the clouds growing darker and more ominous. *I do not want to die. But my training has been to appreciate whatever arises, and that includes sickness and death. This is what I told the Asian man: If you can accept whatever happens—good, bad, or indifferent—that is the best practice. But my vow to save all sentient beings includes myself. If I try to save this life, is that running away from acceptance? But what life am I talking about—this gross physical body that must die someday? Is that what saving all sentient beings means? Maybe not, for we are not simply medical caretakers; we wish to save the physical life so that beings may recognize their own inherent wisdom, and know the deathless reality of unborn awareness. This is the bodhisattva vow: to save all sentient beings from ignorance, delusion, and the misperception that external phenomena are the cause of their suffering, and to bring them to the realization of their own wisdom. This is what I can do if I continue to live. But the bardo texts say that nothing—nothing—provides a better chance for the absolute recognition of enlightened mind than dying. So how can I turn my back on this opportunity? Even if I miss the first chance for enlightenment at the moment of dying, I have a second chance in the bardo of dharmata . . .*

Dharmata is sometimes called suchness, or reality. Within this lifetime, the death of the small self awakens us to the *suchness* of this life, to things-as-they-are: insubstantial, impermanent, and interdependent. We are reborn into reality with the death of the grasping mind. In the bardo of dharmata, we enter reality after we physically die.

At the very end of dying, we pass through the experience of ultimate luminous emptiness. If we do not recognize this, then we enter the bardo of dharmata. The physical body is gone, and we continue in the form of a mental body, like the illusory body we have when we dream. The consciousness of the mental body carries with it karmic seeds. These do not merge with consciousness but accompany it. What also goes forth is our recent experience of spacious emptiness joining spacious emptiness; even unrecognized, this leaves an imprint. We have just left behind our physical bodies and have soared to a peak state of absolute, formless, complete naked awareness, sky without clouds. In this state, we enter the bardo of dharmata. But the entry also initiates the reverse process, and we begin the transformation from absolute formlessness to once again inhabiting form.

In the bardo of dharmata, the perception of dim shapes and pale colors indicates the first signs of form taking shape again. We have just emerged from a state of pure consciousness, and projections and concepts do not yet exist. Slowly, as our experience of ourselves re-forms, we will move toward a future flesh-and-blood body. If we do not wake up and choose our direction, then we will re-inhabit the conceptual mind with the same propensities that have imbued this life.

My father and Saljay Rinpoche had been so optimistic about dying. His Holiness the Dalai Lama has spoken about looking forward to the opportunity that death presents. *But I am too young to die . . . I have not completed my teaching mission. My mother is alive. All my older brothers are alive. My death will be out of order. Even the Buddha would agree. That was his response to the young man who hurried the Buddha to the bedside of a dying grandmother.*

A young man rushed into the grove where the itinerant Buddha and his followers had set up camp. He arrived breathless from running, and with a face full of worry, he implored the Buddha to follow him back to the nearby village because a family member was dying. The Buddha dropped everything to join the young man. On arrival, they entered a house in which an aged woman lay on a mat in the center of the room surrounded by loving children and grandchildren. Someone was holding her hand. A wet cloth was held to her dry lips. The Buddha looked quizzically at the young man, as if to ask, *What's the problem?* And the man turned to the old woman, indicating that she was the problem, that her dying was the problem. The Buddha looked at an old person dying and explained, *There's no problem here.* But those words would offer no comfort to my mother.

By midday the indecision was driving me crazy. I knew that my family members, and the nuns and monks under my guidance, and friends around the world would miss me, and they would miss the benefits of my physical body. *Yet I have trained in awareness and in bardo practices my entire life. I did not know that I would need them so early on. Nonetheless, I believe in my own ex-*

perience, in the words of my father, and other teachers, that aware-ness is deathless, that it will never die, that I will never die. As my illness continued, I gained more trust in my own capacity for rec-ognition.

I have woken up many times within my own dreams. And even if I missed the first opportunity—the mother and child union—I could take advantage of the next one, of waking up in the bardo of dharmata. The obstacles that I encountered, especially in Varanasi, and again through the pain of this sickness, have strengthened my confidence in being able to stay with the recognition of awareness through the dying process. I have glimpsed child luminosity, and that will help me to recognize mother luminosity. Naked awareness is not unfamiliar to me. I know that I can recognize it. This means that I could be able to slip through the gap at the moment of dying and become enlightened, become a buddha, never to return invol-untarily in any recognizable form, and be of immeasurably more help than I can be in this lifetime. Liberation will not be the end of my journey. Without confusion and suffering, I can return to be of greater benefit.

If I had trained in meditation without the addition of bardo teachings, I might become confused at the end. But that will not happen. I have confidence in the teachings, and in the teachers who poured their wisdom into me, and my faith in them will not betray me, I am sure of it. If I do not die, I will continue the life that I have loved, to teach the dharma and continue to practice, and do my best to help sentient beings in this body. Either way I will have nothing to regret. But I must move past this indecision.

A ball of iron stuck in my throat, blocking my breath, stran-gling any capacity for making a decision. Back and forth I went. *This indecision cannot be sustained. I must choose one direction. Either one will be better than this. Go. Stay. Stay.*

Suddenly I saw that I did not have to choose between living and dying. Instead, I had to let my body take its natural course and abide in the recognition of awareness with whatever happened. *If this is my time to die, let me accept my death. If this is my time to live, let me accept my life. Acceptance is my protection,* I told myself, and sought affirmation in a prayer by Tokme Zangpo.

If it is better for me to be ill,
Give me the energy to be ill.
If it is better for me to recover,
Give me the energy to recover.
If it is better for me to die,
Give me the energy to die.

28

•

When
the Cup
Shatters

THE EFFECTS OF this profound acceptance came quickly.
Within ten or fifteen minutes, the agitation I experienced
began to decompress. Tension drained out from top to bottom,
my forehead, jaws, neck, my shoulders, hands—everything
dropped down. The deep sigh that signals the completion of a
tremendous effort circulated throughout my arteries. *Ahhhhhh.*
My mood shifted, and I sat still with opened eyes, enjoying a type
of weather that follows hurricane rains when the sun reappears,
the birds sing again, and the air feels refreshed. Perhaps I would
not die after all.

Assessing that the crisis might have passed soon proved inac-
curate. Making the decision to remain in Kushinagar settled my
mind but not my stomach. I continued to squat in the bushes. By
now every movement confirmed that my body was slipping further toward its irreversible cessation. This brought with it a renewed determination to work with the instructions for the bardo
of dying. The day before, a genuine concern had given rise to
these same contemplations, but I had not yet abandoned a whis-
per that told me, *Everything will be okay.* Now those assurances

were nowhere to be found. I continued to lean against the outside wall of the Cremation Stupa, but my mind felt stronger than it had for the past few days, and I initiated the offering practice. I did not nod off, or lose track, or *think about* the practices, but approached each one with a resolve and devotion that I had not tapped into the day before. I was not preparing to die. I was not in the monastery of my childhood, lying on the floor and listening to guided meditations on dying. I was no longer concerned with the concepts of *living* or *dying*—for what else could they be but insubstantial concepts—but with giving everything I had to whatever was happening right now, to meet the demands of this moment without attachment or aversion, and to befriend any adversity. *Living, dying: two concepts equally distant from this moment. This is who and where I am right now, this being just doing this activity, in this body, making these aspirations. Nothing more. Nothing less. Just trying to fully inhabit the infinite universe of each moment.*

Images came forth, and I did not dwell on any of them. Again Mount Manaslu appeared, which all my life had never been *a* mountain but rather *my* mountain, the defining jewel of *my* hometown, within sight of *my* house, the pride of *my* village. I allowed the image to rest long enough to register the attachment, to taste the glue of Mount Manaslu, to acknowledge the ways that I had adhered to it, and then to be with *just* the mountain, separated from all my associations and attachments. Other natural wonders passed through, but none with the same attachment that I had brought to the mountain: fields of flowers that bloomed near my village in Nubri, the fragrant pines that surrounded Sherab Ling in Himachal Pradesh, redwood forests, and comet showers. I probably spent twenty minutes recalling experiences that throughout my life had made my eyes grow large with disbelief, and that had animated my gratitude for the beauty and sacred diversity of our world. Many of these wonders were appreciated by many millions of people throughout every continent, and the knowledge of that transformed the mutual awe into a conduit of connection.

Seeing clearly, feeling deeply, I reviewed my wealth, returning to my robes. Today they no longer struck me as a valuable possession. What is my wealth right now? *My body is deteriorating. I have no money. No gold coins. No things of value. Even so, I have the possibility of waking up, of realizing the deepest, most subtle aspects of consciousness. My precious human birth is my treasure, in health and in sickness, for it never betrays the possibility of awakening. How could any treasure be worth more than knowing that? How fortunate I am; how truly blessed. My only offering now is how I manifest this dharma treasure, how I manifest living, how I manifest dying, how I live this moment, this only moment.*

If there is no living human witness, does that change the value? I pictured Shakyamuni Buddha sitting in the Earth-Bearing-Witness posture. His left hand rests palm up in his lap; the fingers of his right hand touch the earth. *With the earth as my witness, as my home, with this ground as my support, may I rest in the joy and love of dharma. With the earth as my witness, may I be the joy and love of dharma. With the earth as my only witness; and in the absence of anyone to please or placate, let my activities of body, speech, and mind be pure; cleansed of distortions, unsullied by vanity, true to my own pure Buddha being.*

For offering my body, there was no need to lie down and simulate dying as we did in training. Sitting in this park was an offering of my body. Being sick felt like an offering. I had no control over my physical functions; no control over this sickness. In these circumstances, *offering* my body felt integral to the dying process. I had accepted what life presented. I stopped holding on; that was the offering.

For giving up attachment to friends and family, hundreds of faces passed by as if walking single-file beneath a viewing platform. Family members, teachers, little monks, old monks, friends from home and far away. Every once in a while, a face that I had not seen for decades appeared: a crinkle-faced old nun from Nagi Gompa who used to play with me; a boyhood friend from Nubri; a hermit monk who lived on the grounds of Sherab Ling. As I watched this long procession, I knew that my neutrality would get a jolt when I circled back to the beginning, to my family. Then I focused on offering my mother to the buddhas as a way of placing her in their care. She has lived within a sphere of dharma blessings her entire life, but that made no difference. Aspirations for her protection needed to come from my appreciation. Still, the very thought of leaving my family broke my heart, and tears rolled down my cheeks.

With the completion of this section of the practice, a sense of immense gratitude welled from inside my body. My awareness became very deep, very settled. I heard dogs; I could see people. I remained totally still. I had confidence. *If I die, I will be okay.* Then a surge of compassion and gratitude joined with awareness, and I burst into tears, sobbing, with my shoulders shaking.

After a couple of hours of making offerings, I began to feel a little better. As I dropped deeper into the practice, the anxieties that had swarmed like trapped bees throughout the morning moved on.

By midafternoon, my mind settled into deeper states of resting. Thoughts entered as a gentle breeze passes through an open window, creating no disturbance. Nothing to chase after, nothing to follow, thoughts that had no weight to pull me down, or back, but just continued on their own journey of arising and disappearing. A deep calm spread from the area below my stomach to the edges of my limbs. It felt as if purified air was slowly cleansing toxic fibers, not just in my lungs, but in my bones, my veins, the channels. The circulation of blood dispersed a refined, renewed energy from head to toe. The separation between air inside my body and the air under the trees at the stupa park grew indistinct.

I was leaning against the wall of the cremation site, but trying to keep my back as straight as possible. I continued to sit very still, and to settle deeper. It was still light out when I began to take note of a great heaviness, of being pushed down from the top, and my head falling forward. This was not the same involuntary drooping of the previous days. I could no longer direct my neck. My body became so heavy that its weight threatened to push me down below the surface of the earth. It felt like falling, sinking. I tried to raise my arm but it weighed a hundred pounds. I recalled that these signs indicated the dissolution of the earth element. The foundation was collapsing. The ground beneath continued to open. *If this is the beginning of the end, let it be. Let whatever happens, happen. Stay aware. Falling. Sinking. Quicksand. Remain in recognition of awareness. Dissolution, feelings, senses, let them go and come.*

My mouth became very dry. I rolled my tongue around, but had no saliva. The water element was leaving my body. My body felt like it was opening up and falling away, like the bundles of long grass that are tied together at the bottom; when the tie is cut, every piece falls away from the center. My body was falling apart, dispersing, loosening, melting, and then I began floating on water; but the glue of my conceptual mind had not yet come undone. With my capacity for commentary intact, I intentionally reviewed the bardo map. I wanted to make sure that I was getting this right: that the dissolution of the elements had begun, and that this process would spontaneously dissolve layers of conditioning— leaving the gap through which luminous emptiness would appear with greater clarity than ever before.

I had heard about this luminous emptiness that accompanies the moment of death all my life—the best chance for enlightenment. My experiences affirmed that the dissolution of consciousness freed the mind—and I trusted that sleep and dreams reflected echoes of physically dying. I became excited, eager, and couldn't wait for the next steps to unfold.

My extremities turned cold. It was very hot outside, so I knew that this was caused by losing body heat. The fire element was leaving. As my body became colder, I could not make out distinct forms and saw only reddish flashes before my eyes. The texts say that at this point, the heart area remains warm. I wanted to check, to make sure I was on track. I had trouble lifting my hand, and used one to help push the other toward my chest. Yes! Hands almost too frozen to move, but the heart is warm. *I'm on my way.*

My awareness was becoming clearer and clearer. The conceptual mind was present but beginning to fade, and did not intrude with any force. With the conceptual mind diminishing within the infinite universe of awareness, I moved closer to the utter joy that infuses the awakened moment. My body, which had been so sick, and knew intense pain, was transferring the release of its dissipating energy to my mind, as if saying, *Go, go, go.*

With newfound confidence, recognition of awareness continued. Even as my body weakened, I felt more vigorous. I had no fear. All the confusion and fear had disappeared with the decision to remain here, and to protect myself with acceptance.

The dissolution of air did not have the quality of elimination. Instead, it felt more like being filled up. Each inhalation expanded beyond my lungs, transforming matter into air, making the body lighter, more resilient. The internal air seeped out of the lung channels and into my organs and bones; it went into my blood cells and tissue and marrow. Inhalations blew me up like a balloon, pushing up against the inner edges of bone and flesh until my body imploded. Bits of matter flew in all directions, dissolving into infinite emptiness. I could no longer see or hear. The container had cracked.

With the dissolution of air into space, my body became completely paralyzed. I could not move. Internal physical movement slowed to bare functioning, but my consciousness remained unchanged. With the conceptual mind dimming down, I recalled the dissolution of the body from bardo texts. Up until then I had felt my heart and my lungs. Now I could no longer detect my heartbeat, or feel movement in my abdomen. Yet my mind had become blissful, and continued to expand to fill the entire universe. I took note of what was happening. At this point the lucid mind of meditation was still a state that *I* inhabited. *I* was cognizant of the calm, of the awareness, of the paralysis, of the dissolution of the elements.

Then even the subtlest form of conditioned mind began to fade. As the sensory system and elements dissolved, I had only awareness itself to rest in. With the disappearance of the body structure that stores both gross and subtle perceptions, the mind expanded into realms of boundless spaciousness that it had never known before. The cup that is called child luminosity had shattered.

With the conceptual mind draining away, the uncovered original mind manifested with increasing vividness. Yet at one point, with the pull of the sensory systems and elements withdrawing, I almost lost consciousness. I almost blacked out, and then saw red and white flashes, similar to ones that often appear at the last moments of falling asleep.

Suddenly . . . *boom!* . . . awareness and emptiness became one, indivisible, just as it always is. But the recognition had never been this complete before. The last shred of cohesion slipped away. The entire universe opened up and became totally unified with consciousness. No conceptual mind. I was no longer *within* the universe. The universe was within me. No me separate from the universe. No direction. No within or without. No perception or nonperception. No self or non-self. No living, no dying. The internal movements of the organs and senses slowed way down, to minimal functioning. I still understood what was going on, but not through commentary or voice or image. That type of cognition no longer presented itself. The clarity and luminosity of awareness—beyond concepts, beyond fixed mind—became the sole vehicle of knowing.

I was no longer bonded to any sense of a distinct body or mind. No separation existed between me, my mind, my skin, my body, and the entire rest of the world. No phenomenon existed separate from me. Experiences happened but no longer to a separate *me*. Perceptions occurred, but with no reference back to anyone. No references at all. No memory. Perceptions, but no perceiver. The me that I had recently been—sick, healthy, beggar, Buddhist—disappeared like clouds that move through a sunlit sky. The top of my head came off; *my* hearing and *my* seeing became *just* hearing, *just* seeing. At best, words point to something beyond the conceptual mind that the conceptual mind cannot know.

This must have happened at about two o'clock in the morning. Up until then I had retained some dualistic understanding of what was happening. For the next five or six hours, I had no experience of conceptual mind.

As a drop of water placed in the ocean becomes indistinct, boundless, unrecognizable, and yet still exists, so my mind merged with space. It was no longer a matter of *me* seeing trees, as I had become trees. Me and trees were one. Trees were not the object of awareness; they manifested awareness. Stars were not the object of appreciation but appreciation itself. No separate *me* loved the world. The world was love. My perfect home. Vast and intimate. Every particle was alive with love, fluid, flowing, without barriers. I was an alive particle, no interpretative mind, clarity beyond ideas. Vibrant, energetic, all-seeing. My awareness did not go toward anything, yet everything appeared—as an empty mirror both receives and reflects everything around it. A flower appears in the empty mirror of the mind, and the mind accepts its presence without inviting or rejecting.

It seemed as if I could see forever; as if I could see through trees; as if I could be trees. I cannot even say I continued to breathe. Or my heart continued to beat. There was no individual anything, no dualistic perception. No body, no mind, only consciousness. The cup that had contained empty space had broken, the vase had shattered, extinguishing *inside* and *outside*. Through meditation I had known child luminosity, but never had I known such intense union of child and mother luminosity—emptiness infusing emptiness, the bliss of love and tranquility.

What happened next is hardest to relate: I did not *decide* to come back. Yet I came back. This did not happen independent of choice, although I cannot say who directed the change. Maintaining recognition of awareness allowed for this but did not make it happen. It did not have the influence of a voluntary decision but felt like a spontaneous response to deep connections in this life. The energetic strength of these networks had not come to an end, suggesting that this was not my time to die.

With an acknowledgment that had no language, I recognized that my teaching mission was not complete and that I wished to continue my life's work. As this aspiration became stronger, the infinite spaciousness of awareness slowly withdrew its expanse to settle in more finite form, and this in turn eased the reconnection to my body.

The first sensation was again a sense of gravity, of landing, of falling back down to earth. Then I felt my body; felt the sensation of needing to catch my breath, as if I had just been out of breath. I felt tingling sensations, like electric currents, moving through my limbs, ticklish and pleasant. I still could not see, but I could feel my heart beating in my chest. I tried to move my hand but could not. Everything before my closed eyes appeared blurred, far in the distance and indistinct. As my sensory systems regenerated, my vision felt clearer, even though my eyes were still closed. Soon it became strikingly clear. The air had a crisp quality, and at this morning hour I still felt that I could see for miles. The world seemed boundless, although eye consciousness had not yet returned.

Within another hour I could move my fingers. I touched them to one another, spread them wide, made a fist. Slowly, with effort, they regained some pliability. I experimented with lifting one hand at a time a few inches from my lap, and letting it drop down. I opened my eyes. Blurry forms appeared accompanied by a low reverberation, like the sound from a conch shell held at the ear.

I slowly reoriented myself to place. The grove. The shawl beneath me. The wall behind me. I heard birds. I saw dogs. I felt strong. Refreshed. Light. I had no memory of having been sick during the night. My lips felt parched. My mouth was very dry and I felt thirsty. The sun was up. When I looked around, everything was the same, and utterly transformed. The trees were still green, but shining, pristine, fresh. The hot air felt sweet, the breeze soothed my skin. I stood up to get water from the pump . . . and . . . that is my last recollection of being at the Cremation Stupa.

29

•

In the
Bardo
of Becoming

A large rectangular room. The quality of light suggests that it is late morning. Near-naked figures lie on rope nets set into metal beds in a long row, limbs flung wide, making frail, soft moans. A man reaches for the plastic cup by his side but loses energy, and his arm flops to his side. I recognize this force of gravity. I am in a grave-yard of the not-quite-dead.

I closed my eyes and returned my mind to the Cremation Stupa. I too had not been able to lift my arm. My mouth had felt parched, but I could not lift water to my lips. First earth, then water . . . the dissolution of heat . . . then air . . . When space had dissolved into itself, the cup had shattered. Then . . .

If I had fully realized luminous emptiness, then I would not be here. But where am I? Have I gone past the bardo of dying? If my body had completed its final dissolution while my mind rested in mother and child union, then I would have become a buddha for sure, and transcended the Wheel of Life, never to involuntarily re-turn in any recognizable form. What misfortune that I did not die! But . . . maybe I am in the bardo of dharmata, between dying and becoming. I have recognized my dreams many times in the bardo of this life, so surely I can recognize this dream, and wake up and be-

come enlightened. But I did not experience the collapse of the mother and father energies.

At conception, mother and father energies come together and then move apart; at the time of dying, these energies rejoin at the heart center. This usually occurs prior to mother and child luminosity, which is at the very end of the bardo of dying. That had not happened. I did not know where I was. *Merging with the body of enlightenment would have burned up karmic seeds, and I would not have continued to the next stage. The luminosity is that intense. How regrettable that I came so close to forever inhabiting the clarity of my own buddhahood. I might never again be blessed with such favored circumstances. Until I physically die, I can aspire to this opportunity. I can pray for it. But I cannot know if that will happen. Now I must continue with only mere reflections of enlightenment.*

If I missed reuniting with mother-space and am still alive, then perhaps this might be like waking up in dreams that happen every night in my form-body. Last night I had a wonderful dream. I dreamed that my form-body dissolved and only the purified mind went forth . . . And now my illusory dream has again taken on the appearance of solid form. But I do not feel dense. Nothing around me looks solid. This entire room feels afloat on an iridescent pier; forms rise and fall within rippling movements of radiance. Space and radiance are not separate from form. This is another beautiful dream.

If I did die, and my mind-consciousness is still related to the subtle tendencies of this body, then I am coming down from the peak of consciousness. The reverse process has begun. The experience of ultimate spaciousness is restricting back into waving, translucent shapes that are dancing together and separating, and radiating light and love. But I am not seeing the peaceful and wrathful deities that are supposed to appear in the bardo of dharmata. Perhaps the man lying next to me is a peaceful deity; or the nurses caring for patients are such deities. I see that the room is dirty, but this is not a problem. Deities could reside here.

I could not have entered the bardo of becoming, for I did not visit my closest friends to ask for their advice. Or hover close to family members. For a long time, I have not seen anyone I know and have lived uneasily among strangers. All my life, shades of fear have played in the background, but I do not feel this now. The texts say that we are fearful in this stage; that without being bound to our bodies, the negative reactions we have now are seven times greater. The sounds that scare us in this life become unbearable when the mind is not sheltered by the body; and forms that frighten us in the bardo of this life become much more horrendous than anything we can imagine from within our bodies. Still, I am between one state and another. Perhaps I am in the bardo of becoming within the bardo of this life. These figures emerging from shadow into being are not hostile. They are not rejecting me. I do not feel scorned by them. I am among friends. Maybe these are the friends that one encounters in the bardo of becoming. If I wake up from this in-between dream, I can direct my mind toward new opportunities for realization.

I wonder if the man reaching for water is here to mock my remorse at finding myself alive. Perhaps he's a saint, lying nearby to remind me never to doubt the love that was revealed. If I open my eyes, will the same man even be there? If I have shed the flesh-and-blood body, and exist in the dream body, will I know myself? Is any of my own subtle body recognizable?

I brought my hand to my face to check for eyes. As I raised my arm a cool texture, a surface not skin, brushed against my torso. Through the narrow slit of an opened lid, I saw a plastic cylinder. Machines surrounded the bed. Tubes of liquid dripped into my veins. Needles stuck out of my arms and thighs. The man lying nearby called out for a nurse. I saw old men in bandages. People limping, lurching, walking with crutches. A doctor, identifiable by a stethoscope around his neck, lay sound asleep on a bed. A ceiling fan whirred above.

. . .

I had not died. And I did not know if this was good news or not. I had gotten so close to fully becoming one with my own buddha-being that re-inhabiting this body felt disappointing. While I was trying to put all this together—my location, my body, my reaction—I noticed that the shapes passing through, while beginning to re-semble familiar forms, still seemed to be gliding on water. They appeared more transparent than solid, made more of light than of flesh and blood, more like a dream than a daytime vision.

But I could not tell if I was dreaming from within my everyday waking life or from my illusory body. And either way I had no desire to wake up from this dream. *I am enjoying this dream. The atmosphere feels so gentle, so welcoming and safe. Perhaps I missed both opportunities for liberating myself from the wheel of samsara and have woken up in the bardo of becoming, and have directed my rebirth to a pleasing friendly environment, with loving people that I do not wish to leave or run away from. I want to bend forward, to bow, and to greet them, even though these people do not manifest love with the same enthusiasm that the trees expressed last night. My sight does not have the same piercing omniscience that allowed me to see through forests. Color and clarity only dimly echo the quality of last night, yet I am still resting within the illusory nature of dream phenomena. The experience is familiar through post-meditation states that I have known, but it is more vivid, stronger, and with a more complete presence of emptiness.*

Every form appears and disappears, and moves through and within boundless spaciousness, coming from nowhere, going nowhere, without origin, without destination, spontaneously present. Phenomena within space cannot truly exist separate from space; the duality is not real. All forms arise as magic displays of color and light; a sky of rainbows, there and not there, beyond time, beyond direction, unborn and without end. *I love this new world, this alive brilliant state of suchness—the true nature of phe-*

nomena, without the clouds of substance and characteristics. This is the bardo of dharmata, the bardo of reality, of suchness. If I am alive, then I am in this second stage within the bardo of this life. I have entered this stage because I did not fully die in the bardo of dying.

Trying to figure out whether I was alive or dead seemed like a remnant from a previous life, for whatever had happened had left me knowing that death is not the end of life. There would be no finalities ever; only change and transformation. The experience of the previous night was gone. The days before were gone. Whether I had imagined that I had almost died, or dreamed it, or experienced it—all were gone, not here, not present, as good as dead. The more I acknowledged my ease at this moment, the more living and dying emerged as concepts, one not closer or further from this moment than the other—all held within deathless awareness.

What we call death is not the end. I could see this more precisely than ever; and that awareness continues through what we call living, and what we call dying. *Abdomen rising and falling. Death and rebirth. Now is dying. Last breath is dying. Unborn awareness cannot die. Unborn awareness exists with and beyond our bodies. Death is an illusion and living is also an illusion. Death and dying are only concepts; our perceptions shape differences and distinctions.*

Last night I was dying. This morning, I am an image in a mirage-like state, in a mirage hospital bed. I am dreaming this reality now, with my eyes open. In the train station, with my eyes open and my heart closed, I walked into hell. Last night I had the experience of being in paradise after dying. Now I am alive, I think, and in paradise on earth. Last night's dream and yesterday's life are the same. Both are gone. Both were illusions. It is true, just as the wisdom masters have told us, that life is a dream. Some images hold more meaning than others, but they have no greater substance. What enchantment! Forms rising and falling, breathing in and out, entire universes disappearing and emerging. Last night is gone. Almost-

dying is gone, dream or not. But I love that dream! That dream is paradise. Mother and child union dream is paradise. Real or not real I can still enjoy it, like watching a movie. Real or not real, it makes us laugh and cry. I had enjoyed flying over green emerald fields in Tibet. I like that dream better than the one of boulders crashing down. I like the dream of a healthy body better than the dream of a sick body. I like the dream of the open road better than being hooked up to this bed. All of life is a magic display of light and form, a universe of infinite blessings that invites us to turn our hearts inside out, and to love completely, to love until the inexhaustible end of dreams.

Why have I come back? What was the feeling that reoriented me to this life?

My teaching mission in this physical body had not yet run its course. Some subtle movement of my vow to help all beings had gradually steered me away from leaving. I slowly reentered my functional sensory system, and the paralysis that had enveloped my limbs and organs began to release its grip.

The intense and prolonged experience of absolute luminous emptiness, vast and unrestricted, uncovered a natural spring of boundless love. At that point, the motion of being brought back by karmic forces from the past merged with a present-moment aspiration to return and be of benefit to others as best as I could in this body. With an acknowledgment that had no words or concepts, I saw that I was drawn to continue my life's work. Some recognition of the one called Mingyur Rinpoche wished to both participate in this world and fulfill my teaching mission with compassion and love. As this aspiration became stronger, my conscious mind slowly reconnected to my body.

I still had no idea how I had gotten here, in this transitory dream state in this illusory room. I had been by the cremation site. I had been in a deep meditation state for many hours, deeper than I had ever known. Awareness of this body had slowly returned. The

intensity of the meditation had left me feeling completely restored and revitalized. I had had no memory of being sick during
the night. The inside of my mouth, my tongue, and my lips felt
parched. With the sensation of thirst, I had imagined water. My
mind had followed the thirst, and then my body had stepped
ahead toward the pump. I had not kept any food down for five
days, and the presumption of physical strength turned out to be
wishful. My legs had shaken, then buckled. But when my mind
reached for water, the continuity of recognizing awareness broke.
Because of that break, I could not remember fainting, or what
had come next.

*I am still alive. I wonder what actually happened, I wonder if the
doctor knows how I got here.*

Images of last night's dream slowly flowed by. Nothing moved
quickly. I felt supremely relaxed, and quite content to acknowledge these images without reaching toward them. Yet I was curious. The mind states that I entered are not unique to meditators,
or limited to spiritual seekers. We're talking about recognizing
original mind, the mind emptied of concepts and dualities, beyond time, beyond gravity or direction. One mind, same mind,
just different narratives woven around it. Inherently, this mind
cannot be confined to any one group or tradition. Words cannot
describe it. Nonetheless they are helpful. Without my tradition, I
would not have the language to share anything; and language provides a context for these experiences. Without context, experience alone often does not bear fruit.

On waking up in the hospital, while still trying to figure out
what was going on, I had mused on the language of *mother and
child luminosity.* Such a sweet image, so soft and loving. The
child-cup bursting its boundaries to join its mother. I had studied
this term; I had known enough to trust its meaning, but never
before had I delighted in its visceral warmth. *Mother and child
reunion.* I also felt childlike in that I could not articulate my happiness. Then again, I had no need to try, for I knew no one here.

Now with my eyes open, and knowing that I was in a hospital, I still thought that I was in paradise, along with the man who continued to reach for water, until the nurse came and lifted the cup to his lips. *It cannot be a misfortune not to have died when I have woken up in paradise.*

I dozed on and off, with knowing awareness, with memory and reflection. I felt newly awakened, but not ready to talk. If a nurse walked too near I closed my eyes. This seemed like a nice place to rest, a pleasure garden of comfort, but something started to suggest that I should get on with my journey. If I was in the bardo of becoming and could direct this part of the dream, I wondered where I would go, what I would become. I would look for the realm where I could continue to practice, the human realm. I would look for parents who want to do good in this world, who respect dharma, who are kind and caring, who would encourage and guide my spiritual path. Actually, I would seek a family like the one I had. In the midst of this reverie, I looked up and saw a familiar figure. The Asian man from the Parinirvana Stupa walked through the door of the ward. I shut my eyes.

I felt him standing at my bedside. When I opened my eyes and looked up, he explained that he had come to the Cremation Stupa to make a farewell circumambulation before leaving Kushinagar. He had seen me lying on the ground, looking dead. Even though I was no longer in monk's robes, he had recognized me, and brought me to Government Hospital in Kasia, about five miles from the stupa. He reported this to me in a straightforward tone. Without drama. He made no demand for a response. He told me that he had looked through my backpack and discovered that I had no money. He had paid for my hospital expenses, which included the admittance fees and the cost for medicines that the doctor had calculated for two nights. He explained that he had put money in the backpack, along with his business card. He told me that if I ever needed money, he would wire it from anywhere in the world. He wished me well, and left the hospital to make his travel connections.

This must be a dream.

One nurse brought sweetened juice and milk-tea; another checked the drip bags. I saw that the disorderly ward, with dirty windows and paint peeling off the walls, had its own kind of perfection. I recalled my discussions with the Asian man. I understood that he had saved my life, and yet his kindness did not stand out as exceptional. Nothing did, although some unusual events had just happened. As it turned out, his kindness was one of many instances when people helped me on my journey.

The conversations with the Asian man at the Parinirvana Park had happened a long time ago, as if in a previous lifetime. I had still been wearing my monk's robes, and had slipped easily into the role of teacher. Since then I had new eyes, and new ears. I lived in a new world. I could not exactly depend on help but saw that in one way or another, I would be taken care of by this new world.

The doctor woke up and came to my bed. He hadn't shaved and appeared worn and slovenly. He poked around my abdomen and asked questions. We spoke in a mix of Hindi and English. I told him I was feeling fine, wonderful actually, and asked when I could leave. He explained that I had arrived at the hospital dangerously dehydrated, almost dead. In addition to quarts of glucose water, he had ordered drips of high-dosage antibiotics to cleanse the infection I had picked up. He told me that I would receive bland foods, to eat only small amounts at a time, and that he would release me after two nights. I dozed on and off for the rest of the day and stayed hooked up to the drip bags. All that night, I enjoyed a deep dreamless sleep.

• • •

The next morning, a nurse removed the needles and disconnected the machines. She helped me sit up, and then stand. My legs did not shake. She instructed me to walk in the corridors. In a light cotton gown, I walked slowly down the hallway that led to the exit. From inside, I could see a courtyard and the main gate. Beyond the gate, I saw a wide thoroughfare with fast cars, trucks, tractors, and animals. Loud sounds of honking, yelling, and radio music drifted through the open windows. It was not pleasant. It was not beautiful, not inviting. No problem.

People lined up outside the gate waiting to get into the hospital, mostly barefoot older men. I wanted them to get in, because that was what they wanted. Their scant clothing, unwashed hair, and skinny bodies looked like those of the beggars at Varanasi station, but now I made no distinction between them and myself, between them and men and women in my own family—all of us together in this dream world, seeking happiness, seeking our own ways of waking up.

Before I had gotten sick, everything unfamiliar had made me a little uptight. I had felt separated from the people on the train, from the guesthouse keeper, and from the waiters in the restaurant. Every encounter had some feeling like that of walking into a wall, arriving at a place that stopped me, that pushed me back. Now I could not wait to get past the gate and go out into that noisy, dirty road, to roam through the streets and mountains and valleys of this fleeting world. I could not wait to be of more help to transitory dream people who suffer because they do not know that they are in a dream, and do not know that liberation is waking up to the dream as a dream. I saw beyond any doubt that luminous emptiness is within each one of us. When we talk and walk and think, we are in that state; in our healthy bodies and sick bodies, rich and poor. But we do not recognize the precious treasure that we have. In reality we are dying all the time, but our mind is not letting us know this. If we do not let ourselves die, we cannot be reborn. I learned that dying is rebirth. Death is life.

In the hallway, I met a man from Nepal. He was happy to be able to speak his native language with me. We talked about our villages, he on crutches and both of us in raggedy white gowns, more naked than dressed. He asked why I was here. I told him, *I came to meditate and got stomach problems.* When I returned to my bed a nurse brought me a drink made with powdered milk. It did not taste delicious, but I was happy to receive it. All through the morning my mind remained very fresh and lucid.

When I was a child, I had asked both my father and Saljay Rinpoche questions about this word *enlightenment* that I kept hearing. I had sat in on my father's teachings enough to imagine that *enlightenment* suggested a supreme state far removed from the one we were living in, so a lot of my questions related to physical location. *If I ever get enlightened, where will I be?*

My father had explained: *The location where you stay, where you reside, what you see, what you hear, will not be so important anymore.*

I had persisted and asked if I would be able to stay here, at Nagi Gompa. *Once you recognize the inner wisdom of your true buddha-mind,* my father had told me, *once you become one with the universe, you are everywhere and nowhere. Right now, you are using the conceptual mind to try to go beyond conceptual mind. It is impossible. You have put on a pair of yellow glasses and are trying to see white. Enlightenment is the reality that has no time, no location, no direction, no color, no form. It cannot be known that way. Don't be impatient.*

But I was impatient. Frustrated with his answer, I explained: *If I recognize that my mind and buddha-mind are the same, and I become one with everything, then I can do nothing.*

No, said my father, *when you become one with everything, you can do anything. You are capable of boundless love and compassion, and can manifest in ways that can benefit other beings. Don't forget: Your human form is—right now, just as you are—a reflection of enlightenment, form-body reflecting emptiness.*

This is the part that I had always had so much trouble believing. As many times as my father had repeated that each one of us is buddha, I could not quite comprehend that *each of us* actually included me. What would my father tell me now? I could be everywhere, but not with him—except for the ways that I would always be with him.

A nurse brought a cup of sweet Indian milk-tea. A different doctor from the one I saw the previous day came to my side. He too poked around and asked many questions. He told me that my recovery was going very well, that my blood pressure had returned to normal. I told him that I wanted to leave. He explained that I had come to the hospital more dead than alive, and that my friend had paid for two nights and that I would be best off sticking with that program. I did not wish to do this, and had become curious to be outside, to continue my journey and find my way. *I feel strong and ready to leave,* I told the doctor. He said he would write up discharge papers on the condition that I promised to return for a checkup the following week. I did not say yes; I did not say no. I never went back.

When I left Bodh Gaya I had no backup plan. This became obvious in the first few minutes, when the taxi did not show up. I had not known what to do, and had questioned the judgment of having no alternatives. Now, as I collected my backpack and said goodbye to the nurses, I felt less in need of a plan than ever. No plan A, no plan B. No guidebooks. Within a few weeks, I misplaced the Asian man's contact card.

The illness is over. I had almost died and it had set me free. Free for what? To die again, and again; free to live without fear of dying. Without fear of living. Free to die every day. Free to live without embarrassment. I would no longer rely on enclosures, on shells and

shields, attendants and robes. I would accept impermanence, of
death and of life.

I felt like an animated movie character endowed with super-
natural strength, imbued with acceptance, spacious awareness,
compassion, and emptiness. These were the resources, the shelter and food that would nourish me for the coming days and
years. My heart was expanding with a love that I had never experienced. An infinite appreciation that came from the center of my
being radiated to everyone I had ever known: family and teachers
who had nourished and guided me, friends, the Asian man, the
doctors and nurses, the cremation wall that had supported my
back, the trees that had shaded me. I felt appreciation for every
cloud, every affliction, fear, and panic attack for the roles they
had played in my pursuit of understanding; and I directed special
gratitude for the infection that had blessed my body. *To you, my*
beloved Guru Illness of Infinite Compassion, I bow with one hun-
dred thousand prostrations; to you who guided me to the ultimate
truth, who clarified my understanding, who unlocked boundless
love, I offer gratitude. Forever.

I was free to play in the waves, in-between locations, not
knowing where I would spend the night, what I would eat, where
I would go. The uncertainty no longer compelled me to scurry
toward safety; instead, I wished to rush headlong into the unknown world, to embrace its mysteries and sorrows, to be in love
with love, to be welcomed by love, to live with perfect ease in my
new home. Now that I had embraced this uncertainty, the road-
side seemed as hospitable and safe as the bed in my rooms at the
monastery. My physical body had been saved by the Asian man,
but the decision to return to this life gave me a greater confidence
than I had ever known, and I vowed to use it to live every moment
as fully and joyfully as possible. I learned that unconditional
love—for ourselves and all beings—arises once we allow for the
natural flow of change, and then we can welcome the continual
arising of new ideas, new thoughts, new invitations. If we do not

block whatever comes our way, there is no boundary to our love and compassion.

The whole world opened its doors and beckoned me to enter. I walked down the corridors, through illusory rooms with rows of transient patients, past soft moans, peeling paint, and gentle nurses. This empty body passed through another dream gate—the hospital gate—to continue this dream journey, to help others wake up and know that liberation comes from recognizing the dream as a dream. We are all of us together dreaming ourselves into being. Dying into being. Becoming and becoming. Always becoming.

Epilogue

·

ON LEAVING THE hospital, I felt drawn to return to Kushinagar. Something important had happened there, and I wished to express my gratitude. While the luminous mind never dies, the experience—as with any experience, no matter how transformative—was just another cloud passing by. This particular cloud had helped me recognize the unborn space from which it arose, but I still had to let it go. I checked the money that the Asian man had put into my backpack, then hailed a rickshaw and left the busy town of Kasia. Within an immense joyfulness, it was also with a touch of sadness that I returned to Kushinagar to say goodbye.

I walked through the gates of the Parinirvana Stupa. It was broiling hot, and except for the guards, no one else was there. I entered the building that housed the reclining Buddha. I had not been back since my first day here, almost three weeks earlier. Once again, I made prostrations and then sat on my knees. Before, I had been wearing the robes of the Buddha, and had felt myself to represent the Buddha, offering my devotion, and praying to realize Buddha's awakened mind through his teachings. I had understood that because millions of people around the world follow the Buddha's footsteps, the Buddha of ancient India is alive today.

Now I wore saffron robes. Otherwise, things looked similar to my previous visit: a small human seeker, bowed before a monumental religious figure, and saying the same prayers that I had said before. But everything was different. Buddha was not *dead*, and I was not *alive*. I understood the standard usages of *living* and *dying,* yet these words had no meaning. The continuity and the connection between me and Buddha went beyond time, beyond dualities. Buddha is not *gone.* I am not *present.* We are here, Buddha and me, in the deathless reality that is the true home of us all. The reality of death-beyond-death has no beginning and no end. It is this death that allows our limited time in this impermanent body to flourish, and that enables us to live intimately with ourselves and with one another. Feeling divided from ourselves and the world around us is the deceptive narrative of the grasping mind. But we can learn to let go of false hopes that leave us yearning for ease in our bodies and in this world. We can move beyond our discontent. We can replace longing with love. As I was just beginning to discover, when you love the world, the world loves you back.

I circled the park. I paused at the grove where I had sat in meditation, in heat and in rainstorms. Then I moved on to the Cremation Stupa. I followed the path between the outer wall and the stream until I came to my spot near the Hindu temple. The manifestation of the Buddha, here in the form of a large dun-colored mound, again came alive in a fresh way. The stupa no longer just memorialized the relics of Buddha's body but reflected the unity between the Buddha and me. We were neither indistinguishable nor separate. Not one; not two. Beyond both. I offered prostrations, then sat down to meditate. After a while, I gazed upon the stupa, as I might also have gazed upon my father had he been there with me, and thought, *Ah . . . now I know what you were talking about.*

But how did they know? Shakyamuni Buddha had let go of one life after another, from prince to forest yogi, to teacher and to enlightened leader—but while his forest life left him emaciated, he had never nearly died physically. Neither had my father, nor dozens of other realized masters whose wisdom far surpassed my own. I knew more now than before, yet part of what I had learned in this very place was how much further I had to go.

My dying body had allowed my mind to take a leap forward, as if flying over a stretch that would otherwise have followed a slower and more indirect route. It had provided a potential for pure awareness, for non-dual recognition of emptiness—as it always does for everyone. But the realization was primed by practice. To attain truly superior wisdom, I would have to sustain the same commitment to working with my mind that allowed masters such as my father and Saljay Rinpoche to die before they died; to recognize mother and child luminosity from within healthy bodies; and to inhabit the illusory body of the bardo of suchness within the bardo of this life. Their wisdom came from practice alone, and was not contingent on any particular event. The more that seeds of enlightenment are cultivated, the more the entire field of our awareness becomes fertilized, allowing for deeper levels of wisdom to thrive. But it's a trap to get attached to any particular experience, *especially* those that relate to spiritual awakening.

The biggest challenge to accepting the constancy of death and rebirth lies with our resistance to impermanence, and our hopeless attempts to hold in place what inherently changes. We often express the wish to let go of such disturbing emotions as jealousy, anger, or pride; or to transcend our vanity or laziness. When we think of making changes, our minds often jump to these conspicuous examples; and after decades of repetition, these traits seem immutable, undefeatable, and we lack the confidence to undertake the work of letting them go. The good news is that letting go is itself a way of experiencing change, death, and rebirth; and to affirm this, we don't need to start with our most entrenched and problematic tendencies. We can experiment with everyday activities that we generally do not define as problems at all.

Within the dualistic perception of normal awareness, we can acknowledge that each night when we fall asleep, we're dying to this day, which allows us to take rebirth tomorrow. In ordinary

experience, every moment takes place when the previous moment dies. Every new breath follows the death of the previous
breath. In-between breaths, thoughts, days, events—in-between
everything—there are gaps; and each gap offers the possibility of
glimpsing pure emptiness through the clouds. The point is that
the bardo principle of continuous death and rebirth can be recognized right now, in the midst of our ordinary neurotic patterns
and dissatisfactions and anguish. The view of who we are is transformed through awareness. And this changes everything. Once
we accept the fundamental transitory nature of our minds and
bodies, then we can develop the confidence to dismantle our
most entrenched patterns. Peeling off the outer layers of self is a
form of dying, but the process becomes much more workable if
we can develop confidence in the benefits of rebirth in this lifetime.

Each time we engage in recognizing the mini-deaths of our
daily lives, we become more familiar with the big death that will
come with the end of our bodies. We can use every big and small
experience of letting go to become more comfortable with the
final dissolution of the body. Doing this reduces the fear of future
death, and therefore transforms the way we live in the present.

When I was a child, I listened to stories about the Buddha's
life as if listening to make-believe tales of princesses and dragons.
Once I began to meditate, it occurred to me that these stories
were not just spiritual fictions but might contain a kernel of truth.
By the end of my first three-year retreat, I began to consider that
the Buddha's teachings were truly attainable, and this inspired
my efforts to wake up. Then after another twenty years of meditation and investigations of the mind, I concluded that I knew what
the Buddha was talking about. But at the Cremation Stupa, I
learned that I had mistaken representations of the moon for direct recognition.

In my tradition, we speak of three stages of recognizing the
moon, which signifies our own luminous, empty essence. As with

other stages, levels, and categories, there are no defined boundaries, and many gradations exist within each stage. Still, these descriptions can help us understand something of the process. The stages of recognizing the moon begin only after we familiarize ourselves with different aspects of awareness. We have already learned the awareness meditations of shamata or calm abiding—practices that steady the mind; then we practice Tibetan vipashyana, or insight meditation, to investigate the true nature of things as being impermanent, interdependent, and multiple—meaning lacking singular identity. Then we use these insight meditations to investigate the nature of awareness itself. Here we are approaching the inseparability of awareness and emptiness. We recognize that the qualities of emptiness are not nothing but can be experienced as radiant clarity, luminous and deathless. Through this process we are conditioning our minds to directly recognize the moon. We are getting ready to move beyond relative reality to more fully explore pure perception, beyond permanent and impermanent, beyond interdependent and independent, beyond singularity and multiplicity; beyond living and dying. We have investigated reality through meditation experience, study, and logic. We have dipped into pure awareness, which signifies the beginning of *the path of liberation*. We have gone as far as we can to affirm the limits of conventional understanding and have developed a genuine aspiration to leave behind the world of confusion, and to liberate ourselves from samsara. But so far, we have not directly recognized the moon, unadorned, naked, emptied of concepts and free from grasping.

On our journey of awakening, we have heard others describe this thing called *moon*. We have read about it, and have developed ideas about it. We have enjoyed stories about what it feels like to see it. Then one day, we come upon a picture in a book. It matches the descriptions that we have heard. It's a two-dimensional image of a yellow, round, opaque shape. We are so happy to finally see the moon! At last we know what the masters were talking about. This is our first experience of seeing the essence of our own minds. Compared with just an image in our heads, we see the moon.

Then one night, we see the moon's reflection on the lake. This image appears much more vibrant and translucent than the flat, dull representation on the page. We instinctually recognize that what we saw before was limited, and that this reflection is the real thing. The difference between the first and second stage is huge, like the difference between earth and sky. The quality of light on the lake approaches a vibrancy that cannot be compared to the picture book. Yet the images are similar enough that the more we study the book, the greater our capacity becomes for recognizing the moon's reflection on the lake. Our minds have not been completely freed of habitual patterns, and so our perceptions are still a bit tinted by the past; therefore, an experience of duality—of *me* perceiving something *over there*—separates the mind from the reflection. However, we are still thrilled by this intense experience of the moon.

In the third stage, we look up at the sky and recognize the *real* moon: direct, naked, brilliant. The moon in the book and the moon on the lake can be appreciated for what they are; but they are not direct, unmediated experience. We recognize the moon in the sky with the pure perception of awareness: Our perception and the moon become completely one—the union of awareness and emptiness. The mind has been liberated from conceptual filters and we have perception without a perceiver. We perceive the reflection, but this reflection is empty of any label, any designation or preconception, for it is being perceived by awareness itself. In the third stage, there is no meditator, and nothing to meditate on. We no longer *experience* luminous emptiness. We have become luminous emptiness.

Our minds are now like perfect mirrors, without a hint of obscuration. We neither invite nor reject any image that appears. We see all the myriad reflections. We acknowledge their qualities and characteristics, and know that they are not real. They merely reflect our own unobscured, radiant clarity, and have drifted into the field of our perception like transient, impermanent, insubstantial clouds. Once we recognize that space is our own essence, then we are free, and have no need to make the clouds go away.

The moon is still in varying stages of becoming full. As we continue our path of liberation, the fullness and clarity of the moon increases and the non-dualistic experience of pure awareness becomes ever more constant. This is what we call enlightenment, the full realization of the absolute nature of reality. The spacious mind recognizes that all forms arise from unborn space, and that ultimately, they are clouds without beginning or end.

Our first experiences of directly seeing the moon might be fleeting, as was my own. I was about ten years old, and my father had already introduced me to meditative awareness. This came somewhat easily to me, and I implored my father to teach me about pure awareness, as I had overheard him discussing it with the nuns. He tried to explain this aspect of awareness to me, but I had no idea what he was talking about.

One day I went to his little room at Nagi Gompa to join him for lunch. He was sitting on his raised box facing the large picture window that overlooked the valley. I climbed up to join him, and sat with my back to the window, looking at him. At first, we just made small talk, and then we grew quiet. Lunch was unusually late. As we sat waiting for our meal, I decided to impress my father by showing off my meditation skills. I sat with my back very straight, rigid as a yardstick, held my elbows a little bit away from my torso, tilted my head slightly forward, and lowered my gaze. I tried to imitate what I thought was a state of pure awareness—and waited for his praise.

My father sat in his usual relaxed way, and for a while did not say anything. Then he softly asked, *Ami, what are you doing?*

I am meditating, I told him, so pleased that he had noticed.

He asked, *What are you meditating on?*

I told him, *I am resting my mind in the natural state of pure awareness.*

My father said, *Ami, there is nothing to meditate on. Meditation is fake, the view is fake, the philosophy is fake. None of it is true.*

I was utterly shocked. All the contents of my mind just evaporated; my senses landed nowhere, without direction. No inside, no outside. Just brilliant clarity. I could not put this experience into words, nor could I explain it to myself.

My father continued to watch me, but said nothing. Then we sat in silence together, in a kind of meditation without meditating. When the food arrived, we enjoyed our lunch together. Everything felt normal, but the food tasted exceptionally delicious.

From that day, I knew that I had recognized nature of mind for the first time. I'd had a glimpse of it. After that, my meditation experiences went up and down, and I continued to be plagued by panic. But no matter how dark the clouds appeared, in the depth of my heart this experience had left a newfound confidence. Before that, and despite my panic attacks, I had felt blessed with a wonderful life. Now there was a meaning to my life that I had not even known I was missing. There was suddenly a purpose for being alive. In terms of child luminosity, this was a little chip in the cup, the first faint view of the picture moon. I would continue to hold a lot of intellectual ideas about *moon,* but I aspired to go deeper.

Following my experience at the Cremation Stupa, I saw that many aspects of my bardo training, such as the elements dissolving and the union of mother and child luminosity, had also remained mostly intellectual, more like fairy tales than dharma teachings. After my first experience with my father, I had known subsequent glimpses of emptiness, as well as many prolonged retreat sessions of sun and clouds together—steady and pure awareness coexisting—but all these now felt more like the moon's reflection on the lake, not a profound direct experience. I had never concluded that these previous perceptions were the ultimate, complete realization of awakened mind, but I had thought that they'd come pretty close. It turned out that they paled in comparison with direct recognition. I had known something of the real moon. I had known of the child-cup getting cracked—but not shattered.

I walked to the main road in Kushinagar and waited for the bus to Gorakhpur. There is no ticket office, and there are no specific stops. You just stand on the side of the road and flag down the bus when it comes along. I spent the night in the station dormitory in Gorakhpur, and the next day took a train to Chandigarh, near the northern state of Punjab. From there I made my way farther north to Ladakh, a Tibetan Buddhist region that is geographically within India. This initiated a route that I continued over the next four and a half years: heading north to Himalayan mountain caves for the summers and making my way south to the Indian plains for the winters. I never stayed in one place for more than four to five months. I wished to bring on change and impermanence, and to die again and again.

Up until now my life had contained an element of looking for answers. I had longed for a wholeness that kept eluding me. Often this feeling was so subtle that I barely acknowledged it. But the union of emptiness and awareness that took place at the Cremation Stupa provided a feeling of completion that has never left. I did not remain in a state of uninterrupted bliss for the following years. I knew hunger and cold and fear of wild animals, especially of tigers and leopards. Occasionally, stomach problems returned. But never again have I suffered from longing or loneliness, or from the embarrassment and social awkwardness that I had known previously. Before I left on retreat, I had often lived with contentment and joy; but to varying extents these states had been dependent on circumstances, and my circumstances had been exceptionally harmonious, with very little to challenge my equanimity. Now there was a different degree of stability. My resolve became deeply settled. My sense of well-being outgrew the limits of circumstance—good, bad, it made no difference.

In the letter that I had left behind for my students, I had encouraged them to practice. In light of what had happened, I wondered if my advice had been sufficient. Would I say anything different now? I had advised them *to pause and notice what we already have.* I suppose that now I might emphasize the benefits of noticing how we die every day. But honestly, the essential message would have remained the same. This is because I have complete confidence that with daily recognition of the seeds of wisdom, each of us will eventually arrive at an understanding of deathless awareness, for it is not other than our natural state.

In parting, I would like to give you one small piece of advice to keep in your heart. You may have heard me say this before, but it is the key point of the entire path, so it bears repeating: All that we are looking for in life—all the happiness, contentment, and peace of mind—is right here in the present moment. Our very own awareness is itself fundamentally pure and good. The only problem is that we get so caught up in the ups and downs of life that we don't take the time to pause and notice what we already have.

Don't forget to make space in your life to recognize the richness of your basic nature, to see the purity of your being and let its innate qualities of love, compassion, and wisdom naturally emerge. Nurture this recognition as you would a small seedling. Allow it to grow and flourish.

Many of you have generously asked how you can help support my retreat. My answer is simple: Keep this teaching at the heart of your practice. Wherever you are and whatever

you are doing, pause from time to time and relax your mind.
You don't have to change anything about your experience. You
can let thoughts and feelings come and go freely, and leave
your senses wide open. Make friends with your experience
and see if you can notice the spacious awareness that is with
you all the time. Everything you ever wanted is right here in
this present moment of awareness.

I will keep you in my heart and in my prayers.

Yours in the Dharma,
YONGEY MINGYUR RINPOCHE

Acknowledgments

◦

I N JUNE 2011, Mingyur Rinpoche left his monastery in India to begin a wandering retreat. Once he returned, in the fall of 2015, he expressed his interest in sharing his experiences relating to change and impermanence; and how they might help a general audience in facing our fears and in facing our deaths. He asked for my assistance, and this book grew out of interviews that I conducted with him intermittently between 2016 and 2018.

To expand my understanding of traditional teachings that related to our subject, I relied on *Luminous Emptiness: A Guide to the Tibetan Book of the Dead* by Francesca Fremantle and *Preparing to Die: Practical Advice and Spiritual Wisdom from the Tibetan Buddhist Tradition* by Andrew Holecek. I am grateful for the accessible wisdom that these books provide, and for the encouragement that I received from both authors. In addition, I wish to thank Andrew Holecek for his detailed attention to this manuscript.

For their responses to early drafts, thank you to James Shaheen of *Tricycle,* to Carole Tonkinson of *Bluebird,* and to Pema Chödrön, Dominie Cappadonna, and Glenna Olmsted. Many members of Mingyur Rinpoche's community, Tergar, helped this project in various ways. I thank each one, and in particular Cortland Dahl and Tim Olmsted for their steadfast support and their help in clarifying Mingyur Rinpoche's teachings.

I am grateful to Emma Sweeney, our agent, for her initial encouragement and for steering this book to Spiegel & Grau.

Thank you to Cindy Spiegel and her team. Cindy's respect for Mingyur Rinpoche's journey, her curiosity, and her sensitivity to the material made her an inspiring ally in bringing this book to completion.

Helen Tworkov
Cape Breton, Nova Scotia
August 2018

Glossary

Key: Skt. = Sanskrit; Tib.= Tibetan

ABSOLUTE REALITY Used interchangeably with *ultimate reality,* this is the true nature of all things and is usually equated with emptiness.

AWARENESS The innate, ever-present, nonconceptual knowing quality of mind. There is only one awareness, yet we experience awareness in three different ways: See **normal awareness; meditative awareness; pure awareness.**

BARDO Commonly used to describe an intermediate state between one life and the next; also understood as stages in one's journey through life and death, which can be interpreted as either physical processes or as states of mind during this lifetime; each bardo state provides heightened opportunities to recognize unconditioned reality. In this book, six bardos are referenced: **the bardo of this life; the bardo of meditation; the bardo of sleep and dreams; the bardo of dying; the bardo of dharmata; the bardo of becoming.**

    THE BARDO OF THIS LIFE Existence from first breath until the onset of irreversible conditions that lead to death; considered the best opportunity for becoming familiar with our minds, and awakening to our true nature. Meditation is the most effective way to accomplish this, and in some bardo systems, meditation practice as well as the practices of sleep and dreams are included in the bardo of this life. In others, **the bardo of meditation** and **the bardo of sleep and dreams** are presented as separate categories, but the teachings are similar.

    With **sleep meditation,** the practitioner trains to remain aware of the dissolution of the sensory system as the body falls asleep, an activity that parallels the process of physical death. In the **bardo of sleep and dreams,** one trains to wake up within a dream, which allows for directing one's activities within the dream state; this training emphasizes the impermanent, mutable, insubstantial quality of dream forms, and introduces the essential inseparability between daytime and nighttime reality.

Within the bardo of this life, meditations on emptiness, as well as sleep and dream meditations, reflect mind states that arrive unbidden at the time of physical death.

BARDO OF DYING The stage that marks the onset of irreversible physical decline until the liberation of the mind from the body. At the time of physical death, everyone experiences the dissolution of the elements, as well as the luminous emptiness of mind as it approaches its final separation from the body. Liberation within the bardo of dying comes with the recognition of this luminosity. As a mind state, the bardo of dying refers to the continual endings of all phenomena including breaths, thoughts, forms, situations, and mental states.

BARDO OF DHARMATA A dreamlike state that follows physical death. Waking up in our dreams within this life increases our capacity to wake up within the bardo of dharmata.

BARDO OF BECOMING The mind is released from its familiar physical and/or mental environment and journeys forth in an immaterial form, which is nonetheless influenced by a lifetime of habitual tendencies, as it seeks a new embodiment; a state of mind that, through physical or mental dissolution, loses its familiar moorings, and seeks to re-identify with form.

BODH GAYA A town in the north-central Indian state of Bihar; site of the Mahabodhi Temple and identified as the place where the historical Buddha Shakyamuni woke up under a bodhi tree. Home to Mingyur Rinpoche's Kagyu Tibetan monastery, Tergar.

BUDDHA (Skt.) Enlightened being; one who wakes up to the true nature of reality.

BUDDHA (Skt.) NATURE The fundamental nature of all beings—the empty, luminous, and compassionate essence of mind that is uncovered on the spiritual path.

CALM ABIDING (Skt.: shamata) Refers to a mind that abides in its own steadiness, independent of external circumstances; cultivated through meditative awareness.

CLARITY An inherent aspect of awareness; the knowing quality of mind.

COMPASSION An inherent quality of buddha nature or basic goodness that manifests as a wish to alleviate suffering; its ultimate expression is accessed through the wisdom of emptiness.

CREMATION STUPA Formally called Ramabhar Stupa; located in Kushinagar, India, it is a memorial mound that covers some of the ashes and relics of the historical Buddha on the site of his cremation (c. 483 BCE).

DHARMA (Skt.) This term can refer to the natural law and to phenomena; most commonly, it refers to the Buddhist teachings. It is capitalized when used as one of the three jewels in which a Buddhist takes refuge: Buddha, Dharma, and Sangha.

DHARMATA Translated as "suchness" or "reality." The true nature of things that is beyond all beliefs and concepts.

DILGO KHYENTSE RINPOCHE (1910–91) Born in Tibet, Dilgo Khyentse Rinpoche is regarded as one of the greatest Tibetan masters; following the Chinese takeover of Tibet, he was instrumental in maintaining the continuity of the teachings for the Tibetan communities of monks and laypeople in exile, as well as in bringing Buddhism to the West.

DUKKHA (Skt.) Suffering and dissatisfaction; a state of mind that creates and perpetuates mental anguish by misperceiving reality as-it-is and identifying with a rigid conception of self. Liberation is made possible by recognizing that suffering is created by mental misperception and is not intrinsic to one's basic nature or external circumstances.

EMPTINESS The underlying nature of all phenomena; the recognition that contrary to conventional perception, all appearances are empty of lasting qualities, empty of substance and of independent identity. Despite subtle differences, *emptiness* is often used interchangeably with *absolute reality.*

ENLIGHTENMENT A state of being in which one's buddha nature—the union of clarity and emptiness—has been fully realized.

THE FIRST NOBLE TRUTH The truth that in order to liberate ourselves from suffering, we must first examine its nature and experience its self-created qualities.

GOD REALM See **six realms.**

GURU (Skt.) A spiritual teacher or guide.

IMPERMANENCE The idea that all conditioned phenomena change and that everything that arises will sooner or later dissolve. Our usual attempts to fix in place what inevitably changes denies the truth of impermanence and is one of the main causes of suffering.

KAGYU One of the four main lineages of Tibetan Buddhism.

KARMA The principle of cause and effect: Virtuous actions intended to diminish suffering for oneself and others are the cause of future positive experiences; nonvirtuous actions cause negative experiences. *Future* may be the next moment, year, or lifetime.

KUSHINAGAR aka Kusinara, Kushinagara. A town in the northwestern Indian state of Uttar Pradesh where the historical Buddha passed away c. 483 BCE.

LAMA SOTO (c. 1945–2012) Born in the Kham region of Tibet, he escaped from the Chinese and went to study at Sherab Ling Monastery, where Mingyur Rinpoche was his retreat master (1993–96). From 2001 to 2011, he was Mingyur Rinpoche's attendant.

LUMINOUS EMPTINESS The nature of mind, which is ungraspable and beyond concepts, yet manifests as the capacity to know and experience.

MAHABODHI TEMPLE Temple complex in Bodh Gaya, India, that commemorates the awakening of the historical Buddha, Shakyamuni, in approximately 533 BCE.

MANDALA (Skt.) **PRACTICE** One of the primary practices of Tibetan Buddhism; through a sequence of offerings, the accumulations of merit and wisdom are established. In the bardo of dying, exercises for consciously letting go of our attachments help ease the transition from living to dying.

MANTRA (Skt.) *Man* means "mind," and *tra* means "protection"; a sequence of Sanskrit syllables understood to embody the wisdom of a particular deity; recited in repetitions as prayer, supplication, or invocation.

MARPA (1012–97) Born in Tibet. Known as Marpa the Translator, he made several trips to India in order to bring oral transmissions to Tibet and translated many Sanskrit texts into Tibetan; the teacher of Milarepa.

MEDITATION Working with the mind in an intentional way in order to recognize its inherently wakeful qualities.

MEDITATIVE AWARENESS This state of mind occurs when the mind turns inward and begins to recognize that awareness is an inherent characteristic of mind; the beginning of awareness recognizing itself. The emphasis on outside objects shifts to inherent, internal qualities. With meditative awareness, the mind rests comfortably without reaching toward or reacting to objects of sensory perception. Also called steady awareness.

MILAREPA (1040–1123) Born in Tibet. Tibet's most beloved yogi, renowned for his solitary practice in the inhospitable Himalayan wilderness, for attaining buddhahood in one lifetime, and for transmitting enlightened wisdom through spontaneous songs of realization.

MONKEY MIND The mind that chatters to itself uncontrollably, that grasps after the continuous appearance of forms and cannot let go of self-preoccupation.

MOTHER AND CHILD REUNION The merging of the familiarity of the empty, luminous nature of mind that one experiences in meditation with the experience of the boundless luminosity that accompanies the moment of physical death.

NAGI GOMPA A nunnery in the Kathmandu Valley, and the hermitage of Tulku Urgyen Rinpoche, Mingyur Rinpoche's father.

NAKED AWARENESS A state of mind in which awareness recognizes itself, liberated from thoughts and concepts.

NALANDA UNIVERSITY A Buddhist training center that thrived from approximately the fourth to the twelfth centuries; located in modern-day Bihar, India. Its extensive archaeological remains are now a UNESCO World Heritage Site.

NAROPA (1016–1100) An exceptional scholar, dialectician, and abbot of the legendary Buddhist university Nalanda. Having confronted his imperfect understanding, Naropa abandoned his secure position to study with the eccentric itinerant yogi Tilopa. He later transmitted these teachings to Marpa, his principal disciple.

NORMAL AWARENESS Used for negotiating everyday activities such as texting, driving, cooking, and making plans; the mind faces outward and stays on external phenomena, creating a dualistic relationship between one who perceives and the object of perception.

NUBRI An ethnically Tibetan district in northern Nepal where Mingyur Rinpoche was born in 1975.

NYOSHUL KHEN RINPOCHE (1932–99) Born in Tibet, he narrowly escaped Tibet after the Chinese invasion and eventually settled in Thimpu, Bhutan. He became an esteemed scholar and widely beloved master and was one of Mingyur Rinpoche's four main teachers.

OSEL LING Mingyur Rinpoche's monastery in Kathmandu; also known as Tergar Osel Ling.

PARINIRVANA STUPA Site in Kushinagar, India, that commemorates the passing away of Shakyamuni Buddha.

PURE AWARENESS Perception liberated from the separation between subject and object; non-dual perception unmediated by concepts, memories, associations, or aversion and attraction. Pure awareness rests with the recognition of emptiness; it is the union of emptiness and clarity, and leads to the path of liberation.

RECOGNITION The experiential recognition of a quality that had previously gone unnoticed. In Tibetan Buddhism, this typically refers to recognizing the empty, luminous nature of awareness.

RELATIVE TRUTH Used interchangeably with *conventional truth*; one's ordinary experience of reality in which phenomena are experienced as lasting, substantial, and independent, and existing as entities separate from the mind.

RINPOCHE (Tib.) Precious one; a term of respect.

SADHU A Hindu term for a religious mendicant, or one who has renounced secular life.

SALJAY RINPOCHE (1910–99) The retreat master at Sherab Ling from 1985 to the end of his life. He completed his training at Palpung Monastery in Tibet under the guidance of the Eleventh Tai Situ Rinpoche. Following the Chinese invasion, he fled to Sikkim, where he remained until the Sixteenth Karmapa passed away; he then went to Sherab Ling to be with the Twelfth Tai Situ Rinpoche. Mingyur Rinpoche's retreat master at Sherab Ling and one of his four main teachers.

SAMSARA (Skt.) Literally "going in circles," a cycle of suffering and dissatisfaction kept in motion by ignorance and a lack of recognition of one's true nature.

SANGHA (Skt.) The **noble sangha** refers to the community of enlightened beings; the **ordinary sangha** refers to friends who share a dharma path. Capitalized when used as one of the three jewels: Buddha, Dharma, and Sangha.

SHAKYAMUNI BUDDHA The historical Buddha (c. 566–483 BCE). His renunciation of the conventional world of confusion and his recognition of the cause and cessation of suffering have inspired and shaped all subsequent traditions of Buddhism to this day.

SHAMATA (Skt.) See **calm abiding.**

SHANTIDEVA (685–763) Indian adept whose studies at Nalanda University were considered mediocre until he gave an address to the assembly; these teachings, now known as the *Bodhicharyavatara,* or *The Way of the Bodhisattva,* are celebrated to this day by Buddhists around the world for their brilliance, accessibility, and intimacy.

SIX REALMS The realms of samsaric existence that describe mental states and that reflect a particular type of suffering, these states are not experienced in any specific sequence, but the order in which they are presented signifies increased degrees of suffering: the god realm of pride, the demi-god realm of jealousy, the human realm of desire, the animal realm of ignorance, the hungry ghost realm of greed, and the hell realm of anger.

THE SIXTEENTH GYALWA (1924–81) **KARMAPA** Rangjung Rigpe Dorje. The spiritual leader of the Karma Kagyu tradition of Tibetan Buddhism.

SLEEP MEDITATION The practice of maintaining awareness while sleeping.

SONAM CHÖDRÖN (1947–) Mingur Rinpoche's mother, who was born in the Nepalese district of Nubri and at present resides at Tergar Osel Ling in Kathmandu.

STEADY AWARENESS See **meditative awareness.**

STUPA (Skt.) A rounded structure that represents the Buddha; often built to house relics of enlightened beings.

SUFFERING See **dukkha.**

TAI SITU RINPOCHE (1954–) Recognized as the Twelfth Tai Situ by the Sixteenth Karmapa, who oversaw his enthronement at Palpung Monastery in eastern Tibet, and who shepherded him safely to India at age six (alongside the Sixth Mingyur Rinpoche) following the Chinese invasion. Eventually he settled near Bir in northwestern India and developed Sherab Ling Monastery, where Mingyur Rinpoche began studying at age eleven. Today he oversees a vast network of Kagyu monasteries, retreat centers, and dharma centers worldwide, making an enormous contribution to the continued flourishing of

Tibetan dharma. He is one of Mingyur Rinpoche's four main teachers.

Tashi Dorje (1920–2017) Mingyur Rinpoche's maternal grandfather; born in Nubri, Nepal, he was studying in Tibet when the Chinese invaded. A revered meditation practitioner and direct descendant of King Trisong Detsen, the eighth-century king of Tibet.

Tergar (Tib.) *Ter* means "treasure"; *gar* means "place." The name of Mingyur Rinpoche's monasteries, as well as the name of his international community.

Tilopa (989–1069) The supreme adept and eccentric Indian yogi whose teachings to Naropa were subsequently transmitted to Marpa, and from Marpa to Milarepa.

Tsoknyi Rinpoche (1966–) Born in Nepal, he is the older brother of Mingyur Rinpoche. His teachings draw on deep meditative experience and sustained engagement with the modern world. The married father of two daughters, he travels extensively while overseeing nunneries in Nepal and Tibet, and more practice centers and hermitages in the eastern region of Tibet.

tulku (Tib.) The reincarnation of a spiritual adept; one who is considered endowed with enhanced potential for spiritual development.

Tulku Urgyen Rinpoche (1920–96) Yongey Mingyur Rinpoche's father and one of the most highly regarded meditation masters of the last century. Born in Kham, Tibet, he came to Nepal following the Chinese invasion of Tibet and established two monasteries and many teaching centers, eventually residing at his nunnery, Nagi Gompa, in the Kathmandu Valley. Today his legacy is carried forth by his sons Chökyi Nyima Rinpoche, Tsikey Chokling Rinpoche, Tsoknyi Rinpoche, and Yongey Mingyur Rinpoche. One of Mingyur Rinpoche's four main teachers.

UNBORN Refers to the ultimate emptiness of all things, which is beyond birth and death, and beyond arising and ceasing.

VARANASI Also known as Benares, a historical city on the banks of the Ganges River, in Uttar Pradesh, in northern India; especially sacred to devout followers of Hinduism.

VINAYA (Skt.) Shakyamuni Buddha's collected teachings on discipline and appropriate behavior for the ordained community; a monastic rule book that, to this day, guides Buddhist monasticism.

VIPASHYANA (Skt.) Insight; clear seeing. In the Tibetan system, **Theravada vipashyana** emphasizes impermanence; **Mahayana vipashyana** emphasizes emptiness; **Tibetan** (or **vajrayana**) **vipashyana** emphasizes the nature of mind. In Tibetan teachings, vipashyana meditation works with the recognition that all that appears arises from emptiness and that all form is inseparable from emptiness and dissolves into emptiness. Vipashyana is the direct, experiential insight that while forms appear, they are essentially as ungraspable and groundless as space, and that this quality mirrors the nature of mind itself.

WHEEL OF LIFE A representation of the world of confusion. A complex round image, held in the mouth of Yama, the Lord of Death, it depicts the root causes of suffering—ignorance, aversion, and aggression—which are shown at the center, surrounded by concentric bands that display the perpetuation of cyclical habitual behavior, including the six realms of existence.

WISDOM That aspect of mind that perceives reality as-it-is; that clarity of mind that recognizes emptiness.

ABOUT THE AUTHORS

•

YONGEY MINGYUR RINPOCHE, born in 1975 in Nubri, Nepal, is the youngest son of the celebrated meditation master Tulku Urgyen Rinpoche. He began his formal monastic studies at the age of eleven and two years later entered his first three-year retreat. Today his teachings integrate the practical and philosophical disciplines of Tibetan training with the scientific and psychological orientations of the West. In addition to his role as abbot of three monasteries, he directs Tergar, an international meditation community with one hundred centers around the world, and is well known for presenting the practice of meditation in a clear and accessible manner.

At age thirty-six, he secretly left his monastery in India to engage in a four-and-a-half-year-long wandering retreat, living in mountain caves and village streets. He is the author of the *New York Times* bestseller *The Joy of Living: Unlocking the Secret and Science of Happiness,* as well as *Joyful Wisdom: Embracing Change and Finding Freedom* and *Turning Confusion into Clarity: A Guide to the Foundation Practices of Tibetan Buddhism.* His primary residence is Kathmandu, Nepal.

tergar.org
Facebook.com/tergaronline
Twitter: @TergarOnline
Instagram: @tergaronline

HELEN TWORKOV is the founder of *Tricycle: The Buddhist Review* and the author of *Zen in America: Profiles of Five Teachers* and coauthor, with Yongey Mingyur Rinpoche, of *Turning Confusion into Clarity: A Guide to the Foundation Practices of Tibetan Buddhism.* She first encountered Buddhism in Japan and Nepal during the 1960s, and has studied in both the Zen and Tibetan traditions. She began studying with Mingyur Rinpoche in 2006 and currently divides most of her time between New York and Nova Scotia.